The Prime Minister's Son

The Prime Minister's Son
Stephen Gladstone,
Rector of Hawarden

By Ros Aitken

University of Chester Press

First published 2012
by University of Chester Press
University of Chester
Parkgate Road
Chester CH1 4BJ

Printed and bound in the UK by the
LIS Print Unit
University of Chester
Cover designed by the
LIS Graphics Team
University of Chester

A catalogue record for this book is available from the British
Library

ISBN 978-1-908258-01-4

For Tom

CONTENTS

Contents

LIST OF ILLUSTRATIONS

List of Illustrations

NOTE ON CURRENCY EQUIVALENTS

1870: £1.00 = £45.70 today

1880: £1.00 = £48.31 today

1890: £1.00 = £59.89 today

1900: £1.00 = £57.06 today

1910: £1.00 = £57.06 today

These are the figures for 2005, the latest available.

FAMILY TREES

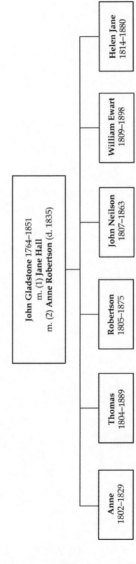

Figure 1. John Gladstone's family tree.

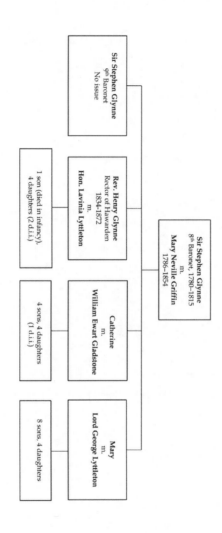

Figure 2. The Glynne family tree.

Sir Stephen Glynne
8th Baronet, 1780–1815
m.
Mary Neville Griffin
1786–1854

Sir Stephen Glynne
9th Baronet
No issue

Rev. Henry Glynne
Rector of Hawarden
1834–1872
m.
Hon. Lavinia Lyttleton

1 son (died in infancy),
4 daughters (2 d.i.i.)

Catherine
m.
William Ewart Gladstone

4 sons, 4 daughters
(1 d.i.i.)

Mary
m.
Lord George Lyttleton

8 sons, 4 daughters

Family Trees

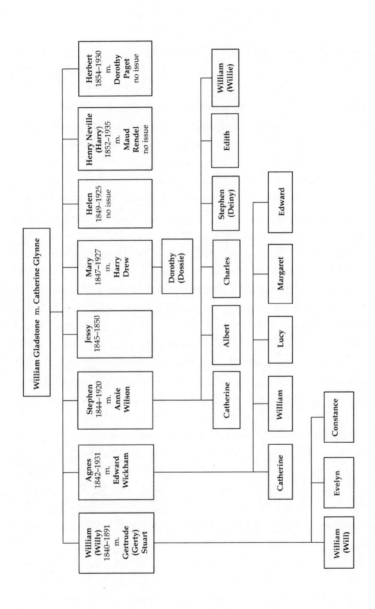

Figure 3. William and Catherine Gladstone's family tree.

ACKNOWLEDGEMENTS

Many people have given me invaluable help in the writing of this book. I should never have embarked on it had I not read the Venerable T. W. Pritchard's article on 'Stephen Gladstone, Rector of Hawarden' in the Journal of the Flintshire Historical Society. Bill not only welcomed my decision to write the book, but generously handed over research materials. Sir William Gladstone, Bt, K.G. has been immensely supportive, showing me round the Castle and lending me a box of family papers which he unearthed when moving house. Eileen de Ville, in Grantham, spent hours photocopying the *Grantham Journal*, shared her knowledge of Barrowby with me, and sent me photographs in her possession. Over the years, attendees at the annual Gladstone Conference at Gladstone's Library (previously St Deiniol's) have encouraged me in my interest in the Gladstone family. Dawn and Julian Bradshaw offered me wonderful hospitality and essential chauffeuring services in Barrowby and Lincoln. My husband Tom has been a rock, offering advice and help with obtaining books and overcoming computer crises, and listening to discourses on Stephen several times a day over many months.

Archivists and librarians across the country have been uniformly willing with their assistance. Online, they have answered queries both esoteric and banal with equal promptness and politeness, and on visits have patiently guided me through their various filing systems and technologies. I owe a particular debt to the Flintshire Record Office, all of whose staff have gone far beyond the call of duty in helping to satisfy my multifarious demands on their time and expertise. Gladstone's Library, where I stayed and wrote many times during my researches, is beyond praise, particularly Patsy Williams, the librarian, who first directed me to the existence of Bill's article. Peter Francis, the Warden, has been a constant encouragement and Annette Lewis has been an invaluable go-between on a number of occasions.

I also wish to thank all the following institutions for their help in various ways: Lambeth Palace Library, the Lincoln Archive, the London Metropolitan Archives, the Institute of Historical Research, the Imperial War Museum and the staff at British Library Newspapers, Colindale, the Minet Library, and Richmond Reference Library. The following archivists have been of particular help: Penny Hatfield and Christine Vickers at Eton, Judith Curthoys at Christ Church, Jacquie Gunn at Cuddesdon, Ian Small, of the Commonwealth War Graves Commission, and Alys Blakeway of the Hampshire Archives. Individuals to whom I owe thanks are local historian Elizabeth Davey, and, at Barrowby: Sarah Cooley, Les Shoebridge, Kate Waghorn and Peter Hopkins. David W. S. Todd, Warden of the College of the Holy Spirit, Cumbrae, gave generously of his time to show me round and let me browse freely in the college records. I apologise to anyone I have omitted and need hardly add that any mistakes in the text are mine alone.

Grateful thanks to Roland Quinault and Peter Francis, again, who made encouraging and helpful comments on my original proposal. Both of them, Sheila Gooddie, Anne Isba and David Bebbington all read and commented on the final manuscript.

At the University of Chester Press, I owe a huge thank you particularly to Sarah Griffiths, my editor, who showed an immediate interest in my book, patiently answered endless questions and offered practical support and suggestions.

PREFACE

Stephen Gladstone first came to my attention when I was researching for a paper on William and Catherine Gladstone as parents. There was no difficulty in finding out about the lives of six of their seven surviving children, but Stephen, the second son, remained a stubborn enigma mentioned, if at all, in footnotes. At first I assumed there simply wasn't much to know, but then I was directed to a solitary published article, concerned mainly with his time as Rector of Hawarden in Flint, filed away in a box in a half-hidden corner of Gladstone's Library (then known as St Deiniol's). Reading this article made me aware that there is just as much primary material about Stephen, mainly in the form of family letters, memoirs and diaries, as there is about his siblings.

Why then has he been so neglected? Perhaps because he was not a trailblazer, like his sister Helen, in women's education; nor someone at the heart of William Gladstone's social and political life, like another sister, Mary; nor even married to a significant spouse, as was his sister Agnes, wife of the Dean of Lincoln Cathedral. Nor was he an MP, like his older brother William, or his youngest brother Herbert, also an MP, who became first Governor General of South Africa. Nor was he an important man of business and a public figure, like his younger brother Henry Neville (Harry), first Baron Gladstone of Hawarden and Lord Lieutenant of Flintshire. Stephen was a country clergyman, but that bland description does him scant justice. The archives are a treasure trove of information about his life and thought; his relationships with his parents and siblings and with his own family; his approach to his vocation; and his attitude to the church of his day. The whole family were prolific letter writers, and the fact that his brother Harry was away in

India for over thirty years is a particular gift to the biographer: there are hundreds of letters to and from Harry as he kept in touch with affairs back in England.

The researcher is faced with a gigantic heap of jigsaw pieces. Some pieces necessary to complete the picture are missing: even addicted letter writers like the Gladstones started using the newly available telephone, an invention of which Catherine was an early fan. The frequent face-to-face family conversations on important matters were not, usually, recorded. Not all letters have survived, some are impenetrably allusive and many are, maddeningly, undated. Catherine's handwriting is particularly hard to decipher, not least when, as often, it is fitted into any spare space on recycled paper such as old invitation cards. Her punctuation and sentence structure are erratic, as are Mary's. Both mother and daughter also on occasion employ Glynnese, a secret language invented by Catherine's family. Constantly recurring names across the generations, in particular 'William', 'Henry', 'Stephen' and 'Mary' can create confusion. Catherine's diaries are irregularly compiled and non-existent for many years. Mary's handwriting as she gets older, and Stephen's as his eyesight deteriorates, are not easy to read, and some letters sent from abroad on flimsy paper are barely legible. Gladstone's diary, regularly and scrupulously kept and available in published form, is an oasis of legibility, but perforce provides a fragmentary and one-sided record of his dealings with his family. All a biographer can do is to complete as much of the puzzle as possible.

As the picture emerges, we see not only an Anglican priest responding to fundamental challenges in the doctrine and organisation of the church of his time, but also, forever at his elbow, his father, a Gladstone often radically different from the great British statesman of popular imagination. At the Gladstone International Bicentenary Conference held at the University of Chester in 2009, the American scholar, Professor Deryck Schreuder, of the University of Sydney, gave a paper on 'Gladstone and the Greater World'. He began with the remark that you 'find your own Gladstone'. The Gladstone whom we find in a study of his son Stephen is only partly the Gladstone we find in the diary, the political records and the published papers. Certainly, we see the same man of prodigious energy, phenomenally wide-ranging interests, intellectual grasp and deep religious faith. Complementing these traits, a wider picture of his personal attributes emerges, particularly his closeness to his wife Catherine and their children. But, significantly, unattractive traits are also manifest, particularly his reluctance to allow to others freedom of action or even of thought. Like many people in positions of power, he imagined he was the only person who knew what to do in any given situation. Worse, he could be a ruthless manipulator, intent on getting his own way. His readiness to equate his own desires with the Providence of God caused him to ride roughshod not only over members of his own family but also over others less powerful than himself, such as the unfortunate Rev. William Dampier of Buckley. We shall probably never form a complete picture of the complicated figure of Gladstone, but a knowledge of his behaviour with regard to his son and his affairs adds an essential ingredient to our understanding.

No one would claim that Stephen Gladstone changed the course of history. The significance of his life lies elsewhere. He himself and his relationships with others offer an interesting study of individual personality and family dynamics, and present us with a prism through which we may view other, much more obviously important, subjects:

not only the character of his father, Gladstone, but also the condition of the Established Church and its priesthood in Victorian and post-Victorian England, and the nature of everyday parish life in Britain over more than half a century. The only comparable source for the life and thought of a country clergyman at this period is *Kilvert's Diary: Selections from the Diary of Rev. Francis Kilvert*, and the latter needs to be treated with extreme caution. Before publication it was severely censored, first by Kilvert's wife, who was widowed immediately after their honeymoon, and later by other family members. By contrast, the Gladstone family letters bear scarcely any evidence of subsequent tampering with the record.

INTRODUCTION

The changing scene, forebears and family

Stephen Gladstone was born in 1844, towards the end of the sixth year of the reign of Queen Victoria, and he died in 1920, ten years into the reign of Victoria's grandson, George V. When he was born, the total population of England and Wales was fifteen million. Convicts were still being shipped to Tasmania. Small boys were regularly sent up chimneys. Railways were in their infancy, motor transport unknown, telegraphic communication just a dawning possibility. British streets were lit, if at all, by gas. In his world, women in crinolines lived lives circumscribed equally by their dress and the rules of society. Entertainment was generally home-made, centred on parlour games and the family piano. Most churchgoers believed in the truth of the book of Genesis, describing God's creation of the world in six days.

By the time he died, the population had more than doubled, to thirty-seven million. The Tasmanian convicts' descendants were citizens of the fast developing state of the Commonwealth of South Australia. All educated Christians had long since accepted the doctrine of Evolution. Those sweeps' boys' grandsons, and their sisters, were all in school. Those crinolined-women's daughters had ridden bicycles in knickerbockers, and their granddaughters were now in short skirts, sitting chatting on the phone or walking, unchaperoned, through brightly lit streets to the local cinema. The modern world had been born.

Although the Age of Empire still survived, during Stephen's lifetime the face of Britain changed almost beyond recognition, mostly for the better. There was a shift of population from the countryside to the towns, creating social problems, but increasing individual wealth and

1

opportunities. Class and gender barriers were challenged and democratic rights extended. Living conditions for the poor improved, as did general public health. Workers' rights started to be recognised, elementary education was made compulsory, travel and communications became easier. Everyday life was transformed. In August 1904, Stephen himself, commenting on life in Hawarden, exclaimed, 'What changes, wrought by development of railways, trade, public law, education, population' and he was referring only to the years since 1872.

For the first sixty years of Stephen's life, he travelled, as did everyone, on foot, or on horseback, in a horse drawn carriage or on the steadily growing railway system. In retirement he owned a motor car; his son flew in aeroplanes. Like all his generation, he began as a Victorian, with all that that implied in the way of inherited certainties, and ended his life in the modern age, with all those certainties, for good or ill, destroyed.

Beyond Britain, the world scene reflected, in far more brutal fashion, the upheavals of change. Stephen's lifespan covered six major military conflicts. The Crimean War and the Indian Mutiny occurred while he was still a child, the American Civil War broke out in the year he went up to Oxford University. The Boer War began when he was in his fifties, the Russian Revolution broke out when he was in his seventies. In his final years, the First World War brought personal tragedy.

The Victorians had not heard of genes, but that did not prevent them from inheriting them. Among his immediate forebears and close relations Stephen could list: a drug addict who converted to Roman Catholicism; a man who bought a white charger belonging to Napoleon; an Anglican clergyman; a commander in the Royal Navy; a merchant who had made money from West Indian sugar cane estates worked by slaves; and several members of parliament. No wonder he was often uncertain and confused about the path he should take.

Stephen's maternal grandfather – he who bought the horse – was Sir Stephen Glynne of Hawarden, the eighth baronet. He died long before Stephen was born, suddenly in Nice, in 1815, the year of the Battle of Waterloo. Stephen's grandmother, Lady Mary Glynne, made her way safely home to Hawarden Castle in North Wales, alone, through a Europe where an escaped Napoleon was still at large. She had four young children: Stephen, who became Sir Stephen Glynne the ninth baronet, Henry, who followed family tradition to become the local Rector, Catherine, who was to become Stephen's mother, and Mary, later Lady Lyttleton. Lady Glynne died when Stephen Gladstone was ten. She had lived with her younger daughter Mary at the Lyttleton family seat, Hagley Hall, during Stephen's childhood. Since the two sisters were very fond of each other's company, he spent much of his time at Hagley, and must have got to know her well. She was a traditionalist, a strongly Christian woman and local patron who had brought up her daughter Catherine to do good works in the village of Hawarden. Duty must come before pleasure, and others had to be thought of before oneself. These values passed down through his mother to Stephen and informed his life.

The Glynnes were a very close-knit family. After Catherine's marriage, her unmarried brother Sir Stephen invited her and her husband, William Gladstone, to share the family home, Hawarden Castle. Stephen Glynne, whose memorial effigy can be seen in the Hawarden church, St Deiniol's, was MP for Flintshire, but his main interest was not in politics but in parish churches: he surveyed and made notes on 5,500 of these during his lifetime. When his nephews and nieces were old enough, he involved them in his antiquarian activities. He was a kind, unambitious man, who like his mother was conscientious and active in the parish. In his role as patron of the Hawarden living, he was much loved for his liberality and he gave generously to the church restoration fund after a fire in 1857. Sir Stephen was to change the direction of Stephen Gladstone's life.

The Rev. Henry Glynne, brother of the baronet, presented with the living of Hawarden by the family, was living in the Rectory, within walking distance of the Castle. He married Lavinia Lyttleton, sister of Lord George Lyttleton, who had married Sir Stephen's sister Mary in a double wedding with Catherine and William Gladstone. The families were therefore doubly bound together and there were frequent Gladstone visits to the Rectory. When Stephen was six, Lavinia died, having borne a short-lived son and four daughters, only two of whom survived. Family visits to his uncle and two surviving girl cousins of course continued.

The Glynne sisters, Mary and Catherine, were soulmates, spending as much time together as possible and often looking after each other's children. Their relationship exemplified the fact that Catherine sometimes showed a stronger loyalty to her birth family than to her own husband and children. When Mary was dying after her thirteenth pregnancy in 1857, when Stephen was thirteen, Catherine left everything to be at her side, and after Mary's death frequently had her sister's children to stay at Hawarden. As a result, Stephen became very close to these cousins. Throughout his life, he had far more contact with his mother's family than with his father's and it is easy to see why.

Introduction

John Gladstone, Stephen's paternal grandfather, was a rich Liverpool merchant with investments in West Indian sugar estates worked by slave labour. A powerful local figure, he had acted as financial backer for the Tory MP George Canning in Liverpool and was rewarded by being created a baronet. In celebration, he purchased Fasque, in Aberdeenshire, a Scottish baronial mansion. He had been an MP himself before the 1832 Reform Act, and put pressure on all his sons to enter politics. Only the youngest one, William, Stephen's father, was to make a success of a political career, and this caused considerable bad family feeling. The Gladstone siblings, unlike the Glynnes, were far from close and as children the older brothers ganged up to bully William. Both William's mother and his favourite sister Anne, who had been his spiritual mentors and who between them might have held the family together, died years before Stephen was born.

When John Gladstone himself died, when Stephen was seven, there was so much ill feeling between William and the new baronet (his oldest brother, Thomas – Stephen's Uncle Tom), that communication between them broke down completely and family visits to Fasque abruptly ceased. Tom inherited the title along with the property, but was nevertheless always in William's shadow, and resented his younger brother's success. The brothers disagreed about religious matters and about William's attitudes to both their sister Helen and their brother John Neilson. It did not help that Tom did not have a son and heir until 1852, by which time William had two sons, a cause not only for jealousy, but fears on Tom's part over the inheritance. Gladstone had, quite unreasonably, hoped to inherit Fasque, on the grounds that he was his father's favourite, and for years after their father's death – all the time Stephen was growing up –

William Gladstone behaved with great coolness to Tom. Stephen did not really have a chance to get to know his uncle until July 1856 when Tom and his wife, with Stephen's aunt Helen, finally paid a visit to Hawarden. Gladstone went up to Fasque two years later, but without Stephen.

John Neilson, the third son and Stephen's youngest uncle, played almost as small a role in his nephew's life. He had a career in the Royal Navy, rising to the rank of Commander before retiring in 1842. By the time Stephen was born John had entered politics, as did Tom, and like Tom he was never more than a mediocre backbench MP, frequently losing elections, much to William's irritation. John Neilson and Stephen saw little of each other, although on at least one occasion John was on holiday with William and Catherine and their family in North Wales. He died young, when Stephen was nineteen.

Uncle Robertson, the second brother, was more of a figure in Stephen's life, even if indirectly. A very large man physically, noted for minor eccentricities, he spent his whole life in Liverpool, the original family hometown, where he became a prosperous and influential businessman and was elected Mayor in the year of Stephen's birth, 1844. He administered, ineffectually as it later turned out, the Trust money left by John Gladstone, and the Seaforth family property which provided some of William Gladstone's income. All his life, Robertson was kind and loyal to his brother. In return Gladstone, though initially appalled by his brother's choice of a Unitarian bride, confided in him and respected his opinions, relying on him in his South Lancashire election campaign in 1861. Even so, Stephen did not see much of his uncle, who only once visited Hawarden, to meet Cobden in September 1859, when Stephen may have been away at Eton. They did correspond. In September 1865, when Stephen was temporarily acting, with a considerable degree of enjoyment and an even greater degree of respect, as his father's secretary in Downing Street, Robertson wrote to him with the offer of a job. Stephen turned it down with polite regrets on the grounds that he was planning to enter the church.

Aunt Helen was by far the most colourful of his Gladstone relations, her eccentricities vastly outweighing those of her brother Robertson. After the early death of her sister Anne she had, perforce, become the family carer, first of her semi-invalid mother and then of her ageing father. Probably it was these restrictive circumstances which encouraged her to behave in ways which shocked and horrified both her brothers and their wives. Catherine Gladstone made no secret of her feelings for her sister-in-law and must have been glad that the scandals were over by the time the children were old enough to take notice. If they later found out about their aunt's escapades, it would not have been through either of their parents. As early as 1835, Helen's erratic behaviour was giving cause for concern to her conventionally minded family. On a visit to Ems in Germany, by coincidence at the same time as Gladstone first met Catherine Glynne, Helen became briefly engaged to a young Polish count. His parents first insisted that she convert to the Orthodox Church and live in Russia, then they terminated the engagement. Helen returned home to her father and gradually became deeply depressed. Soon, having been prescribed laudanum and alcohol as tranquillisers, she became addicted to opium and other drugs, as did many women of her generation, and turned, to Gladstone's undisguised horror, to Roman Catholicism.

Soon after Stephen was born, her addiction caused Gladstone, with some misgivings, to despatch her to Baden-

Baden and Munich for treatment. When he went to Munich to fetch her back, Helen, having tasted freedom, eluded her brother by skipping back to the spa. Here Gladstone found her in a state of mental collapse and tried to persuade her to go home with him, but she refused to go any further than Cologne. By January of 1846 she had temporarily cut herself off from the family, finally returning in her own good time, exhibiting symptoms of paranoia and suffering from fits and delusions. Her father and brothers were totally unsympathetic and wanted her to be confined as a lunatic. She escaped from the family's London house in Carlton House Terrace but was recaptured and virtually imprisoned in a dark room at Fasque, with a nurse and a minder. Rumours of her extravagant behaviour include one about her using the books of Protestant clergy as lavatory paper. However, as her father neared death, Helen's mental health improved and Gladstone became reconciled to such an extent that he called his youngest daughter 'Helen' after her.

By the time Stephen was five, and of a noticing age, his aunt was back in the good books of the family. She maintained an interest in Stephen and his siblings, but saw nothing of them. In 1851 in Rome she had been admitted to a Dominican convent for treatment, and in 1856 she became a novice of the third order of Dominicans in England at St Helen's Priory, which was located in a village on the east coast of the Isle of Wight, near Ryde. She had previously been treated for her opium addiction by the Dominicans and expressed her gratitude by founding a chapel in the grounds. From St Helen's she wrote to Gladstone in 1862 enquiring whether Stephen had made up his mind to be a clergyman, as indeed he had. In the late 1860s she left England and returned to Cologne, dying there of bowel paralysis probably caused by her opium addiction, in 1880, by which time Stephen had been a clergyman for twelve years.

As for Stephen's father, William Ewart Gladstone, he is the major protagonist in countless books. In this book he is not centre stage, although his role is crucial to the action. He entered parliament as a High Tory in 1832, later becoming a Peelite Conservative, and was appointed Chancellor of the Exchequer in 1852, when Stephen was eight years old. Seven years later in 1859, he joined the newly formed Liberal Party and in 1868 became, for the first time, Prime Minister of Great Britain, a post which he was to hold four times before his death in 1898. A dominant figure in public, local and family life, he wielded huge influence over his son, not always for the best.

Stephen's surviving brothers and sisters are all far better known than he is, not necessarily justifiably. One sister, Jessy, sadly died in infancy. He had three other sisters: Agnes, Mary and Helen, and three brothers: William, Henry Neville (known as Harry) and Herbert. William was the firstborn. Usually known as Willy (or 'Willie'), he was much beloved by all the family, though he failed to come up to the high parental expectations, being neither very academically inclined nor very ambitious. He compensated for these deficiencies by having a kind nature and an outgoing personality, and was a close friend of the Prince of Wales. After leaving Oxford with an undistinguished second, he followed his father into politics, but never rose beyond the back benches. He, rather than his father, was made Sir Stephen's Glynne's legal heir to the Hawarden estate. Like all the Gladstone children, he did not marry until relatively late in life, when he was thirty-five, in 1875. His bride was the eminently suitable Gertrude Stuart, daughter of Lord and the late Lady Blantyre. The marriage was happy and

Figure 4. William (Willy or Willie) Gladstone. Reproduced by kind permission of Sir William Gladstone.

soon produced a son and heir, another William. Willy was at his happiest when in Hawarden, rather than in London on parliamentary business. He organised the Castle and the estate and was active in the parish, where his great love of music led to his forming a choral society, and also a glee club, at the time a popular form of amateur music making. He played the church organ and also wrote a number of hymns. His comparatively early death in 1891, when he was only just in his fifties, was a terrible blow to the whole family.

Agnes was the second child. She was a very pretty little girl, unsurprisingly, since both parents were good looking. A brush with death when she suffered a severe attack of erysipelas as a toddler had the effect of strengthening the loving bond between her and her parents. Like all the sisters, she was educated at home by a series of governesses, but, unlike the others, she seems to have found this a perfectly satisfactory arrangement. She attracted an admirer while still in her teens, when she was accompanying her parents to the Ionian Islands where her father was Special Commissioner, and officially entered the marriage market on her reception at court at the age of twenty-one. However, she did not make the presumably expected immediate marriage and, showing considerable bravery, told her mother she wanted to become a nurse. Catherine, appalled at the idea that a daughter of hers should break social convention by taking paid employment, absolutely forbade it. Agnes finally created a new life for herself, in her thirties, by the more acceptable route of marriage. Her husband was Edward Wickham, soon to be headmaster of Welling-

Figure 5. Agnes Gladstone (later Wickham). Reproduced by kind permission of Sir William Gladstone.

ton College, later Dean of Lincoln Cathedral. Agnes was the only one of the siblings who lived a life entirely independent of the Gladstone parents, though she kept in constant touch, and took her children on regular visits to Hawarden. She and Stephen did not have much in common and were not particularly close until relatively late in their lives, when he too went to live in Lincolnshire.

Mary was the second surviving daughter. She was quite different from her older sister, not least in her anger at the poor education she considered she had received. She was musical, highly intelligent, decisive and forthright. Incurring her mother's jealousy, she became very close to her father, acting as his political hostess in Downing Street and attracting the friendship of clever men, such as Lords Acton and Rosebery. When she was nearly forty, she gave up the social whirl of London life to marry a man much younger than herself, a country curate whom she met at Hawarden, where he was on Stephen's staff. This three-cornered relationship was never to be easy. She was the sibling physically closest to Stephen throughout the major part of his working life, but temperamentally, they were poles apart.

Helen was the youngest daughter and, aided by Mary, learned from the experience of Agnes. She was the most academically gifted of all the children, and Mary somehow persuaded Catherine, against all the latter's inclinations, to agree to Helen's having a career in academia. At the age of twenty-eight, Helen went to study at what later became Newnham College, Cambridge and was asked to become the Principal's secretary in 1880. She went on to become Vice-Principal of North Hall in 1884. Gladstone was proud of her and she had his full support. Eventually, she gave up her career, and the chance to become Principal of the new Royal Holloway College in Surrey, to go back to Hawarden and look after her parents in their old age. Stephen shared his father's pride in his sister's accomplishments and was much more attached to her than he was to Mary.

Henry Neville (Harry) and Herbert were Stephen's two younger brothers, very close in age. Stephen was fond of both of them. When they went to Eton, although he himself had by then left the school, he gave his younger siblings help and advice, thus echoing Willy's earlier kindness to himself when they were both pupils there. Harry was the only one of the boys who did not go on from Eton to Christ Church, their father's *alma mater*. Perhaps having learnt the lesson of Willy, Gladstone realised that a classical education was not the best outlet for Harry's abilities. Instead, Harry went to King's College (then a specifically Church of England College of the University of London), lodging for a while with Stephen who was at that time a curate in Lambeth. Harry prepared himself for a career in business, with the family firm run by Uncle Robertson in India. Apart from a brief setback when Robertson died, Harry had a most successful fifteen year career out in India, before permanently returning home to England in 1888. His interest in the business continued, and he eventually employed two of Stephen's sons. Late in life, in 1890, he married Maud Rendel.

After Willy's son's death in the First World War, Harry and Maud moved into Hawarden Castle. Harry purchased the succession to the estate, paid off the outstanding mortgage and made many improvements to the Castle, including moving the position of the front door. He succeeded his nephew as Lord Lieutenant of Flintshire and was to be made Baron Gladstone of Hawarden in 1932 and the Constable of Flint Castle in 1934, the year before he died. He was also at various times a director of P&O and of the B.I. Steamship Company, an alderman of Flint County Council, President of the University College of North Wales at Bangor and a Justice of the Peace for both Flintshire and Cheshire. In the midst of all this public work he found time to keep an eye on the family inheritance, particularly Stephen's share, and support his brother in his many times of trouble.

Herbert was the youngest son, much beloved by Catherine, who called him her 'Benjamin'. He followed Willy into politics and, since his heart was in it, was very much

13

more successful. He progressed steadily, and in succeeding governments, through the offices of Junior Lord of the Treasury, Deputy Commissioner of the Office of Works, Financial Secretary to the War Office, Under Secretary of State for the Home Department and First Commissioner of Works, and was appointed a member of the Privy Council. When the Liberals were voted out of office, he became Chief Whip, then Home Secretary when they returned to power. His perceived lack of judgement in this post ironically led, in 1910, to his being appointed first Governor General and High Commissioner of the Union of South Africa. He was created Viscount Gladstone in the same year. He and his much younger wife, Dorothy Paget, whom he had married in 1901, returned to England in 1914. Not a man to enjoy an idle retirement, he then became involved in various charities during the First World War and was made a Knight Grand Cross of the Order of Bath in 1917. He died in 1930, childless, like Harry. Stephen was very proud of his youngest brother's success in public life and Herbert was, again like Harry, a great supporter of Stephen. The three surviving brothers worked closely together on preserving their father's memory and protecting his reputation.

Even from so brief a summary as this, it is clear that Stephen belonged to a family of high achievers, people of determination and drive, by no means all overshadowed by their famous parents. Stephen was cast in a different mould, more sensitive, more anxious. His battles were consequently more introverted, more protracted, more convoluted, more agonising and, therefore, for a biographer, much more interesting.

CHAPTER 1 – BIRTH, EARLY CHILDHOOD AND PREP SCHOOL, 1844–1856

'The slowest in development of all our children'
(Gladstone's Diary: 1 January 1848)

Stephen Edward Gladstone was born on the fourth day of the fourth month of the year 1844, half an hour after midnight. His mother Catherine, formerly Catherine Glynne, was the sister of Sir Stephen Glynne, ninth baronet and owner of Hawarden Castle on the border of Cheshire and North Wales. Catherine was a beautiful and unconventional young woman. She took childbearing in her stride and thought to record Stephen's birth in her diary only some while later, squeezing the bare fact in between two lengthy and enthusiastic entries concerning the social and political scene. Being in the same room as the Duke of Wellington was apparently more thrilling than giving birth, which she had done, conveniently, at 13 Carlton House Terrace, a prestigious, new, Nash-designed residence overlooking St James's Park in the city of Westminster. Stephen's father, William Ewart Gladstone, the future Liberal Prime Minister, was at that time president of the Board of Trade, a rising star in Robert Peel's Conservative government.

Gladstone was present at his son's birth, not at that time unusual behaviour for a man of his class, and he and Catherine prayed with their firstborn son Willy, now nearly four, for the safety of the new arrival. Their second child, Agnes, now about eighteen months old, was deemed to be too young to join in. That night Gladstone recorded in his diary that the baby was like his own father, John: he was strong, and had a larger mouth and nose than those with which either of his siblings had been born. Catherine

15

believed in breastfeeding and although she had an abscess on one breast, which caused some pain, by 10 a.m. she was suckling the new baby on both sides. Stephen began his life as a wanted and welcome addition to a close, loving, god-fearing, solidly High Anglican, privileged family.

The family's main base was Hawarden Castle, the Glynne family home. Originally eighteenth century, later strikingly remodelled in Regency-Gothic style by Sir Stephen Glynne's father, the Castle has been much added to and changed over the years, but the house Stephen knew is still basically as it was in his day. On either side of the main hall there are interconnecting, beautifully proportioned rooms, not big, but elegantly decorated in Regency style, with mouldings and columns, and hung with family portraits. The library, dining room and drawing room all have large windows overlooking lawns and extensive private gardens, with acres of rolling parkland beyond. It was a wonderful place for children to grow up in. The unmarried and childless Sir Stephen was technically the head of the household, but the Gladstones, whom he came to call 'the Great People', were the owners in all but name.

Gladstone added a special room to contain all his books and act as a study when he wasn't in London. He named it the Temple of Peace, but he was quite prepared to allow the children in when he wasn't working, playing boisterous games with them and measuring their heights against the wall. These marks are still clearly visible. The family's London home in Carlton House Terrace was also large and imposing, and they had access to two other stately homes. One of these was Hagley Hall, in Worcestershire, home of Catherine's sister Mary and her husband, Lord Lyttleton, and their large family, where Catherine frequently took the

Figure 6. Hawarden Castle. Reproduced courtesy of Flintshire Record Office.

children to stay. The other, until the death in 1885 of John Gladstone (Stephen's paternal grandfather), was Fasque, the baronial mansion in Aberdeenshire. There is no doubt that Stephen was born with a silver spoon in his mouth. On both sides of the family there was wealth, earned or inherited, connections and titles, and, at least on his mother's side, Stephen had a flock of caring relatives with whom he was in close touch throughout his childhood.

On 1 May 1844, Stephen was baptised at St Martin in the Fields and, according to his father, 'behaved very well'. Gladstone was occupied with government affairs in the capital but Catherine soon took Stephen to her beloved Hawarden. Fresh country air was much healthier than the closeness of central London. There were still fourteen years to go before the Great Stink was to force Parliament to consider vacating Westminster, but conditions were already far from salubrious. Catherine enjoyed the social whirl of London but was always drawn back to Hawarden.

Ever since Willy's birth, Gladstone's work had meant husband and wife spent much time apart, communicating regularly by letter, often, on Catherine's part, more than once a day. Rather in the manner of a twenty-first century wife whipping out her smartphone, Catherine would seize on the nearest piece of paper, however scrappy, pick up her steel pen, and, with little care for punctuation, grammatical accuracy or even legibility, jot down hopes, fears, instructions and the latest of the children's doings. These missives, a gift to the biographer, were despatched not just from Hawarden but also Hagley and the seaside, mainly Brighton or resorts on the North Wales coast.

She had much to tell. Although she employed nursemaids, Catherine, and indeed Gladstone, believed in hands-on parenting and spent a lot of time with the children.

Several of Catherine's diary entries record taking the young Willy for walks. One assumes, and hopes, that it is due to the perfunctory nature of her diary rather than that of her feelings that there are no records of her doing the same with Stephen. Perforce, she was the parent most involved with the children's discipline, and with their earliest schooling. As soon as possible, she embarked on Stephen's religious training, if we are right to assume that the 'trusty boy' of her letter to Gladstone of 9 January 1846, is indeed Stephen: 'I tried trusty boy at [family] prayers but he is too young for he called "Mama" most innocently so I took him out and there we sat at the door when I got him quite quiet with his hands together and he said "amen".'

Three days later she was complaining that he had a will of his own and she had to punish him, which is 'good training': 'Today he would not sit on the side [of the long dining room table] I told him although I had given him his pet play things – it was from mere disobedience & upon my seizing him to send him upstairs he beat me! showing [*sic*] such decision and such a will – dear child I see he is very determined.' The 'good training' did not have a permanent effect. Four years later she was to describe 'a bout with poor Stephy, & it ended in the necessity of whipping he saw how sorrowful it made me and was very penitent … there is plenty of good ground to work upon – there are the very warmest affections & noble parts & there is much wilful determination'.

It was not uncommon in this era for parents to use corporal punishment, on girls as well as boys, if they had been disobedient, or, equally, reprehensible, told lies. We know from his diary that Gladstone himself beat both Agnes and Willy at least once each, though he regretted it afterwards, and he and particularly Catherine shared the view of their peers, namely: 'Spare the rod and spoil the child.' The woeful lack of determination which Stephen was often to show as an adult, might be traced back to such formative experiences. The idea that he might have a will of his own was beaten out of him at an early age.

Both parents seem to have had reservations about their second son's nature, abilities and even appearance. In his diary Gladstone described him, at three and three quarter years old, as, though very affectionate, a trait recorded also by Catherine, 'the slowest in development of all our children and the most difficult to understand'. As far as we know, the diary was intended as a purely personal record. This must therefore be an honest, if rather sad, assessment. When Stephen was five and a half, his mother described him as a 'curious' child, by which she seems to have meant 'strange', since she went on to say that 'there is much in him for good or evil'. Even allowing for the fact that this was in her own personal diary, the comment suggests an oddly unsympathetic maternal attitude. Catherine also noted how thin-skinned he was, a trait which dogged him throughout his life, and, referring to a friend's admiration of his hair, she commented to his father, 'poor fellow his only good feature'.

She could be touchy, however, if others criticised her son's looks. On 30 January 1846, Queen Victoria, with whom Catherine was, and remained, on excellent terms, asked her to take her four children (another sister, Jessy, had been born in 1845) to Buckingham Palace to meet her own four. The Queen, somewhat tactlessly, told Catherine that she thought Stephen, then still under two, was 'gigantic' and baby Jessy fat. Catherine got her own back privately by recording the 'thick white necks' of the royal children and the Prince of Wales's small stature compared with that of Willy. As he grew up, Stephen lost his puppy fat and turned into a slim, well-proportioned man of middle height. His general appearance, admittedly unremarkable as a young man, improved with age, and by the time he reached his sixties, photographs show him as being almost handsome, with white hair clustered in curls just above his clerical collar.

His unprepossessing appearance might have been one of the reasons why he was never centre stage at home and, being an uncomplaining child, he did not seek to draw attention or sympathy to himself, apparently accepting his very weak eyesight as the norm. Although this problem resulted in frequent poor health in later years, Stephen as a child was, unlike several of his siblings, free from serious health concerns, another reason why he always remained in the shadows.

Catherine was a splendid nurse, according to her husband, and was ever ready with doses of 'grey powder' – name unknown and possibly a home-made family remedy – whenever the children were sickening for something. This panacea was of little use, however, in 1847. Stephen was three, when his older sister, Agnes, had a dangerous attack of erysipelas, a febrile skin disease which had killed Gladstone's mother and from which Catherine also intermittently suffered. For days, the family feared for Agnes's life, but she recovered, and thanks were duly offered up to God. A few years later, at about the time of Stephen's sixth birthday, in April 1850, four-year-old Jessy, the sister nearest to him in age, contracted meningitis. In spite of many prayers, the little girl died after several days of excruciating pain. This death was presented to Stephen and his siblings by the grieving parents as God's will, but it must have severely shaken his childhood beliefs. If God had spared Agnes, why did he let Jessy die? He found it hard to comprehend, as we can see from the wish he expressed to his paternal grandfather, of whom he was very fond: 'I should like to see Jessy again. I mean I should like to see the place where she is.' Gladstone, devastated by his daughter's death, took Jessy's body up to Fasque for burial, but Stephen was never taken to see her resting place in the family vault.

Before Jessy's death, two more sisters, Mary and Helen, had been born, and shortly after Jessy died, Mary became the next child to give cause for concern. She had developed serious eye trouble, and her parents took her to Naples for its reputedly health-giving air. Agnes went with them, because Catherine felt her older daughter was at the age when she needed to be with her mother. Willy was by then away at his boarding prep school, but Stephen and baby Helen were despatched to Hagley to be looked after by their Aunt Mary, Catherine announcing that he would be happier with companions of his own age, that is, his cousins. Stephen wrote to his mother in huge childish handwriting, saying he was sorry he'd been naughty but was now 'a better boy' and so was allowed by his governess to write to her. He can't wait for his mother to come back to him and sounds thoroughly miserable.

The big writing might give us a clue about a problem in embryo: his sight was far worse than Mary's, since he'd been born with a congenital cataract in his right eye, a condition which was to go undiagnosed for years. When the family was back from Naples, with Mary's eyes in a much healthier state, his parents at last got a doctor to investigate Stephen's eyesight. As a result he was prescribed an eye patch to wear during lessons. He must have worn this over the eye in which he had no sight anyway, and although it was presumably intended to make the other eye work harder, it had no effect. Later he was to have numerous operations, but he only ever had the use of his left eye, and suffered increasingly from severe eye strain and sick headaches. He was eventually prescribed glasses, but they were of little more use than the eye patch.

The picture of a solemn, chubby little boy with a big nose, oversized mouth, and one eye obscured by a black patch is both sad and amusing. It would not be surprising if Catherine, badly missing nine-year-old Willy when he was sent to boarding school, felt that the presence of the less favoured Stephen was small compensation. However, she did not neglect his education. Like his siblings, Stephen had some lessons with a succession of governesses, all of whom were closely supervised. A Miss Browne had actually been dismissed some years earlier for being too harsh with Willy over his sums. Catherine herself also taught Stephen, as she did all the children, sharing the subjects with her husband, his specialties being Holy Scripture and Latin.

After one of her early teaching sessions with Stephen, Catherine, with her usual disregard for punctuation, reported to Gladstone, by now busier than ever as Colonial Secretary: 'This morning reading with me about a pony putting his nose into someone's pockets he read pocket. I said look at the s after a pause "it should not be pockets how could the pony put his nose into two?"' A couple of years later he displayed the same kind of considered analytical response. On being asked, 'Stephy do you like plays?' the eight-year-old boy replied, after a pause, 'What kind of plays do you mean?' This scrupulous regard for accuracy was inherited, as were so many of Stephen's characteristics, from his father.

These anecdotes about Stephen are unusual features in his mother's letters. Generally, even after Willy's departure for school, Stephen does not feature so much in Catherine's correspondence as do the other children. Variously over the years, she reported on his improved walking powers; showed some anxiety over his minor childhood illnesses; related his concern over her own health – 'how are you Mama is your throat better let me see your tongue'; and commented approvingly on the 'real interest' he showed in the verses, presumably biblical, she taught him each day. But these mentions of Stephen are often at the very end of a letter and squeezed in, partly illegibly, at the extreme edge of the page. It would be wrong to deduce from this that Catherine necessarily cared less for Stephen than his siblings, but there must be a suspicion that she had more affection for not only Willy, the heir, but also the little girls.

It is symptomatic of Stephen's low profile in the family that his birthday on at least two occasions coincided with big events which distracted attention away from him. Two years after the death of Jessy, his birthday – his eighth – was again put in the shade, but this time by a happier event: the birth of a baby brother, named Henry Neville – to be known as Harry. This brother, and the next one, Herbert born in 1854 when Stephen was at school, obviously played a much smaller part in his childhood than his other siblings. Yet in adult life, he was to be closer to them than to any of the others. There seems to have been mutual respect, they for an older and reliable brother of steadfast if unworldly principle, he for two younger but able siblings, with practical abilities in commerce and politics.

The year before Harry's birth, in 1851, Stephen acquired a new governess, a Miss Pearson, on whom at first meeting, according to Catherine, he gazed in silent awe. There was a mutual attraction between teacher and taught, which caused Catherine to comment, somewhat caustically, and not at all maternally: 'very odd how that child seems to inspire love – she [Miss Pearson] remarked what a dear little fellow he was'. In Catherine's defence, it can be offered that she had within the last eighteen months watched a daughter die, suffered a miscarriage and waved her oldest son off to school. Even so, this coldness is remarkable.

Gladstone also seems not to have been quite at ease with his second son. He was a loving, if often absent, father, seeking to replicate the 'torrents of affection' he received from his own father, and he took a great interest in his children's development. He recorded all their birthdays in his diary and each year wrote a summary of their emerging qualities. On various occasions he praised Willy's skill at cricket and his intelligence – though he 'wanted solidity of scholarship' – Agnes's dancing, and Mary and Lena (Helen's) piano playing, and he recorded in detail conversations he had with Agnes, Mary, and later with Harry and Herbert. It is noticeable, however, that Stephen is mentioned less often than his siblings in his father's diary, just as he is mentioned less often in his mother's letters. Maybe this was because he was more self-effacing, or restricted by his poor eyesight from taking part in various activities. Playing a musical instrument, for example, would not have been possible, since he would have been unable to read the music from the necessary distance. Cricket must have been a nightmare. Moreover, Mary was turning out to be a tomboy, and her activities further eclipsed those of the rather timid Stephen. He must have been grateful for the interest the new governess, Miss Pearson, took in him.

Part of her duty was to prepare her charge for prep school, but Catherine, perhaps remembering Willy's unsatisfactory Miss Browne, wanted Stephen to be tutored in mathematics by a man, and asked Gladstone to find someone in London. This must have been a demand more to his taste than her usual ones such as 'Could you order some toothbrushes and brushes cheap.' Willy, in his holidays, was also conscripted to help his younger brother. Willy, as she reported to her husband, 'is helping a little & thinks Stephy is more intelligent'. This sentiment is wonderfully, though certainly unintentionally, ambiguous. It is not possible to tell if his older brother found Stephen more intelligent than he was himself, more intelligent than when he last talked to him about schoolwork, or just more intelligent than he expected. If the latter, then it reflects rather badly on what Catherine had told Willy about his brother. Whatever the content and upshot of these lessons, Stephen was never to enjoy mathematics. He infinitely preferred the classics, and here again, the older brother was called on to assist. Two years later, Catherine reported that Willy was correcting his brother's Latin 'very steadily'. This might mean either that there were a lot of errors to correct, or that Willy is a conscientious tutor, or both. In either case, it seems that the tutor-pupil relationship was not resented by either boy.

Whether thanks to Miss Pearson, or the maths master, or Willy, by 1853 Stephen, aged nine, was deemed ready to go away to school, and the first and best part of his childhood ended. He was sent to join Willy at his prep school in Geddington, near Kettering in Northants. Presumably to boost his confidence, his father gave Stephen a series of Latin lessons in the months before he started school. Gladstone was glad of the opportunity to get to know his son better, and according to his diary, he found Stephen diligent, with good reasoning powers, although he had a poor memory and was slow to grasp new ideas. It was typical of Gladstone that he should so clear-sightedly describe his son's strengths and weaknesses. But in spite of his reservations, by then he seemed to have warmed to Stephen far more than had Catherine. Gladstone liked what he was learning of

Stephen's character: his tenderness and humility, and his growing intelligence.

Not long before he began school, his father had Stephen with him at dinner *à deux* one evening. During the meal the little boy admitted that the manliness he was displaying was only a front; he was actually scared at the thought of leaving home. Gladstone was sympathetic, but of course there was no question of Stephen not going away. All boys of his social class were sent to prep schools, and his cousins, the sons of Catherine's sister Mary and Lord Lyttleton, as well as his brother Willy, were already at Geddington. Between them, the Gladstones and Lyttletons made up about a quarter of the total school roll of twenty or so boys.

On the face of it, the parental choice of Geddington School, Kettering, is odd. Kettering is near neither family home, being well over 100 miles from Hawarden and sixty-seven miles from London. The headmaster, a Rev. William Montagu Church, was known to have a furious temper and the school was not academically renowned. There were better schools in existence, which the Gladstones surely knew of. There was, for example, one in Hammersmith, which would have been within easy reach of the London home in Carlton House Terrace. That school was run by Edward Wickham, father of the other, more famous, Edward Wickham, who was later to become headmaster of Wellington School, Dean of Lincoln Cathedral and husband of Stephen's oldest sister, Agnes.

Geddington seems to have been chosen not for academic reasons but because of the Gladstone family association with its founder, the Duke of Buccleugh. He had business connections with Gladstone's father and social connections with Catherine, who was on visiting terms with the family in London. She noted in her erratically kept diary an occasion when she had taken Willy and Agnes to breakfast with the Duchess.

Throughout Stephen's time at Geddington, Mr Church wrote regularly to Catherine, reassuring her about the healthy climate the school enjoyed – a popular ploy in epidemic-fearing Victorian England – and the special help he was giving her son because of his sight problems. At first, Church gave Stephen one-to-one tuition at the times of day when the light was best, and allowed him to read out his classical translations rather than writing them. He seems to have left off these practices as soon as possible. He told Catherine they were no longer necessary, thus cunningly emphasising the success of his personally tailored pedagogic methods while ensuring that he didn't have to spend any more time pursuing them.

Mr Church found Stephen quiet, conscientious and obedient. These traits were no doubt cultivated by Stephen in order to avoid the beatings received by his fellow pupils, which were violent, frequent and public. His cousin Neville Lyttleton later remembered how one boy was boxed savagely on the ears before being thrashed black and blue, for making a single grammatical error. Neville himself and his brother Spencer were thrashed regularly every day for a week for not finishing set tasks on time. Stephen wrote to his parents saying, 'I have not been flogged yet.' He clearly did not expect to escape permanently.

Gladstone seems to have accepted severe corporal punishment as a necessary, perhaps even desirable, part of school life, even if he was less happy about resorting to it at home. Catherine, though she herself was not slow to employ the whip, may have been more concerned. When the time came for the two youngest sons, Harry and Herbert, to go to the school, which Mr Church had by then moved to

Hunstanton, she tried, though without success, to persuade her husband to let them remain at home with tutors. Both boys were as miserable, and as ill-educated, in Mr Church's school at Hunstanton as had been their older brothers at Geddington. Incidentally, Hunstanton is even further away from both family homes, being nearly 150 miles away from Hawarden, and 100 miles from London.

Right from the start Stephen wrote home regularly from school, individually to both parents, who were still perforce frequently apart, with Gladstone, now Chancellor of the Exchequer, in London and Catherine at Hawarden or Hagley. Although she later sometimes grumbled about the contents of Stephen's letters, Catherine was delighted over the first one she received, realising he had 'taken enormous pains' over it. A year later, she forwarded one of his letters to Gladstone, describing it as 'excellent ... some part of the writing is more like Willy's'. As usual, she was comparing Stephen with the heir and favourite, although she also noted proudly that Stephen's letters were better than those of one of her Lyttleton nephews who was older than their own son.

From these letters we know what Stephen endured. The school day began at 6.30 a.m., a particularly wretched time in the cold dark winter months, with exiguous heating, light only from candles, and breakfast nearly two hours away. Before they were given anything to eat, the boys had to learn and be tested on Latin grammar by the irascible, cane-wielding Mr Church, then attend prayers. The rest of the day was spent on a variety of subjects, including scripture, history, 'arithmatic' as Stephen spells it, and 'geaghraphy' which he found particularly difficult because of the small print on maps. There were some periods of recreation and some treats – he writes about fun scrambling over rocks, possibly on the Buccleugh estate, nearby Boughton Park –

but on most days schoolwork went on till 6 p.m., by which time in the winter it would long have been cold and dark again.

He tried to put a brave face on things, particularly at the beginning of his time there. He worked hard and on one occasion came top of his class, but he found school frightening at worst, dull at best, and constantly longed for the holidays, counting the days, sometimes starting as far as six weeks ahead, to 'joyous joyous HOLYDAYS [*sic*, and always spelt thus by the Gladstones], hurrah, hurrah, hurrah, hurrah'. In his letters home he endlessly repeated how happy he was, either in a desire to appear manly or to stop his mother from worrying, and presumably Catherine was ready to believe him. His gratitude for parental letters, and his admission that he kept all his father's letters in his desk, belie his assurances. The keeping of the letters in his desk seems especially sad. It suggests that he had nowhere else of his own to stow his treasures. It is hard from a modern perspective to see how such bleak conditions could ever have been thought to be essential character training for life. Maybe Geddington was exceptionally brutal, but if this is the case, its selection does not reflect well on the Gladstone parents.

Certainly the school run by Edward Wickham in Hammersmith was both far more humane and more educationally effective. A Hammersmith old boy remembered his headmaster, Wickham, as not unkind, if austere, and his teaching as lively and stimulating. Only Sundays were apparently 'dull'. Wickham's school prepared boys well for public school, unlike Geddington, where Neville Lyttleton tells us the necessary skills for Eton entrance – writing Latin verse – were poorly taught. As can be seen from his letters to Catherine, the sycophantic Mr

Church was more interested in the aristocratic backgrounds of the boys on roll, than in their academic achievement.

In Stephen's yearned-for holidays from school, he was free to roam the grounds of Hawarden and Hagley with Willy and his sisters and cousins, and there were regular visits to the elegant, recently developed seaside resorts of Rhyl in North Wales and Brighton on the south coast. Catherine, always looking for a chance to bathe, took the children away even if her husband was too busy to be with them. In March 1856, the usual situation was reversed. Catherine was at the fashionable seaside resort of St Leonard's, near Hastings, with the younger children, escaping a scarlet fever epidemic in Hawarden, while Stephen and Willy stayed with their father in London. Willy wrote to their mother saying how much they were enjoying the 'cozy' [sic] dinners and she admitted in a letter to Gladstone to being jealous, while making it clear that 'it is such a great advantage any moment they see of you'. Catherine was always torn between her desire to have her husband with the family in the country or at the seaside and her wish to see him promoting his political career in London. That year, when Stephen's birthday came round at the beginning of April, she asked Gladstone to advance him half a sovereign on her behalf. Birthdays were enormously important in the Gladstone family. In his diary, Gladstone himself noted every one of his children's birthdays, however busy he was, and wherever he might be, and all the family wrote birthday letters to each other, forever apologising if they were for any reason late in marking the occasion.

In the holidays spent at Hawarden and Hagley, there was cricket, which Willy especially enjoyed, and the poor-sighted Stephen gallantly joined in. When he was nine, which must have been during his first holiday from

Geddington, Catherine wrote to Gladstone telling him that 'cricket goes on high gee [*sic*, Glynnese, the private Glynne family language] and ... Stephy & Agnes are wonderfully improved in the art'. As well as cricket, the children enjoyed less structured pleasures. There were extensive grounds at Hagley, but the Park surrounding Hawarden Castle was even bigger. There were trees to climb, or help their father to cut down, a stream to dam, a lake to skate on in winter, muddy ponds to paddle in and acres of grassy slopes to race around. When Gladstone was there, Stephen went walking and riding in the park with his father who, when down from London, spent as much time as he could with his children, taking pleasure in their company and discussing their hopes and plans. One day, on a visit to his uncle, the Rev. Henry Glynne, at the Rectory in Hawarden, Stephen, then eleven, first announced his own hopes, declaring that he wanted to be a clergyman when he grew up, if he 'could see how to manage the sermons'.

CHAPTER 2 - ETON, 1856-1862

'There is much yet to grow out of him.'
(Gladstone's Diary: 4 November 1856)

Soon after that pronouncement, Stephen went to Eton, again following in Willy's footsteps, as well as those of his father, who recorded in his diary 'with cheerful confidence' that he believed his younger son would flourish there. Stephen set off armed with a series of admonitions, a later copy of which, in what may be his niece Dossie's handwriting, is to be found in a box of effects recently unearthed by his grandson, Sir William Gladstone. The demands bear all the marks of Catherine's stern but maternal concern, not to mention her disregard for the rules of punctuation and sentence structure:

> Never omit your prayers, night and morning, in Church always behave reverently. Be brave and always tell the Truth, to lie is very cowardly & greatly injures your character. Make some good friends – passing by any bad boys, though not with any unkindness to them. Keep your hands and your heart pure from sin: and do not utter any words you know are bad. When tempted – Remember that God's eye is now watching you. Try and always act worthily of your father, your mother, your happy home.

It is likely that Stephen committed this charge to memory: he certainly tried to abide by it, both at school and well beyond boyhood.

He signed the Eton Admissions Book on 17 April 1856, in nervously shaky copperplate: 'Gladstone, Stephen Edward'. Eton, with its impressive buildings, spacious courtyard, vast playing fields, and over eight hundred boys

33

in the Upper School, must have seemed enormous after Geddington. Fortunately, the custom was for brothers to be put in the same house – in this case Mr Coleridge's – and to share rooms. There is no extant photograph, as far as I am aware, of Mr Coleridge's house, but there does exist a group photograph of the Rev. W. B. Marriot's house, taken in the early 1860s. A three-storey, ivy-covered brick building provides the background. The top-hatted housemaster sits in front, correcting the work of one of his boys. About twenty-four other boys, all dressed in light trousers, black jackets and Eton collars, a few with top hats, are ranged in rows to his right. It is to be supposed that, as with official school photographs today, this does not capture a real situation, but it does give us some idea of what things were like. It emphasises the way in which the school population consisted of a series of small units – the houses – each with its housemaster, who was not only the figure *in loco parentis* but also an individual tutor for the boys in his charge.

Each house contained both communal rooms and study bedrooms. Every study had a table, chairs, beds, an ottoman and a bureau. There was an open fire which a maid usually lit in the morning. The fire was not only a means of heating: kettles were provided which the boys could use for brewing tea. This must have been good fun for youngsters whose catering needs had previously been provided by servants, both at prep school and at home. As at Geddington, the only light, apart from the firelight, was from candles, and Stephen wrote home saying how hard it was for him to see to read. This was surely a constant worry for him, since by now he can't have had much hope that his sight would ever improve. Apart from this personal anxiety, the quality of life was much better than at prep school. The boys rose at 7 a.m. in the summer and 7.30 a.m. in winter, much more humane hours than those at Geddington, and they were not expected to be in bed until between 10.30 and 11 p.m.

We do not know if Mr Coleridge was one of those housemasters who insisted on attendance at morning and evening prayers in the school chapel, but even if he did not, Stephen probably went: he was a devout child. With all the other boys, he attended compulsory Chapel on Sunday morning, when he might or might not have been able to hear the sermons. These, often largely inaudible, consisted, as one former pupil who could actually hear them wrote, of 'scholarly expositions of texts which read like footnotes from our Greek Testament'. According to this pupil, the boys were also on these occasions 'instructed in mild general terms about the higher moralities'.

It doesn't sound very inspiring, and there was often poor behaviour in Chapel, though not from Stephen, except accidentally: not long after his arrival, as he confessed in a letter home, a kneeling mat slipped, provoking uncontrolled giggling fits. It seems that he was kneeling with a group of friends, and although boys were not supposed to form friendships outside their houses, out of the forty-five or so boys in his own house (the maximum allowed was fifty; Marriot's was smaller than average), Stephen would have had quite a number of boys of his own age to choose from. He spent his leisure time with these friends in the House, where the main midday meal and light supper were eaten in the communal dining room, and breakfast and tea in their bedrooms, where boys often met to share rations and make their own tea.

Out of doors, to develop corporate spirit and physical fitness and channel surplus energy, there were plenty of activities such as bathing, rowing, cross-country running and field games, including cricket, and the Rifle Volunteer

Corps. The poor-sighted Stephen did not write about participation in any of these activities, not even rowing, although, to his intense pleasure, his own sons later participated keenly and with great success in this sport. Indoor activities appealed to him more. We know he belonged to the debating society, because some years after he left, he described in a letter to Herbert, by then at Eton himself, an occasion when he, Stephen, spoke against fagging, 'the only one on that side'. That must have taken some nerve.

Stephen had not himself suffered from the fagging system, thanks to his older brother. Willy, who was a kind boy by nature and remembered how unhappy he himself had been when he first arrived at Eton, took Stephen under his wing and acted as his fagmaster, employing him to perform such tasks as boot cleaning and the running of errands. This meant that Stephen was protected from bullying, and in any case there was mercifully less of that than there had been in their father's day.

There had been a number of other changes for the better too: various pointless ancient rules, such as the one making streets on the way to the river out of bounds, while the river itself was not, had been scrapped. Masters were more friendly and less strict, and there was less flogging, which must have been a relief after Mr Church's violent regime. There were official school trips, including one to the National Gallery, during which their tutor bought them all ice creams. There were also unofficial trips, to the nearby annual Windsor Fair, which was strictly out of bounds, not least because of the gambling which took place there. In theory, boys caught in any part of the town during the Fair were flogged, and if they were found actually in Bachelor's Acre, where the roulette tables were laid out, they could be sent down to a lower division (form). In practice, much greater leniency prevailed, and some masters even lent boys money to go to the fair. Masters would often chase boys they saw breaking the rules, but not always follow things up if the boys got away, as we have to assume Stephen did, the year he went to the Fair and witnessed the 'gamboling', as he described it to his father.

The education Stephen received at Eton was very different from that on offer in most state or even public schools today. There was no Science at all and the emphasis was still on the Classics, although other subjects were taught, including Divinity, History and the recently introduced Mathematics. Stephen retained his dislike of Mathematics, possibly because the masters who taught it had less authority than the others and consequently found discipline more difficult to maintain. This would have upset Stephen, who needed peace and quiet in order to concentrate and learn: people who cannot see well need to hear clearly. Modern languages were also on offer, but were extracurricular, with a low take-up. Stephen did not opt for these lessons, nor did he need to, since Gladstone taught all his children some Italian and he and Catherine both taught them French.

The general standard of teaching seems to have been surprisingly low, and indeed the 1861 Royal Commission into public schools found more to condemn at Eton than at all the other schools put together. Stephen spent most of his time learning lessons by heart and then repeating them over and over again. Cribs were much in use in the initial preparation of Greek and Latin texts, which took place in the boys' studies in their House, with the younger boys made to stand on guard to warn their seniors of potential discovery. We don't know if Stephen, or Willy, used cribs, and it is probable that they did not, since their rigid moral training at home would have induced strong feelings of guilt, and Stephen certainly would have felt obliged to admit such wrongdoing in a letter home: no such letter exists.

After this initial private study, with or without a crib, each lesson was gone over in the Pupil Room in the House, perhaps twice, with the tutor, and then repeated twice more. As if this wasn't boring enough, there was a relatively narrow range of authors, represented mostly through extracts in anthologies rather than complete texts, so there was no sense of engaging with a work of literature. Worse still, the three successive divisions of the Fifth Form all studied the same texts. Every Friday morning, sixty lines of Horace had to be prepared. On Saturday, everyone did thirty to thirty-five lines of Theocritus. There seems to have been a mind-numbing lack of imagination on the part of the school authorities. It is tempting to think that the Latin lessons his father had given to Stephen years before were far more entertaining. Gladstone had a lively and lifelong interest in classical literature, feeling a particular affinity for Homer. He was still working on an edition of the Odes of Horace when in his eighties.

Stephen's lessons, as opposed to preparatory sessions in the House, were in Upper School, a large hall in which the eight hundred or so boys were taught all at once, by several masters, with curtains between the divisions (classes). These divisions were large, with anything from sixty to seventy-five boys. Anyone with any experience of schools will not be surprised that Old Etonians writing later about their schooldays record masters turning up late and 'sheer chaos in some quarters'.

Apart from Mathematics, which was taught not in Upper School but in separate rooms, no written work was done in class. Indeed it would not have been possible. The benches were close together and the boys held their books on their knees. Lessons each lasted an hour and must have been physically very uncomfortable. Greek lessons consisted simply of parsing, that is, describing the grammatical function of each separate word. As the divisions were so large, time constraints meant each boy mumbled his way through just a few lines. Since the same order was always observed, it must have been possible to work out in advance how likely you were to be called on, and which bit of the text you would have to present. 'To take care of the few and let the many take care of themselves was as much as any master could be expected to do', wrote an ex-Etonian, and since Stephen was inconspicuous, we may assume he was one of those who had to take care of himself.

In Latin, matters were slightly more interesting. A weekly theme was set, for example the character of Julius Caesar. The master would throw out a few headings about which he would then discourse generally while Stephen and his classmates scribbled frantically in pencil on the flyleaves of their books. The master followed a similar procedure when setting the Latin verses for his pupils to compose. When the boys had written their themes and verses, it was their tutor in the House who initially went over their work with them and corrected their efforts. After that, the boys wrote out fair copies which they presented in the hall to the division master. As often as not he would glance briefly at the work and then simply consign it to the waste paper bin, unless it merited being 'sent up' to the Headmaster, as happened to Stephen a couple of times.

Another weekly exercise was 'maps and description' which sounds like a change from the Classics, but wasn't really. Each boy was handed an outline map of a classical country, on which he had to fill in the details, which he could look up in the school library. As at Geddington, such close work was especially difficult for Stephen with his poor eyesight. The dreary scholastic routine occupied the whole day, until 6 p.m., on Mondays, Wednesdays and Fridays. Tuesdays were half holidays and Thursdays and Saturdays ended at 4 p.m. Sundays were free after compulsory morning Chapel. The work was unremitting and there were few creature comforts, but it was better than Geddington and Stephen was not unhappy at Eton.

Every term ('half') ended in examinations ('trials') which, since there was no room in Upper School for written work, were mostly in the form of orals, and consisted of construing and 'saying lessons', that is, repeating yet again what they had done already. This suited Stephen, as it saved him from straining his eyes with reading and writing under pressure of time. At the end of trials, a list was published in merit order, and prizes awarded, but the business was relatively unthreatening, since advancement to the next division was unaffected.

More important were the end of year examinations, on which promotion depended and in which there were written papers in Classics, Divinity, History and Mathematics. To make writing possible, scores of little brown desks were placed about a yard apart amongst the benches in Upper School. The second set of large red curtains, which divided the hall into three, were drawn back. Masters stood on rostra, invigilating. The boys wrote with steel pens and many, though surely not Stephen, cheated with cribs. As his first set of examinations approached, Stephen wrote home saying he believed his parents knew he would do his best, and he did do his best, but the poor light coming in from the high windows made it hard for him even to read the paper, and he was grateful when on one occasion another boy seated in better light kindly offered to change places with him.

Stephen seems to have failed one early set of examinations, perhaps his first, 'chiefly from his Greek', according to an older Lyttleton cousin, who was quick to add, to Catherine, that 'excepting this & his holyday task he did very well'. Stephen survived this setback and in March 1857 his housemaster gave him 'a very good character' stressing how he was 'working gallantly with his impediments', but expressing the fear that 'he might be crushed were he unkindly or impatiently used'. This is a much more astute assessment by Mr Coleridge than anything ever offered by Mr Church. Coleridge expressed the hope that a Mr Marriott, whom Stephen liked, might become his tutor, and this did indeed happen, with Marriott giving Stephen 'an excellent character' a year later. There is an area of confusion here. If this Marriott was the same Rev. W. B. Marriot, with only one 't', as was photographed with his house in 1860, then either Stephen changed houses, which is unlikely and certainly not mentioned in letters, or, more likely, Marriott, with or without a second 't', was an undermaster in 1858 and was later promoted to a house of his own. Whatever the actual circumstances, the main inference is the same: Eton cared about Stephen's welfare.

The end of the half did not mark the end of schoolwork. Holiday tasks were set, consisting of the writing of sixty lines of Latin verse on a biblical subject. Stephen's family also made sure his education continued in the holidays. Catherine gave him some French lessons and he went up in her opinion, partly because he outshone his cousin Albert Lyttleton in both French and English, and partly because, as she admitted, he had 'improved in figure and general looks'.

Stephen was also coached in the holidays by Gladstone in Horace and Virgil, on one occasion voluntarily, or so his father said, doing a double lesson. He was always a conscientious worker and it was obvious to him and to his father that as he lacked natural academic brilliance, a lot of hard work, mostly of course involving reading, would be necessary if he were to succeed. Anxious to help him with his eyesight, in his first long holiday, on the afternoon of 26 July 1856, his parents arranged for him to have an operation to divide an eye muscle. This operation was performed in London, mercifully with the relatively newly available chloroform. Stephen was left with pain, depression, little appetite in the evening and the prospect of another operation the next day. Neither, since his condition had been misdiagnosed, did much good.

Not all the holidays were taken up with study, and happy days were spent at Hawarden and Hagley. The cousins all played together, usually harmoniously, for example digging a deep hole in the garden, but of course there was naughtiness too: on one occasion Stephen let Agnes's canary out of its cage. Mary told their mother about this misdemeanour, whether in a spirit of amused tolerance or sisterly spite it is hard to tell. Astonishingly, in view of his eyesight, Stephen took part with the others in shooting matches.

In 1858, their parents were in the Ionian Islands where Gladstone was acting as Special Commissioner, and with the exception of the now teenage Agnes, the children were left behind. Letters from both Mary and Stephen tell us how much they missed their parents, and the parents also missed their children. Catherine, particularly, wanted the children with her whenever possible. An undated letter from Brighton, possibly written in March 1858 and so just before the Ionian trip, gave Stephen instructions about train times, cheap tickets and so on and continues 'don't think me tiresome if I beg you to come on the Friday ... there is a little room where you can write undisturbed far quieter than in London ... dying to see you in our lodging and you will save a cake. Bless you. Your own mother who longs to see you.' This letter is not self-explanatory, and the cake is a total mystery, but it seems to imply that Stephen, on holiday from Eton, is staying with his father in London, while Catherine is with the other, or some of the other, younger children at the seaside. We don't know if he joined her there but he probably bowed to the maternal will. Catherine's influence over her second son was at least as strong as was that of his father.

Apart from the official holidays, Eton boys could be given special leave to attend important events, and this must have been granted to Stephen in May 1859, when he was confirmed at Cuddesdon in Oxford by a great friend of his father, Bishop Samuel Wilberforce. Gladstone prepared his son for this significant step in his religious life both by having a long conversation with him the month before, and by writing him a letter, which was, perhaps to save time, identical to the one he had written years before to Willy for the same purpose. Gladstone also attended the Confirmation service, with Catherine. Nearly ten years later, Stephen was to write to Harry saying that 'no moment is so important to one as confirmation'.

Gladstone's letter stressed the centrality of Holy Communion in Christian worship, the importance of resisting temptation, and his own readiness to answer any questions his son might have. No doubt he was aware that Eton at that time, in spite of compulsory Sunday Chapel, was not much concerned with spiritual development.

Throughout Gladstone's life, he and Stephen were frequently to discuss, in conversations and letters, matters of faith, with the father directing the son's reading, though not necessarily his thinking. (In 1917, when Stephen was reading his father's diaries, he told Herbert, somewhat cryptically, that 'I am rather a heathen in the domain especially of the moral and religious part of them.')

Eventually Stephen tired of Eton and announced, in February 1861, that he wanted to leave school early, not proceeding to the Sixth Form. He gave his father various reasons: recurrent problems with eye strain, particularly bad in the dark winter months; a desire to concentrate on Classics and History, rather than the detested Mathematics; and the noise and distraction from building work which had just begun. He also thought that he would simply be repeating the same work over again and in this he was certainly correct. Willy and his father tried to make him change his mind but finally, on 8 January 1862, that is, nearly twelve months later, Gladstone recorded in his diary: 'Conversation with S. Settled his leaving Eton at Easter, on his own wish.'

CHAPTER 3 – CHRIST CHURCH, CUMBRAE AND CUDDESDON: PREPARATION FOR THE PRIESTHOOD, 1862–1868

'You do well not to let your mind rest on anything beyond what may lie fairly within your reach.'
(Gladstone's Diary: 17 July 1866)

Stephen now had a private tutor to prepare him for entrance to Christ Church, Oxford, where, as at Eton, he followed Willy and his father. He passed the written examinations and, armed with practical fatherly advice on the use and value of money, went up to the University in October 1862. Henry Liddell was Dean of Christ Church. In his thirty-six years in office, Liddell made many changes, all for the better, but Stephen's years there were not a particularly glorious time in the college's history. One of his contemporaries later referred to 'dull apathy' among the undergraduates and 'sullen discontent' occasionally breaking out in rowdyism. Another contemporary remembered card-playing for high stakes and almost nightly wine parties. The majority of the approximately 250 (male) undergraduates were from wealthy noble families and they dominated the college, even sitting at the doctors' table on the dais in Hall at dinner. Stephen would have felt little in common with these riotous rich young aristocrats, who belonged to various 'sets', but he found a niche in 'one strong and quiet set who held their own'.

Stephen was thrilled to be at Christ Church, partly because he was proud to be following in his father's footsteps, and partly, one imagines, because of the character and history of the college itself. In the heart of the city, bound by its meadow and the rivers Cherwell and Isis, it

45

was, and still is, one of the largest and most prestigious of the university colleges. Its beautiful buildings date back to a ninth-century monastery which was transformed into a college by Cardinal Wolsey, who created Tom Quad, the largest in Oxford. When the college was re-founded by Henry VIII in 1546, the old monastery church, a gorgeous Romanesque building, became the cathedral of the diocese of Oxford. The college is rich in history. During the Civil War, Charles I, driven out of London, lived there and held his parliament in the Great Hall. Christopher Wren designed a new bell tower in 1682 to house 'Great Tom', and a magnificent library, begun in Elizabeth's time, was finally completed in the eighteenth century, specifically designed to attract aristocratic students with its elegance. It clearly succeeded.

Stephen seems to have been no more troubled than was Gladstone that, as at Eton, the spiritual life of the college was somewhat low key. Daily chapel attendance was not enforced and Holy Communion was celebrated only once a month. In the year before Stephen went up, the old Latin prayer book with which his father had been familiar had been superseded by the English version. Otherwise, things were much the same. He wrote ecstatically to his father saying that he 'felt sure that with God's blessing, this will be the happiest part of my life'. Gladstone must have been delighted.

Although he was certain of his vocation for the priesthood, Stephen chose to study not theology, which was in any case not to become a regular degree subject until the 1870s, but Greats, like his father and brother before him, and indeed like most aspirant churchmen. The syllabus suited his temperament and abilities well. The emphasis, as at Eton, was on the minutely accurate preparation of set texts, which was laborious, but favoured earnest and consistent effort, which Stephen never shied from, in spite of his poor eyesight and still uncertain health. This was before the days of intercollegiate lectures, and the teaching, mainly of ancient literary, historical and philosophical works, and commentaries on them, was in small groups, with only occasional larger scale classes.

Henry L. Thompson, who went up in 1858, four years before Stephen, recorded in 1900, 'with the help of a somewhat treacherous memory', that there were 180 graduates in his time, under the care of six classical tutors. Thompson describes a typical tutorial session. Six or eight students, all of whom had arrived late, sat not at a table but scattered round the tutor's room holding their books in their hands, while the tutor himself reclined in his armchair by the fireplace and listened to them construe. A satirical drawing made in about 1849, and so nearly ten years before that, shows a group of young men, albeit in this case sitting round a table, holding texts and making notes. A don stands in front of them, reading aloud. It seems likely that Stephen experienced a very similar teaching method.

Stephen was aware of his comparative academic shortcomings, telling his father, over-modestly, in November 1863, that he had a poor memory and was slow to take in new ideas. This summary is an uncanny repetition of the description Gladstone wrote of his younger son's mental abilities back in Stephen's early childhood. It is improbable that his son had seen the diary entry, so the suspicion must be that his father had never made any secret of his estimate of Stephen's abilities. Self-fulfilling prophecy, a concept not then recognised, nevertheless seems to have been at work.

Fortunately, Stephen did not 'depreciate what capacities [he had]' and was determined to develop them. So although

Figure 7. Stephen as a young man. Reproduced by kind permission of Sir William Gladstone.

it became clear that, like Willy before him, he would not achieve academic distinction, he worked hard. On one occasion he even received a warning from his workaholic father that reading for seven and a half hours a day in the vacation was over-doing it. The Glad-stone family has a photograph of Step-hen taken either at this time or a little before. It shows an earnest young man sitting, legs crossed, on a hard-backed chair, reading a book. Though posed, the photograph suggests a habitual attitude.

His mother as well as his father was concerned for his welfare, and she worried about Stephen when he was away from home. Thanks to the family habit of passing on to one member information received from another, Catherine discovered that her son was 'not sleeping without morphia'. This is information which Stephen must have disclosed in supposed confidence to a sibling, forgetting that it was likely to be forwarded to his mother. Immediately, Catherine, perhaps mindful of her drug addicted sister-in-law, Helen, wrote to him in something of a panic. He hastened to reassure her that he was not suffering from sleeplessness due to overwork, and explained that 'there is noisy building work going on overhead'. This would have been the construction of the Meadows Buildings, necessary to provide more accommodation, as the college population was expanding and at this time all undergraduates still had to live in.

Stephen needed his sleep, because there was plenty of work to get through. He had to study for three sets of examinations, mainly written papers, involving both questions on set texts and composition in Latin and Greek. At the end of each term came the 'Collections'. The Dean sat at the north end of a green baize covered table, examination results and a register of attendance at lectures in front of him. The tutors were ranged in a row along one side and the student sat on the other. The conscientious Stephen had little to fear from these interrogations, but they must have been intimidating experiences. Still, at least these were formal occasions with an agenda, unlike the regular breakfasts held in the Deanery, which were times of dreaded social embarrassment: Liddell was not one for small talk.

Stephen survived his Christ Church experiences more happily than Willy had done, because less was expected of him. In his first year he successfully sat Responses, which were internal examinations whose results were not published, then in 1865 he obtained a second in Greek and Latin and, in 1867, having warned his parents that he would not get a first, he was awarded a second in *Literae Humaniores*. This was a very creditable result for a young man of not the highest academic ability, hampered by chronic physical problems. Gladstone was satisfied that his son had done his best. More significantly, Stephen felt that he had acquitted himself well.

In the summer of 1865, at the end of his second year at Christ Church, Stephen and a few college friends went for a month to read and study at Cumbrae College in Millport, Scotland, which acted as a retreat house, partly for students and partly for clergy. As well as spiritual guidance and refreshment, the college offered, according to the seasons of the year, the physical relaxations of walking, football and skating, all of which Stephen participated in. Cumbrae is the smallest island – bar Lesser Cumbrae – in the Firth of Clyde, only about twelve miles in circumference. Today, it is reached by ferry from Largs, and a bus has to be taken from the terminal round the coast to Millport. Stephen almost certainly went direct to Millport from Glasgow, up the Clyde by paddle steamer. Millport is the only settlement, and the island has many of the qualities of a nature reserve. A tranquil spot, it consists mainly of green upland covered with brilliant yellow gorse, dotted with occasional rocky outcrops, stands of trees and clusters of sheep. Seagulls wheel incessantly inland from the sandy shoreline. There are glorious mountain and sea views, even on the blustery, rain soaked spring day on which I visited. It is not surprising that Stephen was to return to this idyllic place on several occasions, including twice in 1866, once again before he was ordained in 1867, and finally, after he became Rector of Hawarden, in 1874.

Not only are the surroundings beautiful, but so are the buildings. The college is part of a small complex, commissioned in 1849 by George Boyle, later the sixth Lord Glasgow, a Christ Church friend of Gladstone. After Oxford, Boyle returned to Scotland inspired with a mission to inject some life into the Episcopal Church there. He concentrated on the family-owned island of Great Cumbrae and employed William Butterfield as his architect. Adjacent to the college is a tiny church, popularly known since 1876 as the Cathedral of the Isles, which has an interior glowing with stained glass and variously patterned white, green, black, brown and orange tiles. Viewed from the north, its spire rises high above the Gothic structures of the college itself and the choristers' lodgings, now turned into residential accommodation. The approach is up a tree-lined path leading from a gate in College Lane. In Stephen's day, the grounds on either side the path, now a mass of wild garlic and bluebells, were formally landscaped, and the overall effect, unsurprisingly, given its founder, was that of an Oxford college, which must have seemed a home from home to Stephen. Also, it had the added advantage of a deeply religious atmosphere, something which was notably absent from both Eton and Christ Church.

Up a narrow staircase from the ground floor of the college, are the small study bedrooms, one per student, each with a desk positioned to discourage gazing through the window at the lawns and trees beyond. Below, there was – and still is – a cosy common room, a small library, and a refectory with long, sturdy tables, lancet window and a high arched ceiling. All the fixtures and fittings in both rooms and corridors were designed by Butterfield, and the dark oak, frequently carved with his trademark trefoil motif, creates a pleasingly homogenous effect.

On the common room wall is a picture showing a group of five students formally attired in caps and gowns, chatting in the grounds. These could well have been Stephen and his friends in the 1860s. There was not in fact much time for such socialising. Among the college records is a printed set of house rules and timings of the day dating from 1886, which cannot be far different from those existing in Stephen's time. On weekdays, a call bell at 6 a.m. was

51

followed by matins, prime and Holy Eucharist (Communion), all before the half an hour allocated for breakfast at 8.30. Terce and meditation, reading, study and Sext then followed before dinner, for which three quarters of an hour was generously allowed. At last, at 2.30 p.m., there came 'recreation and freetime' before Evensong at 6 p.m., followed by tea and then a further two hours of reading and study before compline and preparation for more meditation. Light refreshments were available before lights out at 10.45 p.m., by which time they must have been exhausted. On Sundays there was an extra hour in bed, but no recreation or free time.

The rules state that: 'Silence is observed every day until after the reading of some spiritual book at the commencement of breakfast ... and is also observed at all times in the corridors and on the stairs.' Smoking was forbidden both inside and out. It tells us much about the young Stephen that this ascetic monastic regime had such a strong appeal. He took full advantage of his time there and fitted easily into its routines. The Rev. J. G. Cazenove, Vice Provost, then Provost, under whom he studied, described him as 'a very nice, modest, unassuming person'. It is possible that Stephen conceived his ambition to work in the mission field as a result of his visits to Cumbrae, since mission was very much part of the college culture.

When he finished at Christ Church, in the summer of 1866, Stephen paid a second visit to Cumbrae, and then travelled to join his parents, his Uncle Stephen and his sisters Mary, Agnes and Helen in Italy. He stayed on in Rome, having been joined by Willy, when most of the others moved on to Naples. Agnes and Helen, who also remained in Rome, were staying with friends, but the brothers, as Stephen wrote to Herbert (who with Harry had been left at home), lodged 'in the very top of a house in rather a narrow dirty street'. They apparently lunched on chestnuts and ate all their other meals in cafés or restaurants. In typical Gladstone family fashion, no time was wasted: 'All day long we spend in seeing buildings, churches, ruins, pictures, statues, gardens, villas or palaces ... last night we went to hear the opera of *Norma*.' They went riding in the surrounding plains, visiting the ruins of the aqueduct and seeing the quarry which supplied the stones for the Colosseum. It must all have been enormous fun for the two brothers. Once back home, the demands of real life began again.

Stephen's decision to become a clergyman, taken as a boy, was now to be acted upon, but he was very aware of the current problematic state of the Church of England, and this worried him. The Church was embroiled in controversy within its own ranks, as a result of the spreading influence of the Oxford Movement. This clerical group, originally called Tractarians (because they published tracts explaining their beliefs), wanted to return the church to what they saw as its true medieval spirituality. This implied the reintroduction of catholic – though not Roman Catholic – rites, practices, fittings, art, music and architecture. Some High Churchmen, notably Newman and Manning, both friends of Gladstone, did actually go over to Rome, which further inflamed the debate. Gladstone himself, and Stephen, embraced High Churchmanship, but were totally opposed to its more extreme manifestations, as embraced by the Ritualists, the advance guard of Anglo-Catholicism. The church authorities were not only suspicious of, but adamantly set against, Ritualism.

Apart from this internal dissension, all churchmen, of whatever leaning, faced a challenge from the growth of the new Liberalism, which had spread from Germany. This ethos encouraged the questioning of Christian beliefs which had been long held to be inviolable, and which therefore had never before been examined, at least, not by most Anglican clergy and their faithful congregations.

In March 1860, a group of seven scholars – six ordained, one lay – contributed to a publication entitled, with deliberate blandness, *Essays and Reviews*. Its note 'To the Reader' urged an open minded response to the questions currently being raised about the nature of biblical evidence: 'The volume, it is hoped, will be received as an attempt to illustrate the advantage derivable to the cause of religious and moral truth, from a free handling, in a becoming spirit, of subjects peculiarly liable to suffer by the repetition of conventional language, and from traditional methods of treatment.' In other words, it was to be seen not as an attack on faith, but as an aid to it. Baden Powell's 'Study of the Evidences of Christianity', the second essay, encouraged the belief that no threat was intended, stating optimistically: 'The present discussion is not intended to be of a controversial kind, it is purely contemplative and theoretical; it is rather directed to a calm and unprejudiced survey of the various opinions and arguments adduced. '

However, other articles dared to suggest that there might be something in the idea that the first chapters of Genesis should not be taken literally (Frederick Temple, the Queen's Chaplain); that the story of Adam and Eve might be read as 'a form of narrative', that is, as a myth, (H. B. Wilson); and that differences of interpretation of scripture are 'inevitable' (Benjamin Jowett, the Master of Balliol College, Oxford). To many readers, and, one suspects, even more to those who had not actually read the text themselves, these ideas seemed heretical.

Baden Powell's optimism was misplaced. Such was the strength of feeling that two of the contributors were actually tried for heresy and suspended from their benefices for a year. The church hierarchy, backed by the known views of Queen Victoria and the Prince Consort, found it unacceptable that authority should be thought to lie with individual judgement. The response of many of the rank and file clergy is reflected in the attitude of the Rev. Charles Kingsley. When his new curate asked him if he should read *Essays and Studies*, he responded: 'By no means. Do not darken your mind with intellectual puzzles, which may breed disbelief, but can never breed vital religion, or practical usefulness.' Gladstone certainly read the book, and annotated his copy heavily, so it can be safely assumed that Stephen read it too.

This creeping secularism, as some saw it, was actually not new. As early as 1851, a census had revealed that nearly 38% of people did not attend church at all, and nearly half of those who did were Dissenters (Nonconformists), not Anglicans. In practice, less than a quarter of the population were regular attenders at their local parish church. Church doctrine had long been under attack from rationalists, who did not believe in the supernatural elements in religion. As historical and scientific studies advanced, well before the publication in 1859 of Darwin's *On the Origin of Species*, secularists, or religious sceptics, had been questioning the date and authorship, and by implication the validity, of the scriptures. Darwin's book simply reinforced the views of many people who read it. Inevitably, it was seen, particularly by many who had not read it, as a direct challenge to the existence of God the Creator and, through his son Jesus Christ, Saviour of the World.

The authenticity of the biblical record was also being questioned by scholars, not only outside but also within the church, as more early texts, such as the *Codex Sinaiticus*, were discovered, deciphered and compared with the King James Bible. (Interestingly, the *Codex Sinaiticus* was found in the Monastery of St Catherine, built below Moses's mountain, in the year of Stephen's birth.) In 1862, the year Stephen went up to Christ Church, Campbell Tait, Bishop of London and later Archbishop of Canterbury, aware of all these developments, warned his clergy that the church had three main problems: the spirit of free enquiry and criticism, which was alienating educated people; the difficulties of an established church in an age of freedom of worship and a state no longer wholly Anglican; and an ever growing population, including a generation of the working class with no knowledge of the church, or even of Christianity. These difficulties were only to increase with time.

While Stephen was at Christ Church, Arthur Stanley, Regius Professor of Ecclesiastical History, a man in tune with developing scholarship, had preached a sermon on the evils of theological controversy, during which he had advised the students: 'Never condemn a book unless you have read it.' Perhaps mindful of this advice, Stephen felt that before taking holy orders, he should not only study traditional theology but also come to grips with all the various arguments currently raging in and outside the church. Ever the perfectionist, he estimated that this would take him two or three years, and he was in something of a quandary. He wrote to his father, in July 1866: 'It may be said that to attempt to face the difficulties of controversy before entering the Church is only to endanger one's ever entering it at all.'

Gladstone was alarmed. He assured his son that 'ripening of the mind' would occur naturally over the years, and aggressively stated: 'I do not see what advantage is gained by delay [in ordination.]' He made it clear that he wanted his son to commit himself immediately to the priesthood, and was anxious that he should go as soon as possible to Cuddesdon, the increasingly famous theological college just outside Oxford. Cuddesdon had recently emerged from its own period of controversy, stoked by the wild exaggeration of supposed popish practices resulting from the strongly Ritualist influence of its first Vice-Principal, Henry Liddon. The college, housed in a picturesque if chilly building on a hill in the village of Cuddesdon, had been founded in 1854 by Samuel Wilberforce, currently Bishop of Oxford. He was yet another friend of Gladstone, and had actually christened Stephen.

Edward King was the principal of Cuddesdon in Stephen's time, and he kept the Ritualist element under control. It was certainly High Church in its leanings, however, which commended it to both Gladstone and his son. King shared in the growing realisation that simply being an educated gentleman was no longer a sufficient qualification for becoming a parish priest. The role was now seen as one demanding skills which had to be taught in institutions. At Cuddesdon, men were trained specifically for parish duties at home, not in the mission field, although there was a Cuddesdon Missionary Exhibition fund designed to provide finance for missions, and an increasing awareness that the mission field needed a supply of able graduates. King actively encouraged missions in South Africa and in India, where he helped to found the Oxford Mission in Calcutta, a venture which came to figure large in Stephen's imagination. (At one time, King thought of going out to the colonies himself.) But the chief aim of the college was to teach the essentials of effective priesthood in British parishes.

Stephen applied for entry to Cuddesdon in October 1867, making it clear to his father, and maybe to the college authorities, that he was in no hurry to be ordained. He wanted time not only to read and think, but if possible to gain experience as a layman in parish work. Percipiently, he realised that once he was ordained, he would have little time for study. In the event, Cuddesdon proved a disappointment to Stephen, falling well short of his beloved Cumbrae. He complained that the day was too broken up, the system irksome, too organised and too communal. In view of what we know of the regimes at Cumbrae, these comments might suggest some unexamined prejudice. A group photograph, taken in Lent 1868, shows him standing slightly aloof from the couple of dozen other men, and this physical distance is indicative of the mental and psychological gap he was aware of. However, the college was to prove a formative experience. Years later he was to be praised for setting an example to his Hawarden curates of how, as a working parish priest, it was possible to implement the high standards set at Cuddesdon.

There does not seem to have been much attempt made by the college to fulfil Stephen's need to come to grips with the various controversies threatening the Church. Indeed, the previous Vice-Principal Liddon had proclaimed that: 'The first function of a theological college is to teach Theology' and build 'an intellectual basis for the priestly life, focusing on moral and spiritual growth.' Its job was specifically not to raise problems of criticism and speculation. Nor was the college at all interested in Stephen's idea of gaining experience as a lay worker. So he considered a desperate measure, both to escape the controversies and to build up his own confidence: going out to India as a missionary for ten years. Gladstone was strongly opposed to this idea, for a mixture of reasons, both personal and disinterested, which came together: he did not want to lose close contact with Stephen, for whom he felt a deep affection, and he thought the church in Britain was desperately in need of good quality clergy (though he knew the same was true of the mission field).

By May 1868, partly because of pressure from his father and partly because he felt stronger in his own faith, Stephen was prepared to seek ordination, and by August he was considering not one but two offered vacancies, one in Leeds and one in Lambeth. He chose Lambeth, in South London, across the River Thames from Westminster. This was a brave decision. Urban posts were considered far less desirable than those in rural areas. Firstly, there were far larger numbers of parishioners, many of whom were uninterested in, if not actively hostile to, the church, and, secondly, having no patrons, the livings were much poorer. Of course, Stephen had private means, courtesy of his father, so a small stipend would not worry him, but his experience of society consisted of a close family unit, the residents of a virtually feudal country village, and a handful of like-minded school and college friends and tutors. This was not much of a preparation for sprawling urban Lambeth.

CHAPTER 4 – LAMBETH, 1868–1872

*'Our dear Stephy's demeanour was full of modest
concentrated devotion.'*
(Gladstone's Diary: 13 March 1870)

Gladstone had been overjoyed when Stephen chose to enter the church, declaring that his son was one 'whose shoe's latchet I am not worthy to unloose'. In religion, as in all else, Stephen was strongly influenced by his father, who had himself considered becoming a clergyman until apparently dissuaded by his own father. Gladstone maintained a strong, practising, Anglican faith throughout his busy political life, whenever possible attending church at least twice every Sunday and three times when there was opportunity to do so, and always listening particularly attentively to the sermon. He had been brought up as an Evangelical, influenced by his Episcopalian mother, Anne, but while at Oxford he had begun to attach far more importance to the Communion service than did the Evangelical wing of the church. This brought him closer to High Church doctrine. The Oxford Movement was not to begin until after his days at Christ Church, but he was certainly later influenced by it, and although not himself a Tractarian, he did envisage the Anglican Church as being the true Holy Catholic Church in England. Throughout his life he remained outspokenly hostile to Roman Catholicism, and was appalled by the defection of his two friends, John Newman and Henry Manning.

Stephen's own High Church leanings had been further fostered by his experiences at Cumbrae and Cuddesdon. In the prevailing climate of suspicion, such tendencies were, a few years hence, to cause him some problems, but they were not an issue at St Mary the Less, Lambeth, where the Vicar, since 1853, was Robert Gregory, himself a High Churchman. Nonetheless, an initial hurdle had to be jumped. Not long before, Gregory had been driven to threaten resignation when a High Church candidate for curacy had been rejected, and he was afraid that Stephen's candidature would be equally unacceptable to the authorities. Happily, this time – perhaps influenced by the fact that the candidate was the son of the new Prime Minister – the authorities did not let their prejudices stand in the way, and Stephen's application was duly accepted.

In Gregory, Stephen found a churchman he could both admire and strive to emulate. He described his mentor as 'always busy but never in a hurry … broad-minded and ready to learn as well as to rule … the organiser of all sorts of parochial good works … His whole heart was set on the good of the people … All was done, not only with the highest purpose, but with his irrepressible brightness, humour and tact'. This is a description of the kind of parish priest all High Churchmen aspired to be, and Stephen did his best to achieve this ideal throughout his own career. Not all of Gregory's practices were within Stephen's reach. A man of immense energy, Gregory once told Stephen that he never went to bed leaving a letter unanswered. It is doubtful if Stephen was able, or would even have wanted, to emulate this behaviour, in the face of the barrage of letters he received from his own family.

A photograph of Gregory in his middle years shows a simply dressed man with a strong face and a firm but compassionate expression, and a hint of a suppressed twinkle in his eye. Of comparatively humble origins, never forgetting what he owed to his own various mentors, he was a modest man. His autobiography is typically self-deprecating: 'At the request of friends, I am about to note down a few particulars of my life. Probably no one will think it worthwhile to publish them, and with that opinion I should perfectly agree.' From a man who ended his career as a highly respected Dean of St Paul's, this is an astonishingly self-effacing statement. It is no wonder he was so greatly and so widely liked.

Gregory's church in Lambeth, St Mary the Less (not to be confused with the ancient parish church of St Mary the Great, not far away), was in Black Prince Road, in the north of the Borough. Lambeth was socially diverse, and St Mary the Less served what was then one of its least privileged districts. Living conditions, nevertheless, were better than when the church was first built, forty years before Stephen's appointment. The 1848 Public Health Act had brought about some limited improvement in general health, although householders were often reluctant to allow inspectors in: compulsory fumigation after the discovery of infectious disease was expensive. Acts of Parliament in 1866 and 1868 had resulted in some slum clearance, improved sewerage and regular rubbish collection, which also improved public health. However, these advances were relative. Many people still lived in overcrowded, insalubrious accommodation, and sub-letting meant that it was not uncommon for two or three families to live under one roof. Frequent flooding of the River Thames increased the incidence of fever, coughs, congestion of the lungs and rheumatism; caused unemployment, when working premises were wrecked; destroyed meagre furniture, bedding and clothing; and weakened the structure of the shoddily built houses.

The construction of the Thames Embankment between 1866 and 1869, which resulted in the wharves being moved down water, had thrown many labourers out of work and caused a serious loss in trade. Some of the very poorest people, the beach-pickers or mud-larks, had been particularly hard hit. However, the baptismal records suggest that the majority of Stephen's parishioners were in some kind of employment, in the Lambeth Pottery; in a huge variety of other local trades, particularly chair-making and bricklaying; as shopkeepers and as car-men, delivering goods; and, more surprisingly, as musicians.

There were also a number of police constables, clerks, artists and even an architect and a professor, and one clerk who got married in 1870 described his father as a 'gentleman'. So did his bride, but these pretensions to gentility were far outweighed by the number of people who were illiterate and simply made their marks on parish registers and other official forms. Stephen, and his fellow assistant curates, regularly baptised the babies born to unmarried girls living in the Lambeth Workhouse. A lot of people struggled to survive and many, including children, were underfed and sickly, with little resistance to disease. There was an epidemic of scarlet fever, then a potentially deadly illness, in 1870, part way through Stephen's time there. The local papers in the 1870s were full of reports of murders, rapes, abortions, domestic violence, baby farming, child abuse, dread of smallpox, theft, begging and animal cruelty. Although many strove against the odds to lead respectable lives, Lambeth was emphatically not Hawarden.

Gregory himself had been ordained in the 1840s, at a time when pastoral work was still little practised, but, like most High Churchmen, he always had concerns about the living conditions of the poor. When he first came to Lambeth, after his wife's early death, he immediately set about alleviating the immediate needs of his most impoverished parishioners. He set up a winter soup kitchen and organised clothing work for the women. Next to food, clothing was one of the greatest problems for the poor, who were often forced to buy second hand garments. These had often already been remade, enlarged and patched by a series of unscrupulous middlemen, which greatly increased the risk of the clothes being infected by contagious diseases.

The fabric of the church also needed Gregory's immediate attention. The 1828 building was now dilapidated, and had been in a state of decline throughout the late 1840s, in spite of having been granted its own parish in 1842. The energetic and devoted Gregory, then assisted by a single curate, improved the buildings, built a parsonage house and persuaded the richer surrounding parishes to give financial support. Sadly, St Mary the Less did not survive a further decline in the twentieth century and the land on which it stood is now covered with a housing development, but descriptions and photographs show that it was very attractive, inside and out. Built in Gothic style with a small spire, it presented a generally welcoming appearance.

But Gregory knew that people were not likely to come to the church, however attractive its appearance, of their own accord. The church had to be taken to the people, many of whom were either indifferent or inarticulately hostile. Believing that the best way to reach parents was through their children, he built schools and an art school. He tried hard to get to know his parishioners personally, a difficult task since they were frequently moving house, either trying to better themselves or fleeing creditors, and he was aware of the need to create a strong group of lay visitors. He built up good relations with all his lay workers, consulting them and listening to their views. He believed that the proper task of the chief pastor in a parish was to recruit, train and supervise both clerical and lay people, of both sexes, to help the priest to extend his ministry to everyone in the parish. These ideas were to inform Stephen's own ministry. Gregory's insistence on reverence in worship and his awareness of the duty of the church to promote teaching and missionary work (his own son became a missionary in Madagascar and Mauritius) were also key elements in Stephen's own practice.

Stephen was lucky not only in having Robert Gregory as his mentor but also in having previously received some relevant training in parish work while at Cuddesdon. A more typical experience for a new ordinand was that of one John Sandford in 1863:

> I was dismissed from the schools of the university on the Friday and was ordained on the Sunday week, and then put in sole charge of a parish of between 7,000 and 8,000 souls, to whom I ministered for 2 years, till my health was so impaired that I had to leave the charge.

No wonder there were few men eager to serve in the towns and cities.

The church had woken up to the severe shortage of clergy in urban parishes in 1836, and the Evangelical wing had formed the Church Pastoral Aid Society to pay for more curates and lay workers. This initiative was followed in 1837 by the setting up of the wider based Additional Curates' Society (originally, but sensibly briefly, entitled 'The Society for the Employment of Additional Curates'), with Gladstone as one of its earliest subscribers and most active committee members. In London in 1844, the year Stephen was born, there was only one clergyman to every 16,000 people. Even with the best efforts of the Society in providing grants to pay for extra curates, including some at St Mary the Less, the number of clergy in England and Wales barely increased between 1851 and 1901, while the population doubled. It was calculated that a typical single-handed priest in a huge urban parish, working a twelve hour day, seven days a week, could just manage the routine work. He had no hope of contacting the thousands of non-churchgoers, entirely ignorant of religion, to whom he desperately wanted to reach out. Not only would he be swamped with duties, but he would very likely be living in poverty. Unsurprisingly, there was a shortage of men seeking to serve in such gruelling circumstances. To compound the problem, because of the growing number of other professions on offer, a much smaller proportion of the male population was now opting for the Church as a career. In 1862 only half as many Oxford graduates were ordained as had been the case twenty years previously.

The crisis in recruitment to urban parishes meant that few candidates ever failed the examinations. However, aware of Gregory's earlier problems over a High Church applicant, and, as ever, personally diffident, Stephen confided to his mother that he feared the Bishop of Winchester might reject him as an ordinand. He was also anxious over the bad publicity for his father which he thought such failure would bring. A less unconfident young man might have found it inconceivable that a son of Gladstone, devout, well educated and keen, would be turned down. He was duly ordained deacon in 1868 and priest in 1870. In the event, the ordination in December 1868 was performed not by Charles Sumner, Bishop of Winchester, who had suffered a stroke in the previous March, but by Bishop Vincent William Ryan of Mauritius. Ryan had left Mauritius in 1867 and become a commissary of Winchester, which means he was 'entrusted with the performance of an absent bishop's duties.' Sumner was presumably not back to full health – he was to resign in August 1869 – and was being helped out in his duties by fellow bishops.

Before he went to Lambeth, Stephen went on a Scottish walking holiday. He may have been preoccupied with thinking about his new life, for he managed to lose both his purse, containing £10, and his railway tickets, all of which were fortunately found and returned to him. Arrived in Lambeth, he had similar good fortune, immediately finding lodgings with a kindly widow at 98 Upper Kennington Lane, spacious enough for his brother Harry to share when he became a student at King's College, which was within easy reach, in the Strand. The name of the road has changed, and, like the church, the house no longer exists, but if houses on the opposite side are anything to go by, it was in a terrace of solidly built, pleasant-looking properties.

Stephen was happy there. When his parents dined with him in December 1871, Gladstone described the household as 'a most satisfactory little menage.' It was near enough to the family's home in Carlton House Terrace, retained though his father was now Prime Minister, for Stephen to visit them, and vice versa, whenever time permitted. All the family delighted in his curacy and involved themselves with his work. Gladstone himself on at least one occasion went out of his way to give personal help to one of the poorest parishioners, Jacobus Parker, who later recorded how in June, 1871 he:

> was mainly indebted for my rescue from the Workhouse to the kindness of the Ex-Premier, Mr. Gladstone. I wrote to him, and he replied at once to me, a pauper, in a manner so kind that it brought my heart to my mouth.

He also sent his secretary to inquire into my case, and the result was a prompt grant of £10 from the Queen's bounty.

With this money, Jacobus was able to set up as a licensed bootblack and earn his living, which, incidentally, he supplemented by giving recitations of Shakespeare.

With less spectacular results Harry and, on at least one occasion, their sister Agnes, assisted in the parish by helping out at the night schools in which Stephen enthusiastically taught, where 'the crowds were almost overwhelming'. His mother Catherine helped to decorate the church at Christmas, and, of course, whenever members of the family were up from Hawarden, his services were attended and his sermons listened to.

His boyhood hope that he would learn to 'manage the sermons' was fulfilled. 'Strong and high-toned' was his father's view on one of them, and he was an expert. Agnes agreed about the high tone and added: 'beautiful, and yet very simple but so earnest'. She wrote to Herbert telling him the congregation had been touched and delighted, and that one old lady had told Stephen afterwards that 'he had the face of an angel'. (This is the only complimentary comment I have found on Stephen's looks.) Mary told Harry she was delighted with a sermon she had heard, hiding herself away in the back of the church. The sole occasion we know of when his preaching was below par was when he attempted to speak extempore. Harry described the results to Agnes as 'not first rate' and excused his brother on the grounds that it was about St Luke, 'about whom so little is known'. Unfortunately, it must have been on some kind of special occasion because Harry wrote, 'the hard part is that the clergy must have thought that he had not prepared it at all, whereas he had thought about it for two whole days'. He records how Stephen 'had to repeat the same thing over again and hesitated rather, but at the end he got alright'. It sounds like a nightmare.

Sermons at that time were considered to be of great importance. Yet another friend of Gladstone's, Dr H. P. Liddon (the first Vice-Principal of Cuddesdon appointed a canon of St Paul's Cathedral in 1870) was an enormously popular preacher, and one whom Stephen must have heard. Liddon was able to command the attention of a vast middle-class audience on Sunday afternoons for an hour at a time, not so much through his arguments, which were unexceptionable, but his skill in oratory. He gave a famous series of lectures at St James's Piccadilly during Lent of 1870. Stephen may have been too busy with his own duties to attend these, but it is hard to imagine that they were not discussed by the Lambeth clerics.

Like Stephen and Gregory, Liddon, in common with many contemporary clergy and certainly their congregations, believed literally in the Virgin Birth, miracles, the resurrection, and Heaven as at least in some sense an actual place. In his sermons he sought to counter current attacks on fundamental aspects of Christianity, such as the idea of a personal God who answered individual prayers. His approach in the Lent series of lectures was to examine the whole question of what constituted the Christian religion. For Liddon, the most important aspect of God was not his omniscience nor his role of creator, but the moral guidance which he provided for humanity. As for man, because he was inevitably sinful, he could enjoy the love of God only if he repented and sought forgiveness through prayer. Through the intervention of Jesus Christ, God in his mercy would then bestow his grace on the suppliant.

Liddon's lectures were expressed in sophisticated language, appropriate to his audience, but the faith they presented was a simple one: Christians were to follow God's will, and to confess and be sorry if they failed to do so. They would then receive forgiveness and eventually be rewarded by bodily resurrection on Judgement Day. Stephen's own faith was of a similarly straightforward kind, and he publicly taught these beliefs throughout his ministry. It is possible that as time went on his position may have changed – we do not know. The Clerical Subscription Act of 1865 freed up the Anglican clergy to hold their own individual views on liberal interpretations of the Bible, except for the Virgin Birth, but like many educated, thoughtful clergy, Stephen would never have considered unsettling the cherished beliefs of his parishioners.

Two years before his 1870 Lent lectures, speaking at an anniversary festival at Cuddesdon, Liddon had, appropriately, concentrated specifically on the role of the priest, providing a practical blueprint for Stephen. He urged priests to follow Christ's teaching in the Sermon on the Mount. They were to aim at the relief of the ignorant, the erring, the suffering and the poor, showing that 'in Jesus Christ, Incarnate, Crucified, Interceding, given to us in the Sacraments, presented by us again and again to the Father, there is grace which can more than cure all human woes'. The priest's job was: 'to show Morality is important, as are practical self-discipline, self-forgetting love, uniform brightness and joy of heart and soul, true inward peace amid troubles and distractions, longsuffering, self-improvement (in the higher sense) and personal culture of moral truth'. The gloss on self-improvement – 'in the higher sense'– makes it clear that Liddon was not thinking about the concept in the usual Victorian sense of worldly betterment.

His stress on morality is typically Victorian, reflecting the preoccupation of the middle classes with guilt and duty, and the description of the priest's job is strikingly in accord with Stephen's later description of Robert Gregory's work.

Throughout his own ministry, Stephen strove to achieve these ideals, whatever difficulties he experienced in his personal life, arising from ill health, outside pressures, disappointments and his tendency to self-doubt. Always highly self-critical, a trait inherited from his father, he wrote to Gladstone in September 1869, saying that although he felt a sense of working for God and with God, 'it is a great trial to feel no certainty or actual assurance that one is working in the truest way'. This self-doubt, coupled with a lack of worldly ambition, led to his being in no hurry to leave Lambeth, where he thought he was doing the work God had called him to do. His father, who always felt the need to encourage, indeed, push, his son, urged him to apply, as early as May 1870, for the vacant living of St Mark's Horsleydown, in Bermondsey.

Stephen found the courage to tell him that he felt unfit for such a post and would prefer to wait for two or three more years. He thought that after 'a spell of steady and patient labour in Lambeth' he would be better fitted to take on more responsibility elsewhere, and less likely to get disheartened and break down. In this Stephen showed a peculiar prescience, in view of what was to happen a few years later. He was sure in his own mind that a living was something to look forward to, not to embark on immediately. This brave response to his father's urging shows not only his diffidence about his own abilities, but also his self-awareness: he knew he was a perfectionist, putting too much pressure on himself. The greater the responsibilities became, the greater the pressure would be.

Over a year later he was still considering what form his future in the church should take. In a letter to Herbert, who at the time was considering his own future, he wrote about the varied choice of work that a clergyman's life offered. He saw his curacy as a time of training, testing what work he was best fitted for.

> I don't know yet what I shall do when I leave Lambeth: but I am trying to discover what I can do best ... There are troubles and perplexities about, I know: but to occupy a post in these times is a thing of no ordinary honour – and it may be that a golden age is dawning for the Church of England.

This optimistic view may have been a cover for concerns that internal divisions might even destroy the Church. His future was, after all, at stake.

By then he was thinking seriously about life after Lambeth, but was still not sure he was ready to take on more demanding duties. Writing to his father he analysed his own weaknesses, as he saw them, stating that the difficulties of his current work were far greater than he had expected, and blaming his own over-sensitive nature and a 'sort of restless & defiant intolerance' in his character. Restlessness and over-sensitivity were certainly part of his nature, and became more pronounced with the years, but of 'defiant intolerance' there seems to be no evidence at any stage in his life. Either he was exaggerating this trait to stop his father from pushing him where he did not yet want to go, or he became very good at disguising the supposed shortcoming in both his public and private life.

It is certainly likely that the work in Lambeth was more difficult than he had foreseen. Even with the support of

Robert Gregory, Stephen, an Eton and Oxford educated young man from the upper echelons of society, comfortably off financially and brought up in a stately home, must have had a shock when confronted with the realities of trying to connect with overwhelming numbers of the uneducated, naturally irreligious, urban poor. Granted, he had before him the example of his mother, with her hospital work in the 1866 cholera epidemic in the East End of London. However, at the time she had been much older, better established, and far more self-confident than was Stephen, and she was focusing on just one problem.

By providing pastoral care for the patients and their children, Catherine had freed the nurses to get on with their professional job of curing the sick, and freed the patients from worries that were impeding their recovery. She saw positive results every day. Stephen was concerning himself with the less tractable problems of providing spiritual and moral health for hundreds of not necessarily grateful parishioners. He seems to have enjoyed at least the occasional success in persuading people of the relevance of the church to their needs, if we are to judge from the baptismal records. It is not uncommon for the register to show several children of one family being baptised on the same day, as on 20 November 1870, when he baptised no fewer than five children of a painter and his wife, or 25 October 1871, when he baptised six children of a bricklayer. Behind both these entries there must surely lie much effective pastoral work.

CHAPTER 5 – THE APPOINTMENT TO HAWARDEN, 1872

'If the greater station and higher are a trial, they are a
trial of that kind … which may be boldly encountered
when it has not been sought.'
(Gladstone's Diary: 14 August 1872)

Whatever the difficulties he experienced in Lambeth, Stephen never felt he had made the wrong decision in going there. Back in the summer of 1866, he had told his father that he intended to take work in London, and 'if I find it suitable, to settle there for good'. Now, uncertain though he may have been about the form his future would take, of one thing he was sure, as he told his brother Herbert:

> I do not mean ever to take on a country parish – as I feel
> my own tastes for work are for town work & as I am
> being trained in a town. Country work is just as
> interesting and engrossing but it is of a different sort: & I
> do not think I would ever be suitable for it.

Shortly after Stephen wrote these words, an event occurred which changed his life irrevocably. This was the sudden death, on 29 July 1872, as a result of a freak lightning strike, of his Uncle Henry, brother of Stephen Glynne, ninth baronet and owner of Hawarden Castle. The Rev. Canon Henry Glynne had been Rector of the Church of St Deiniol's, Hawarden, for thirty-eight years – in other words, since ten years before Stephen was born.

The church had a long history, and a long connection with Hawarden Castle. Since 1770 it had been, like half the benefices of England and Wales, in the gift of a private patron – in this case, the Glynne family. Henry himself had no surviving son and Sir Stephen had no offspring, let alone a second son, who would otherwise have been the obvious candidate for the rectorship. In the absence of a Glynne heir, it was inevitable that Stephen should be expected to take over the living. Not only was he the second son of the elder Glynne sister, Catherine, but, conveniently, he was already in holy orders.

Many a young clergyman would have jumped at the benefice on offer, which was an ecclesiastical plum. The Rectory of Hawarden was worth the enormous annual sum of £3,000, more than some bishoprics, and more than seven times the income of most Anglican clergy, thousands of whom somehow subsisted on the perceived minimum of £100. In every conceivable way, the parish was the exact opposite of Hanmer, only twenty miles to the south-east, the deprived Flintshire parish described by Lorna Sage in her memoir, *Bad Blood*. By then part of the diocese of St Asaph, up until 1849 Hawarden had the status of a 'peculiar', outside the jurisdiction of any bishop, even empowered to hold its own ecclesiastical courts. It still retained some of this aura of power and independence.

Not only Stephen Glynne, but the whole family, felt it right and proper that Stephen should, in spite of his youth and inexperience, succeed his uncle as Rector of Hawarden. Agnes, his older sister, summed up the general view when she wrote to their brother Harry, on 8 August: 'I have mingled regrets that such a load should come on his young head so early – However that no doubt is part of the Providential ordering of [events].' There is an echo here of her father's cast of thought and terminology. The Providence of God was often cited by Gladstone, and was not easy to argue against.

Figure 8. Hawarden Church and Rectory. Reproduced courtesy of Flintshire Record Office.

The day after this letter was sent, Stephen had a long talk with his father, who although he was his usual strongly persuasive self, surprisingly failed to convince his son that he should take on the rectorship. After deep thought over the next few days, Stephen wrote his father a letter which set out all the reasons for and against his acceptance. He gave only three reasons for, as opposed to six against. These latter included not only his own youth, inexperience and lack of aptitude for the type of work involved, but also what he called 'some special difficulties of working at home'. Again, he showed prescience. Stephen was aware that his family, in particular his parents, would expect to be a strong influence on him and, clearly, this is not what he wanted in his first living. Nonetheless, by 14 August, he had bowed to the inevitable, putting his parents' wishes before his own, and going against his own better judgement. Gladstone, delighted, and with no misgivings at all, expressed in his diary this hope: 'May God guide him in this and all his ways.'

It was not to be as simple as that, however. The family, and indeed God, may have wanted Stephen installed as Rector, but the parishioners were not so keen, fearing that he would introduce changes, and worse, be too High Church for their tastes. His Uncle Henry had been on the Evangelical, or Low wing of the church, and this, coupled with the fact that he had held the living for so long, meant that the parishioners were very set in ways which they realised were different from those of Stephen. In fact, Stephen was relatively moderate in his views. Like his father, he was strongly influenced by the Oxford Movement, and, under his mentor, Robert Gregory, his practice had become firmly rooted in High Church theology, with particular regard to the central significance of the sacrament of Holy Communion in worship. However, he was certainly nowhere near the Anglo-Catholic persuasion of some clergy.

Rumour exaggerated Stephen's position: the parish dreaded the arrival of a 'Ritualist' who would introduce hated 'catholic' practices. Soon after Stephen was officially instituted as Rector of Hawarden on 14 September, Holy Cross Day, 1872, an apprehensive letter appeared in the *Chester Chronicle*. The letter was particularly concerned with changes which might be made to the conduct of the Holy Communion service. The writer stated that he did not think that the new Rector 'would actually turn his back on the people' (as did Anglo-Catholic and Roman Catholic priests during the rites.) But the letter clearly implied that the Rector might indeed 'turn his back', and, what's more, if he did, he might expect serious trouble. The people of Hawarden were not alone in their fears of 'catholic' practices. The Establishment shared their view: two years later, with the backing of Prime Minister Disraeli and Queen Victoria, Archbishop Tait was to introduce the Public Worship Regulation Bill in Parliament, in an attempt to put down Ritualism. Five clergymen were actually gaoled. Feelings were running high.

Gladstone, although busy with prime ministerial duties in London, was, as always, in touch with local affairs. He read the *Chester Chronicle* letter and warned Stephen, still in Lambeth, that there was 'murmuring in the air'. According to Stephen, he sent his son 'an alarming account'. Gladstone's memory may have gone back to the 1850s and 1860s, a time when many parishes were riven on the issue of Ritualism, suspicion was rife and observers were actually sent out as spies.

There were riots in various parts of London protesting about the introduction of 'catholic' practices. The rioters were not the parishioners, but rent-a-mob, organised by malcontents who encouraged talk about papists in disguise and chalked graffiti on walls – 'No Virgin Mary', 'No Wafer Gods' (a reference to the elements in the Communion service), 'No Creed Worship', and so on. Over 100 police had been required to prevent a mob from storming St Barnabas' Church in Pimlico and clergy residences had to be given police protection. At St George-in-the-East in Cannon Street Road, there were ten months of violent episodes. On one occasion the Ritualist Alexander Mackonchie had to be rescued from his pulpit by five policemen when he was attacked while preaching his sermon. On another, the choir stalls were seized by a mob shouting, 'Let us attack the choir boys!' They had to barricade themselves in the baptistery, waiting for the police to rescue them. The curate Charles Lowder was followed, attacked and narrowly escaped being thrown off a bridge. Twice, in February and March 1860, the mob pelted and defaced the altar hangings with orange peel and bread and butter and threw down the altar cross. At St Barnabas', the clergy and parishioners won the day. At St George's the mob, supported by Bishop Tait, prevailed. Lowder's biographer described the rioters as 'the vilest of the vile, the very scum of the most degraded parts of London', but local magistrates, aware of the sympathies of the church authorities, were disinclined to punish them.

Alerted by his father to the possibility of such violent horrors occurring in Hawarden, which would hardly have been good publicity for the Prime Minister, Stephen panicked. Believing 'there was very little time to think', he immediately wrote and had printed a circular letter to the churchwardens and parishioners with the object of allaying their fears. Dated from Lambeth in October 1872, the letter was prefaced by a title page announcing to whom it was addressed and from whom it came. The letter proper began by saying that the new Rector would use the time before he arrived to prepare for 'the arduous labour' to come. Having expressed a desire to get to know them all personally, he announced that 'to win your respect and confidence, will be my greatest anxiety'. He paid tribute to his deceased uncle but referred to 'the fresh energies and new hopes of younger years' which he had to offer, and 'the blessings of health and strength' which he averred he possessed. If Stephen believed, as he surely did, that he was speaking the truth here, then we might conclude that the erosion of his mental and physical health over the succeeding decades was a direct result of 'the arduous labour' of being Rector of Hawarden.

The preliminaries out of the way, the letter got down to the matter in hand, with Stephen freely admitting to being a High Churchman, although 'it is not pleasant for a churchman to call himself by any party name'. He probably felt that the less often differences were advertised, the better it would be for church unity. He reminded his readers that he could not hope to please everyone all the time, but reassured them that he did not wish to meddle with their traditional routine: 'It is my desire to keep up the existing services in their present form.' However, he laid out three proposals: 'to begin every Sunday and Holy Day with an early celebration of the Holy Communion', which they were clearly unaccustomed to; to introduce daily evening services; and to change the nature of the Sunday afternoon service in the direction of a Sunday school. Finally, and he must have assumed, less controversially, he asked for help in developing the charity work of the church. All these intentions reflected the practices at Lambeth introduced by Robert Gregory and enthusiastically followed there by Stephen himself.

Gladstone had not been consulted about the letter. When he got to hear about its existence, from a letter Stephen wrote to his uncle Stephen Glynne, he objected to it sight unseen. Having got hold of a copy, he immediately wrote to Stephen enumerating a number of 'suggestions' for changes, even on the title page, where the word 'introductory' was struck out before 'letter', 'Church District' was removed after 'Hawarden' and 'Their Rector' was changed to 'The Rector'.

These changes, all adopted by Stephen, had the effect of making the letter more authoritative. Other changes, also adopted, generally made the meaning clearer, though at least one seems simply pernickety, adding in the word 'these' after 'propose to begin' when it is perfectly obvious that the unstated object of the verb is 'services'. One change, however, seems aimed at giving the new Rector greater freedom than the original version had implied, 'keep up the existing services in their present form' became 'adhere in full to the spirit of the existing services'. The mind of an experienced politician as opposed to that of a simple young curate can be clearly discerned here. Stephen noted these changes in his own handwriting on a copy of the already printed letter and had it reprinted before it was put out on the pews.

Right from the start, in other words, Gladstone was the power behind the pulpit.

Stephen took up the rectorship of Hawarden in December, after preaching his farewell sermon at Lambeth on 24 November 1872. He was not to see his mentor Robert Gregory again until he invited him to take the Harvest Festival services at Hawarden in September the following year. His principal feeling must have been not joy or even excitement, but rather, apprehension.

The Hawarden parish church, dedicated to the somewhat obscure sixth-century St Deiniol, was, and still is, an imposing building, with a square tower and a spire, central nave and side aisles. Dating back at least to the fourteenth century, it was restored in 1855–1856 and again after a fire in 1857, when Sir Stephen and the Rev. Henry Glynne provided much of the necessary money. The interior was redesigned by Gilbert Scott, who was also responsible for the spire. There was a new organ chamber, with a new organ to go with it, a new pulpit of Painswick stone and Devonshire marble, new piers supporting the old arches in the nave, new oak seats and a new eagle lectern. The chancel was paved and a reredos of tiles constructed behind the altar. All was in the handsome Gothic style.

The church was approached by gates (originally just two narrow ones) leading to paths through the tree-filled churchyard, which slopes down to fields and has an extensive view across the Dee Estuary and the Wirral beyond. In Stephen's time, some of what is now the graveyard was still a hayfield, which directly abutted the church. The then chief path to the church led through the graveyard from opposite the Rectory, which is directly adjacent. It is a short stroll in fine weather, or a quick scurry in the rain. The south gate, now the main entrance, was built in 1877 as a memorial to Sir Stephen Glynne.

When Stephen came to Hawarden, it was decided that some minor work needed to be done on the Rectory before he moved in. It was ready furnished, but with the Henry Glynne family furniture, most of which Stephen did not want but which would remain there for another year, a constant reminder of his uncle's presence. While the refurbishment was in progress, Stephen stayed for a couple of days with his parents in the Castle, a brisk walk away

Figure 9. Haymaking in front of Hawarden Church. Reproduced courtesy of Flintshire Record Office.

from the church. In the second week of December he moved into the Rectory.

This impressive red brick edifice still stands, with some later additions, and currently houses the Flintshire Record Office and a library. It was, for a single man like Stephen, enormous. To the left of the main entrance, just across from the churchyard, and to the right of the stables, was his uncle's library, a beautifully proportioned room with fitted shelves and full-length windows opening on to what was then four acres of grounds. Above this was a spacious drawing room, which shared the view over lawns, bushes and flowerbeds towards groups of mature trees, several of which were rare species. There were also kitchen quarters, a dining room, a small sitting room and rooms for meetings. There were no bathrooms of course, since maids brought water up to the many bedrooms – more than had been necessary for Henry Glynne and his wife and their two surviving children, let alone a bachelor. Stephen valued the library and spent his time there and in the cosy room he used as his study, with its fireplace and, as photographs show, cluttered mantlepiece, desk (also cluttered) a screen to ward off draughts from the door, and a small occasional table covered with heaps of books. Although one of the curates usually lodged in the Rectory, the first being his cousin Albert Lyttleton (described by descendant Penelope Gladstone as 'tactless and vague'), the house must have seemed reproachfully large. Stephen felt increasingly that his parishioners would have preferred a married Rector with a family.

When he arrived, the widespread parish included seventeen townships, with a total population of 9,500, and several small hamlets. The village of Hawarden itself, built along a windy ridge rising above the Cheshire plain,

Figure 10. A sitting room at the Rectory. Reproduced courtesy of the Flintshire Record Office.

principally comprised one wide main street. This was lined with cottages, built of local stone, some thatched, some painted white. There were also various small shops and businesses, including three butchers (one of which is now a bus shelter), two saddlers, two foundries for shoeing horses, a chemist, several public houses, the Institute, which was later to be rebuilt, and, in Rectory Lane, a telegraph and post office. There was a weekly market on Saturday and two cattle fairs each year. It was busy and relatively prosperous.

At the start of Stephen's rectorship, and for some years afterwards, the population was involved mainly in agriculture, with fifty farmers still being listed as late as 1886. The marriage registers for the 1870s illustrate both the wide social range and the extensive range of occupations:

Figure 11. Stephen's study at the Rectory. Reproduced courtesy of the Flintshire Record Office.

labourers, gardeners, engine drivers, potters, shoemakers, blacksmiths, a civil engineer, a parish clerk, a chimney sweeper, a ship owner, a piano tuner, a tobacconist and dozens of other jobs. During his rectorship the balance between agriculture and industry, as in so many rural parishes, shifted inexorably towards the latter. There had been coalmines in the area since the first half of the nineteenth century, and the Aston Hall colliery in particular was booming in 1874. Ratcliffe's Engineering Works had been in the village since the 1800s and there was also a brickyard, an iron works and an iron-founder's. The year 1886 was pivotal: a new coalmine opened and there was a big influx of workers. The 1891 census lists page after page of coalminers and railway workers, albeit with an admixture of farm labourers, craftsmen and tradesmen, dressmakers, a handful of white collar workers and several pupil teachers. The early 1900s marriage registers carry the same story, with a far higher proportion of the population employed on the railway than had been the case thirty years before.

The station was opened in 1890, and throughout Stephen's final years, Hawarden become gradually more urbanised. As a result it achieved greater administrative importance, as the centre for the Rural District Council, with petty sessions held monthly and a House of Correction for those awaiting trial. Even in 1872, it was already the largest rural parish in England and Wales. There were four churches, including nearby Buckley, about to become a separate parish, and a number of voluntary Church of England schools. In Hawarden alone, there were three schools, one for girls, one for boys and one for infants, with a total of 358 children in 1872. Stephen, *ex officio*, had financial and managerial responsibility for all the Church schools in the parish. Although this greatly increased his workload, he saw that part of his job as essential. The Education Act of 1870 allowed for the setting up of School Boards to fill any gaps in educational provision, and a School Board would inevitably mean secularisation.

Stephen was twenty-eight years old and had been ordained for just four years, for only two of which he had, as an assistant curate, performed the full range of clerical duties. To put it another way, his experience, prior to taking over this important and extensive rural parish, was four years working in a junior capacity in a relatively unknown church in south London. No wonder he felt anxious and unprepared, no wonder the parishioners were suspicious of his appointment. What is surprising is his father's apparent

Figure 12. Hawarden Village. Reproduced courtesy of Flintshire Record Office.

total certainty that this son of his, with his low self-esteem, indifferent health record and chronically weak eyesight, would make a success of the job.

In the event, his father's trust was vindicated, and for most of the thirty-two years of his rectorship of Hawarden, Stephen proved himself to be not only an able priest, deeply concerned with the pastoral care and spiritual development of his flock, but, more surprisingly, a competent administrator: he oversaw the work of six curates, whose salaries he paid, and over 300 lay people. However, this success came at great personal cost. Long hours of work at tasks for which he was not by nature suited, twelve years of domestic loneliness, until he married in 1884, and the worry and physical effects of his deficient eyesight, combined to result in regular bouts of depression and despair.

He felt trapped by the strength of the family influence. Living a short walk away from him were, for the majority of his time there, his mother and father, two brothers and one, often two, sisters, all of them active in the parish. Their support, both financial and psychological, was welcome, but the sense of obligation this generated, and their commitment to the parish, sometimes indistinguishable from interference, was hard to bear. In another time, in another place, in 1910, he was to refer in a letter to his younger brother Harry, a letter in which he was generally unburdening himself, to his inability to 'open to anyone of the family', which at Hawarden 'was one of the troubles – in one way or another – beginning with December 1872'. He owed his position to them, he had their co-operation. How could he begin to explain his doubts and insecurities to them without seeming to be a discontented, self-obsessed ingrate?

At first he felt reasonably optimistic, writing to Harry, who was in London working for one of the Gladstone commercial interests: 'All has so far gone smoothly; although I see here and there traces of past uneasiness and surprise, I don't think it has been much, & is certainly passing off. Those I have visited have been most friendly, and altogether things are looking pretty bright and hopeful.' He had introduced some minor changes in service times, as posited in his introductory letter, but avoided doing anything remotely controversial. The parishioners were obviously prepared to give him the benefit of the doubt, even though it was soon clear that their new Rector was intent on influencing not just the pattern of their churchgoing, but their whole lives.

Keen to put into practice what he had learned under Robert Gregory, by February 1873, he had started up a night school. Sadly, at first, this was nothing like as successful as the one in Lambeth, where the 'crowds [had been] perfectly overwhelming'. Agnes sensed his depression over the night school venture, and sounded off in a letter to Herbert about how 'dense and slow' the 'folk here are', and how they 'don't half appreciate all the efforts that are made for them'. Things had improved by March, with twenty-seven men attending, and two lay parishioners assisting. Mary and Helen took some sessions, and Agnes herself helped on a couple of occasions, before her marriage took her away. She taught basic reading and writing and told Herbert she found it interesting: 'the men are so anxious over their pothooks [the looped heads and tails of letters] etc'. Some of the men in question were, according to her, quite elderly '& great drunkards'. It says much for Stephen's powers of persuasion, and pedagogic skills, that they were prepared to spend their evenings bending over books rather than pints. Extant handbills show how over the years, the classes grew in popularity, with subjects expanding to include not only reading and writing, but arithmetic, elementary drawing, the elements of singing and music, the Bible and elementary science. Separate classes were created for men, young men, lads over thirteen, and lads over eighteen, meeting on different nights in different venues. The subscriptions were low, and there were prizes for regular attendance.

Stephen gradually got to know his flock, although the division still normally perceived at the time between the laity and the gentleman parson must have been compounded by his being not only the nephew of the lord of the manor but also the son of a great public figure. Slowly he adapted to the differences between a city and a country parish. He wrote to Herbert: 'it is so different to London', but one of the differences which struck him most seems to have been the alacrity with which young people in Hawarden came forward for Confirmation. In some ways it was surely easier being a priest in a widespread rural area than in a congested urban parish. There was to be one big problem, but this was still far ahead in the future. Hawarden, although close to the English border, was actually in Wales, and the parish was part of the Welsh Bishopric of St Asaph. The fact that his parish was under the jurisdiction of the Welsh Church would create its own special difficulties for Stephen. The issue of Welsh Church Disestablishment – that is, severance from parliamentary control, with the consequent loss of endowments – was one on which he was eventually to find himself at odds with not only some of his parishioners but also more importantly, his superiors. He was pro, they were against.

CHAPTER 6 – HAWARDEN: THE PATTERNS ARE SET, 1872–1876

'It is very comforting to feel that I am doing what you and Mama wish.'
(Letter from Stephen to his father: 15 August 1872)

In December 1873, Stephen's older sister Agnes married Edward Wickham, then a fellow and tutor at New College Oxford, and soon to be, with Gladstone's active backing, headmaster of Wellington School. Stephen took part in the wedding ceremony 'with immense emotion strongly and repeatedly suppressed', according to his father. This was the first of many times when Stephen officiated on family occasions, and to a man like Gladstone, used to being in control and holding firm religious convictions, it must have been a delight to have a son so conveniently on hand to perform the rites of the church and administer the sacraments. Four years earlier he had described Stephen as one 'whose shoe's latchet I am not worthy to unloose'. He now became keen, if not actually to untie his son's shoelaces, to be closely involved in almost all aspects of his life. He often accompanied Stephen on his pastoral visits; enjoyed frequent visits to the Hawarden Rectory, which he described as 'truly noble, truly holy, and truly priestly'; and even when up in London, made sure he was *au fait* with everything that went on in the parish.

The inexperienced Stephen was at first very grateful for this support, and from the start he co-operated by keeping his father fully informed on all aspects of his work, often asking for, and taking, advice. It must be said that he was also not slow to ask him for money, whether for a fund for curates or for new schools, and Gladstone usually obliged.

He had always been generous with money and time where Hawarden and the Glynnes – Catherine's family, the patrons of the living – were concerned. In the 1840s, he had rescued the Estate from a parlous financial crisis, and after the serious church fire in 1857 not only joined Sir Stephen in contributing money for the necessary rebuilding but also acted as treasurer of the fund.

The Glynnes had always been at the heart of parish life. Catherine's mother, Lady Glynne, had brought up her daughter to visit and succour the poor, and there were close ties between the Castle and the village. Gladstone enthusiastically embraced this culture and, like Catherine, took an active interest in all village events.

This family tradition was valuable to Stephen, but he was also keen to make his own mark on the parish. In January 1873, he introduced the first issue of a parish magazine, which was to come out every month throughout, and beyond, his rectorship. As he wrote:

> The first object is to supply every month a printed sheet containing all the information as to the churches, schools, charities & sundry other matters which it may be useful to know ... We think ... it would be very acceptable throughout the parish, and would help us all to feel that sense of unity and concord within our fold which ought to prevail among us.

He saw the magazines not only as a means of communicating information and fostering a sense of common purpose, but also as a corollary to his sermons, and he wrote regular articles under the general heading: 'Are you a Churchman?' including rules about fighting against the three enemies – Satan, the World, and the Flesh – and asserting the importance of believing in all the Articles of

Faith. By this he might have meant either the creeds or the Thirty-nine Articles. In either case, the stress is principally on unquestioning acceptance of the church's traditional teaching on the one everlasting God, maker and preserver of all things; the dual nature of Christ; the importance of knowledge of the Scriptures in achieving salvation; the existence of original sin and free will; and justification by faith rather than works. Dr Liddon and Robert Gregory, two of his strongest influences, would have heartily approved of these epistles.

For us, the magazines offer not only a source of information about the Rector's spiritual beliefs and his aspirations for the parish, but a fund of amusing trivia, such as his and his wife Annie's endearing absent-mindedness. Between them, over the years, they managed to lose a bunch of keys, a leather bag of books and a silk umbrella. Slightly more worryingly, the issue of January 1908, asks: 'Who gave 6/6 [six shillings and sixpence] to the Rector during last month, & for what?'

The magazines also provide a picture of the daily round of parish activities. It is clear that in the early years, Stephen's mother Catherine was partly filling the much needed role of Rector's wife, hosting mothers' teas, running stalls at bazaars, handing out prizes at the annual flower show and so on. This was a function which later she would not find it easy to relinquish.

To return to the first issue: in it Stephen can be seen grappling for the first time with what was to become one of the recurring themes of his rectorship, education. The 1870 Education Act had effectively taken away the automatic right of the Anglican church to provide all local schooling. In future, if the church failed to show that it could provide satisfactory elementary education for every child in the parish, a School Board would be compulsorily set up to raise money to build and run local schools. These schools, although they would still teach religion, would no longer teach Anglican doctrine. (Edward King, Bishop of Lincoln, was later to state, somewhat provocatively, that non-denominational religion was itself a denomination.) When and where such School Boards were set up, a local rate would be levied to replace the traditional voluntary contributions.

Stephen explained all this in the magazine. He made it clear that if Hawarden was to avoid the formation of a School Board with the ensuing rate rise, and was to keep control of how religion was taught, then the parish would have to erect two new schools (he later realised this would have to be four), improve the school in Buckley and enlarge and re-floor the school in Shotton. All this would cost money and involve an increase in the voluntary subscriptions. Although in the following September Hawarden, like the majority of parishes, opted for continuing voluntary education rather than for Board schools, the parish was slow to subscribe the necessary money. The Gladstone family and other local landowners and industrial magnates were consistent benefactors, but many people had to be constantly reminded that if they did not pay their promised subscriptions, there would be no alternative to the setting up of a Board, with a subsequent rise in rates. Furthermore, the new rates would far exceed the existing voluntary payments, which were, and would continue to be, supported by Government grants. (It should be noted that the very successful Hawarden Grammar School, in which the Gladstone family was much involved, was governed by an entirely separate organisation, the National Society for

Middle Class Schools Committee, and not covered by the Education Act.)

The church schools, though voluntary, were not unregulated, and diocesan inspectors regularly visited them. The magazine was able to report that the inspectors were satisfied with all the existing schools except the one at Broughton, which for some years hence was to suffer from far more problems than any of the others, mainly because the parents kept their children away in order to send them out to work as young as twelve. This circumstance may have reflected the relative poverty of the residents of Broughton. The question of regular attendance at both day and Sunday schools constantly haunted Stephen. The idea of compulsory education was not popular with many parents and was slow to catch on not only in Broughton but in Hawarden too. People were disinclined to realise that in their now swiftly changing world, education was to become a necessity for economic survival in a way which had not been so before.

As well as education, the first issue of the magazine also dealt with another potential and more immediate awkwardness: the church services. Stephen had increased the number of these, and was aware that this might be interpreted as a criticism of both the previous Rector and his parishioners. With great tact, he assured them: 'We do not wish in any way to disturb the minds of those who already have settled rules for living close to God; nor to cast any kind of disparagement on the past ... it rests with each individual to have his own rule of life.' The Rev. Henry Glynne had not in fact been particularly Low Church in his leanings, and years before Stephen's arrival had changed the focus in the church from the pulpit to the chancel.

In April, Stephen again used the magazine to praise his uncle for his work in the parish: 'His heart was in his work.

He loved his people.' This was followed in May by a long and detailed account of Henry Glynne's last hours and death, which had followed soon after a freak lightning strike, and this issue also included a tribute to Henry from Stephen's older brother, Willy.

Determined to make his mark early on in his incumbency, in June 1873 Stephen decided to set up a Temperance Society. He himself was a very moderate drinker and, like many of his generation of churchmen, Anglicans and Dissenters, especially the mostly teetotal Methodists, he saw alcohol as the scourge of the working classes, threatening religious obligations and personal and family happiness. Drink wasted time and money. Young men in particular had to be constantly wooed away from its temptations by being offered more worthwhile opportunities for spending their leisure time productively. Stephen's night schools for young men were a big part of this plan. Hawarden had long had two men's Friendly Societies, the Ancient Shepherds and the Druids, which held regular festivals and performed works of charity, but they were interested in group support, rather than issues of personal betterment or temperance. Night schools had more far-reaching benefits.

Another of Stephen's constant concerns which arose early in his incumbency was the music in the church. All his family was musical. His mother and sisters, Mary and Helen, were competent pianists and Willy, who wrote hymns, had formed a Glee Club in Hawarden some years earlier. Stephen, keen to persuade the congregation to join more enthusiastically in the hymn singing in services, provided hymn books and singing practices for them, but the choir and the organist were at least as important. Over the years he spent much time on appointing a succession of the latter,

Figure 13. William Gladstone. Reproduced by kind permission of the Flintshire Record Office.

most of whom were perfectly able but, or perhaps, therefore, soon moved on.

In May of 1874 there was a difficulty over the church music, involving 'as on some previous occasions, ... an imperfect understanding between the organ and choir', as Stephen described it to his father. Whether this refers to a catastrophe in the middle of a hymn or a muddle over the time of choir practice is not clear. Whatever it was, Gladstone wrote to Stephen on behalf of Sir Stephen Glynne. Sir Stephen believed, or was thought by Gladstone to have believed, that his nephew had taken the church music, which he considered was his province, out of his hands. This was not the case, but, as ever, Gladstone could not resist intervening. Being now in opposition after a recent General Election won by Disraeli and the Conservatives, he must have had a little more time on his hands. (Sir Stephen was to die later in that year, mourned by family and parish alike.)

The church music affair was just one of many occasions when family misunderstandings arose and had to be patiently and time-consumingly sorted out. Small wonder is it that in November 1874, Stephen was ill, and unable to go to Southampton to see Harry off to India to work with one of the branches of the family firm in the sub-continent. Stephen told his parishioners that he had strained his voice preaching in a large London church back in June, and when he finally saw a doctor, he'd been told to rest his voice at least until Christmas. In a letter to his brother he put his problems down to either 'past carelessness', by which he could be referring to the straining of his voice, or, as he adds, 'to my experience at Hawarden ... mental worry'. This possibility suggests something rather different, more private and less easily curable. Whatever the cause, he clearly needed a break, and in December he went up to his beloved Cumbrae. Even while he was there, Gladstone did not let up, writing to him about the arrangements for Holy Communion in Hawarden and the dissatisfaction of some of the congregation, a matter which was in any case on his son's mind.

By January 1875, Stephen felt much better and, after three months' rest, his voice was strong enough for him to preach again. He returned home, although by no means completely recovered. Mary reported to Herbert on 1 February that 'Stephy preached a long sermon yesterday and was [rather] worn', and shortly after this he briefly left the parish again, for a walking holiday in Wales. Like all his family, Stephen loved walking. His sisters thought nothing of walking into Chester and back, a total distance of some ten miles, for a shopping trip. Catherine walked incessantly between Castle, village and church. Gladstone went on vigorous walking holidays with his sons in Scotland. Stephen covered long distances well into old age.

He seems to have found this Welsh holiday both physically and spiritually refreshing. Refreshment was certainly needed, for in December his father, briefly retired from politics, was interfering again, objecting to Stephen's plans for a new altar cloth, which he thought was in some way inappropriate. Firmly, for him, Stephen wrote back saying that 'in my opinion the prospect of any organised opposition here is most unlikely. There was a time, but that is past.'

Indeed, a working compromise seems to have been reached between High Church Rector and comparatively Low Church parishioners. In December 1875, the parish magazine included a long letter from Stephen, reviewing the situation after his three years as Rector of this 'important place'. It was indeed important, even if size were the only criterion. The parish now comprised about 6,000 people, including about 4,000 attached to the Mother Church. His parish letter begins, in typically self-deprecating style, by recalling an early setback. He had wanted Sealand to be a separate living, an idea for which he had gained no support. But triumphs are also mentioned: three new schools have been built and the poorly attended Sunday early evensong of his uncle's time has been turned into a 'plain and bright service for children, together with catechising', a change he had planned to make right from the start.

These preliminaries out of the way, the letter turned to a much more significant matter, concerning the still vexed question of Holy Communion and, specifically, the physical position of the priest, the very matter which had been raised back in 1872 by the writer of the letter to the *Chester Chronicle*. Central to the sacrament of Holy Communion is the altar, or Holy Table. Before the Reformation, the celebrant (the priest), while he prepared the elements (or bread and wine), stood with his back to the people, facing east, towards the altar, which was usually stone and very elaborately decorated. After the Reformation, the altar, now seen as a focus of remembrance rather than sacrifice, became simpler, usually basically a rectangular table, often placed democratically in the domain shared by celebrant and recipients, sometimes in the middle or even at the back (west end) of the church. In the mid-1800s, High Churchmen were suspected of wanting to restore pre-Reformation practices. In some Anglo-Catholic churches, the altar had been moved and actually fixed to the rear east wall of the church, so that the celebrant perforce kept his back to the congregation.

Stephen had decided that he wanted to stand facing east, and took the opportunity to defend his decision as an interpretation of the Prayer Book which was 'nothing new'. He drew attention to the rubric of the then regularly used 1662 Book of Common Prayer, which says that after the prayer 'We do not presume to come to this thy table ... ', 'the priest, standing before the table, hath so ordered the bread and wine'. He interpreted this as meaning 'facing the long side', that is, eastwards, the same way as the congregation and therefore with his back to it. In fact, the rubric is, probably deliberately, deeply ambiguous, but the parishioners appear to have accepted that the Rector had made his decision in good faith, and no more fuss was made.

Stephen's letter also referred to two further innovations, the first of which was relatively minor. The previous system of voluntary giving to the church had now been changed to a weekly offering, which had made the church's financial position more secure. Of far greater consequence was a related change of which he was personally very proud –

almost all the seats in the church were now free and open to all. The old system of pew rent, which went back in Hawarden to at least 1766, meant that the well-off members of the congregation paid for the privilege of sitting in the same pew at each service. Just a few, badly positioned, seats were left free for the poor.

The abolition of the system of pew rent had become a contentious issue in the Church as a whole. Stephen had the Chester Diocesan Open Church Association on his side, but abolishing pew rent meant not only that an offertory had to be introduced to make up for the lost income, but also that the better-off literally had to rub shoulders with the potentially dirty and smelly. This caused outrage in some churches. As late as 1885, the Incorporated Free and Open Church Association had to defend three parishioners who were served with writs of trespass by a pew-holder; and also had to appeal on behalf of a young man who, having attempted to sit where a church warden did not want him to, had been convicted of violent behaviour under a Brawling Act. The goal of the abolitionists was to encourage greater numbers of the poor to attend church, and though this did not always happen, the principle was important to Stephen.

On a more personal level, the December 1875 letter comments honestly and openly on his relationship with his flock. He writes,

> Of personal unkindness I have met with none. Of difference of opinion I have had some experience ... But I would suggest that when anyone is disturbed he would do best to talk the matter over with me; or with the Clergy who are working with me ... let there be mutual forbearance and mutual explanation.

This implies that people had been criticising him, or his views, behind his back and that he both knew about this and was hurt by it. Later in the letter he lists a string of criticisms of his own of the local people: licentious keeping of company; violent language and drunkenness; dishonouring of parents by sons and daughters who refuse to support them in old age; slanderous gossip; recklessness of parents as to what becomes of their children, and particularly of their daughters growing up; insincere profession of religion; double-facedness; petty stealing and injustice; personal enmities; want of courage. One has to assume either that he thought his readers would welcome his openness, or that they would take these accusations as being levelled not at them but at the non-churchgoers of Hawarden, who also had access to the magazine.

The letter gave him an opportunity not only to review the past and the present, but also to set out his future aims. The first of these concerned attitudes to worship, which he wants to become more reverent and fervent, with the congregation kneeling in the prayers, singing the hymns, and making their responses audibly. His stated hopes that people will also arrive punctually and regularly, be quiet and collected, and give alms readily, suggest that a somewhat lackadaisical attitude was still prevalent. These points must have caused offence to some diehards. The second set of aims would have been taken less personally: he wants to reach out to more people in the area by building more schools and churches and setting up more church-run institutions. Church clubs, and in particular, Institutes, were seen as an essential part of the work of the church at this time, since they provided opportunities more varied than those presented by night schools, for working men, and later women, to better themselves. In Institutes, they could read, attend lectures, enjoy constructive – and free – relaxation, and, should they so wish, meet the clergy on an informal basis.

In Hawarden itself, largely because of the patronage of the Gladstone family, there was already a large number of church activities, some preceding Stephen's rectorship, some recently started by him. The Institute, originally called the Hawarden Literary and Scientific Institute, had actually been set up as early as 1854, when it was known as The Mechanic's [sic] Institute and Literary Improvement Society, with Gladstone as president. It was soon to acquire a bagatelle table, a smoking room, where talking was allowed, and refreshments. The activities were supplemented by a huge range of other opportunities: the society for intercession, Sunday schools, night schools, mothers' meetings, an afternoon school for young women, a church book shop, a choral society, a horticultural society, a clothing club, and a Young Men's Society. A tea, coffee and cocoa room, promoting temperance and offering facilities for games and general recreation, was also now set up.

But if Hawarden was well provided for, elsewhere in the scattered parish there was a lack of facilities for people, which effectively at this time still meant mostly men, to get together. Stephen, schooled by Robert Gregory in Lambeth, equated an increase in such places and activities with a desirable extension of the influence of the church. Hence his enthusiasm for setting them up. Numbers at least were looking healthy. Over 1,000 people attended the church-sponsored Hawarden Festival in July 1875 and there were fifty-two candidates for first Communion in December.

In general, the December 1875 magazine presented a picture of harmonious relations between parishioners and Rector, partly thanks to the tact of the latter. However,

Stephen had been less successful in his dealings with the local Nonconformists. Methodists of the New Connexion had been established in Hawarden since the beginning of the century and had built a new and larger chapel in 1862, capable of seating up to 300 people. Elsewhere in the parish there were several flourishing Primitive Methodist chapels. Perhaps unaware of how strongly rooted these congregations were, in an earlier magazine – in June 1874 – Stephen had begged the local Nonconformists to return to the Church of England, suggesting that their own religion was 'in vain'. This was perhaps the inevitable position for a man who believed absolutely in the Thirty-nine Articles, which imply, while they do not state, that only by embracing the beliefs of the Church of England can salvation be achieved. (They do actually specifically denounce Roman Catholic belief.) However logical his position seemed to him, however, Stephen's public suggestion that all non-Anglicans would go to Hell had, unsurprisingly, not been well received by the local Nonconformists themselves. Eventually, now, he humbly printed their strongly worded reply to his damning statement. He exonerated himself as well as he could.

His lifelong tolerant and understanding attitude to Dissenters, which was to become particularly significant in the 1890s, when the issue of Disestablishment was under discussion, began now.

CHAPTER 7 – HAWARDEN:
RELAPSE AND RECOVERY, 1876–1880

'Conversation with SEG on future punishment. His mind
does indeed grow in strength and wisdom.'
(Gladstone's Diary: 8 May 1878)

The months passed, and Stephen worked on, running the parish with outward efficiency but inner turmoil. In May 1876 he thought of going to America, for reasons we don't know. His father recorded in his diary: 'Conversation with the Rector on his projected trip to America: it is to be tested as being or not being a recreation.' Presumably if on examination the idea turned out to be for 'recreation' it would not have been undertaken, which is perhaps what happened, since Stephen remained in Hawarden. The first World's Fair was held in 1876 and it is just possible, though improbable, that Stephen had considered a visit to that. There were no family connections in America and it is unlikely that he was attracted by the idea of work in the church there – America was as riven as England over the issue of Ritualism. Perhaps he simply felt the need to get away. Gladstone was putting overt pressure on his son, by now thirty-three years old, to get married, but there seemed to be no obvious candidate. It is a curious fact that all the seven surviving Gladstone children, girls and boys, married comparatively late in life, except for Helen, who didn't marry at all. Stephen was not the sort of man to spend time actively searching out a bride, but at the same time he was acutely aware that married rectors, with wives devoted to parish work, were the norm. The America plan might have been seen as a temporary escape from pressures. It is hard to imagine him harbouring any idea of bringing home an American bride.

The next year his sister Helen became only the second sibling to break free of the family when she went off to begin a very successful academic career at what became Newnham College, Cambridge. In so doing, she was acting in defiance both of received opinion on the function of young upper middle class women – to stay at home preparing for marriage, as her older sister had done – and of Catherine's horror at the idea of any daughter of hers taking on paid work. To Stephen, Cambridge must have seemed an enviable distance from Hawarden. At this point his health broke down again, almost certainly due to the combination of stress from the demands made upon his time, and worry about his personal future.

There was, once again, a looming problem over the church music: 'as you may know there is nothing gives so much trouble in a Church as the choir', Stephen wrote to his father. Much later, in 1891 he was to become so frustrated with the men's poor attendance at choir practice that he proposed setting up a supplementary choir, including women singing, not robed in surplices, from the body of the congregation. For now, a new organist had to be found and meanwhile the choir was disbanded. Looking on the bright side, Stephen optimistically hoped this would encourage the congregation to sing the hymns, which was fast becoming an obsession with him. Naturally, Gladstone had a possible candidate for the organist vacancy already lined up, and 'Mama is going to see him, and write to you further on this matter.' There were over fifty applicants, and Stephen conducted many interviews, on top of all his other work. He drove himself hard and everything he did was planned down to the last detail. There is extant a handwritten order of service for a special twenty-minute children's service he held in Lent 1877. It ends: 'Take off surplice & go & stand in the mid aisle to see the boys out, seat by seat, beginning from the pulpit end.' These detailed instructions, more suitable for a grand civic occasion than a short children's service, suggest almost neurotic insecurity.

He suffered some blood spitting and it was decided that what was needed this time was not a retreat in chilly Scottish Cumbrae but a trip to the sun of the Cape, as South Africa was referred to at the time, which had a climate supposedly good for all kinds of physical ills. (His cousin and curate, Albert Lyttleton, was also not long afterwards to leave Hawarden for South Africa for health reasons.) The family felt that Stephen should not make the journey alone, and Herbert, who was experiencing something of a hiatus in his own life, was the obvious choice to accompany him. Herbert had finished his studies, and, having failed to gain a coveted fellowship at All Souls, Oxford, was preparing to take up a post as history tutor at Keble College, Oxford. No difficulties were raised about not starting his duties there till the autumn, and the brothers left England on 20 March 1877.

The voyage began well, with good weather, and the two brothers enjoyed the care of a stewardess who, Herbert wrote to his mother, took a deep interest in their welfare. Two eligible young men must have been quite an incentive to attentive service. They suffered bad storms in the Bay of Biscay, but things improved as they neared their destination, and shipboard life started up again. Herbert won a chess competition and there were various amusements on deck, including dancing. Stephen does not report whether he himself indulged in the latter and one suspects he did not. Although he certainly did not disapprove of dancing, and throughout his ministry cheerfully attended events which included it, he never wrote anything suggesting he participated in it himself. His mother loved dancing when she was young, and in her old age frequently played the piano for others to dance to, and she and Gladstone often danced about the house at home. But Stephen was after all in holy orders and must have read some of the various books of advice for clergymen being produced at the time. These conveyed, at best, an ambivalent attitude to clergymen taking to the dance floor. He, if not Herbert, may have disappointed the attentive stewardess.

Safely arrived in Cape Town, the brothers were received at Government House by the quaintly named Sir Bartle Frere. Frere had just been appointed as the first High Commissioner by Lord Carnarvon, Disraeli's Colonial Secretary, in an attempt – doomed, as it turned out – to impose a confederation on South Africa. The difference in political allegiance did not prevent Frere from treating the Gladstone sons with unbounded kindness and they much enjoyed his hospitality. They later stayed with the bishop and then travelled up country, uncomfortably, by train. Stephen regretted not seeing more of the countryside, but he had to get back to Hawarden and there was not time for very extensive travel. The British annexation of the Transvaal during their trip, an action inevitably seen by the Boers as an act of aggression, would not in any case have encouraged a longer stay.

Apart from a brief attack of asthma, Stephen's health was good in the Cape, probably due to lack of stress as much as the climate. Indeed, he realised that Andrew Clark, the family doctor, had recommended the trip as much in order to get him away from Hawarden as for the sake of his health. He wrote to his parishioners of enjoying 'repose and freedom from responsibility', but he also appears to have treated the whole expedition as a fact-finding mission, gleaning information on the local church, education and social conditions. He found the colony rather dull and backward, for which he blamed the Dutch (Boer) majority, but he was pleased with the church activity, particularly its missionary work, an area always dear to his heart. He himself preached to a small black congregation and to a large group of 'coloured' convicts. He shared the unthinking racial prejudice of the time, describing the male Kaffirs in a family letter as 'idle layabouts', but in an account mailed home for the newly created Children's Corner of the parish magazine, in which he described a children's service at the Cathedral in Cape Town, he told the Hawarden youth that 'There were 200 there; half of these were native children, with black and brown faces, and bare feet. But they all sang so nicely.' Patronising, maybe, but appreciative too. To the adult readers of the magazine he expressed his feelings of guilt at this, his second compulsory absence.

Stephen arrived home in June, after fifteen Sundays away, and at first took things easily. There was a new organist, although he was only to stay a little over two years; the choir had been duly revived; there was an increase in the number of baptisms; and a bazaar raised much-needed money for the schools. With renewed zeal, Stephen set up an Association of Communicants, with fixed rules concerning almsgiving, fasting and guarding against 'occasions of sin'. By the end of the year he was completely back in harness and on the third Sunday in Advent preached a keynote sermon which his father considered so significant that he paid to have it printed. The sermon began by pointing out how much the parish had grown in recent decades, with three new centres of worship and eight clergy at work instead of the five curates of twelve years previously. It then abruptly changed tack, turning into something of a harangue: 'What are the men of this Parish doing? If not found in Church, nor helping in Church works, what then do they do?' Offering some answers to his own questions, Stephen suggested that what they were mainly doing was eating and drinking too much, leading to slothful neglect not only of the Church but also of their own families. Many of these criticisms echo the ones he made in his parish letter two years earlier, so either things had not improved or his standards had risen.

Such strictures were not uncommon in the sermons of his contemporaries but it is hard to believe that this homily endeared him to his audience, although he is careful to 'take my own share of the blame'. Since he himself was regularly in church, did not drink and had neither wife nor children to neglect, it is not clear exactly how he was to blame, but this is not to say that he therefore felt free from guilt. He worried constantly about almost everything: church regulations and their interpretation, his own conscience, and, inevitably, his father's attitude on any given matter. When he did not seek his advice in advance, he hoped for his *post facto imprimatur*, as in the case of a recently widowed parishioner co-habiting with a widow whom he (the parishioner) wished to marry. Stephen neatly solved that one by refusing to marry them in church but telling them to go to a registry office.

He now began to turn his attention to the needs of the female members of the parish. In February 1878, a Girls' Friendly Society, which aimed among other things to help its members find and keep suitable employment, was set up with twenty-one members. A Miss May Vincent was holding regular cookery classes, which presumably were inexpensive. (An offer by a Mr Gothard, on his wife's behalf, of two lectures on cookery for six guineas, was declined.) In

111

June, a weekly afternoon class was introduced specifically to teach girls reading and writing. These girls would have been those who had missed out on elementary education before it became compulsory. In view of his sister Helen's active interest in women's education, these developments are not surprising, and she may even have suggested them. Mary, too, was keen on the concept, still relatively new, that girls of all social classes could benefit as much as boys from education, and indeed it was she who had first suggested that Helen should go to Cambridge. All the Gladstone girls had been taught at home, and Mary in particular felt they had been short-changed compared with their brothers, both in having received only a second-rate education and in being made to feel inferior by a series of incompetent governesses.

Some clergymen would by now have been congratulating themselves on their achievements in the parish, but not Stephen. In April 1879, he wrote to Harry:

> Well six and a third years spent here is a serious hole in my life. I wish I had right [*sic*] to feel more satisfied with the way they have been spent. Outwardly they make a very tidy show – in such a large parish & with so much 'going on' it looks well enough. Yet I fear from time to time you would scarcely note a difference inwardly. Still one hopes seeds may be sown here and there for future good. [Underlining in source.]

Harry, who understood his brother well, sent this letter on to another, unidentified, family member, scribbling on the bottom: 'How thankful and glad [?] I should be if Hawarden would respond better to his untiring efforts for indeed he cannot but feel often discouraged & out of heart.'

The 'tidy show' to which Stephen referred included, among other things: his recent raising of money to make the

Hawarden church bells safe; winter mission services in school chapels in outlying Sandycroft, Ewloe and Shotton; regular lectures, illustrated by the latest in magic lantern technology, on a range of topics from 'Darkest Africa' to bee-keeping; Sunday schools in Hawarden and Sandycroft; night schools for boys and men not only in Hawarden but also Ewloe, Broughton, Sandycroft, Shotton and Sealand; countless mothers' meetings and various other societies, including a Mutual Improvement Class; and the development of lay involvement in sick visiting. All of these activities, significantly, benefited from the patronage of various members of the Gladstone family.

It is easy to think that Stephen simply underestimated his achievements, and the reason is not far to seek: he had not one but two high achieving parents of prodigious energy who enjoyed countrywide fame and affection. They and his siblings were ever present in his life in Hawarden. He may have found it difficult to judge his own efforts fairly or even know how far he was responsible for his own successes. Or he may have been worried that he was failing in what he would have seen as his first duty as Rector: reaching the inner souls of his parishioners. He was catering for their bodies and minds – they were happy enough to make use of the Institute's bagatelle room, attend education classes, take advantage of the penny bank, and gather to drink coffee, smoke and read the newspapers and books freely provided, or learn to cook and sew. But could he be sure that their lives were fully committed to God? He was particularly worried about his Association of Communicants, set up two years previously, whom he must have seen as the core of his congregation, and he wrote to its members to express his dismay: 'We need a little more zeal... we need a little more regularity ... It is pitiful that the male members have been the least regular … we want a little more self-sacrifice.' These pleas imply serious backsliding.

In August of that year, 1879, he went on another walking holiday, this time with Herbert in Norway, and it must have been a welcome relief from the pressures which were once again building up. Walking for pleasure is a great aid to clear thinking and forward planning, and perhaps it was while tramping up and down the craggy mountains and gazing at the spectacular views along the fjords that he conceived the notion of organising a Mission in Hawarden, since he announced it soon after his return. High Churchmen had taken over the idea of missions from the Evangelicals. Their basic purpose was to save souls for Christ, an ideal fitting well with the zeal of the Oxford Movement, with its desire to return to the (supposed) spirituality of the Middle Ages. The accepted mission method was for the organising parish to hire visiting preachers who were experienced in leading people away from the works of the Devil. Special services were held at times when working people could attend. The preachers' job using, among other tools, extempore prayer, was to urge people to commit themselves publicly to the Lord. The belief of many that Hell was an actual place, where those who turned their backs on God's mercy would suffer fire and torment in perpetuity, was a strong motivator, for both preacher and potential convert.

Stephen, undeterred by the received wisdom that missions were of no use in country parishes, announced his plans for such a Mission in the parish magazine, seeking publicity, requesting helpers, and, above all, asking for prayers for its success. Although missions were no longer a new concept in the Church of England at large, they were new to Hawarden, and Stephen realised he needed to tread carefully. Not so Catherine, who immediately sprang into action on his behalf, preparing to visit all the public houses before the official Mission began. Stephen commented wryly to Harry: 'If wisely done it will do good.' At least Catherine was in tune with her son's intentions. By contrast, his father, according to Mary, took 'long walks with Stephy, spitting fire at the Mission, and says he only likes prayers out of the Prayer Book'. Ever keen to advance Stephen's interests in ways he himself understood, rather than in ways which Stephen actually wanted, Gladstone chose this inappropriate moment to raise the possibility of his son's becoming Diocesan Proctor. This appointment would have involved Stephen in representing the St Asaph Diocese in convocation and consequently would have raised his profile in the Church, something his father wanted far more than did Stephen. Perhaps fortunately, Gladstone's idea, which would surely have distracted Stephen from his planning for the Mission, and involved him in administrative work of the kind he least enjoyed, came to nothing.

Mission plans were advancing fast, and they were ambitious. With fervour, Stephen explained to his parishioners what would be involved in this opportunity to 'rouse people from their sins and their neglect, and enable them to make a new start on the great journey of life'. He described the preachers he intended to bring in as 'appointed messengers of God', who would preach daily in all the churches in the parish to 'win souls for God'. He suggested suitable Bible passages and methods of self-examination to be used by way of preparation. The Mission was to begin on the evening of 23 January 1880, with a service in the parish church, and last for six days. No less than five missioners were to hold special services, preaching, leading prayer and administering Holy Communion. There were to be separate services, at appropriate times, for various groups such as working men, children and women.

The people responded in enthusiastic droves and Stephen was overjoyed with the results, which must have surpassed his wildest dreams. His sister Mary was more sceptical. She had been supportive from the start and admitted that her expectations had been far exceeded. She was impressed by the closing service in the parish church at, unbelievably, 4 a.m., with more than 100 worshippers. However, she thought that much of the preaching had been over the heads of most of the congregation and that any effects on the community at large would be short-lived. On a personal level, she feared that Stephen would inevitably suffer a disappointed reaction when the effects wore off. It is not easy to tell if in expressing this sentiment Mary was genuinely anxious for her brother's psychological and spiritual well-being, or if she was giving vent to less attractive emotions of spite or sibling jealousy. The Gladstone children always maintained a united front publicly and there seems to have been a strong and genuine bond of affection between Stephen and Willy and both his younger brothers, but his relationship with Mary became more and more problematic. Waspish, domineering and confessedly outspoken by nature, she grew ever more critical of her brother, even when he was at his most needy, as in the affair of Constance West, which was soon to dominate him for over a year.

Mary's doubts about the success of the Mission proved to be unfounded. The first fruits were a new Temperance Society, which was set up in February, not, surprisingly, to insist on total abstinence, but to encourage people to drink less. This practical idea appears to have originated at the grass roots, rather than having been Rector-led, and suggests that people were genuinely keen to live more sober and god-fearing lives. Not long after, a new cocoa and reading room was set up with a bar. If, perhaps a big 'if', this bar sold alcohol, it must have served as a place where the menfolk could gather with their wives and families, and been a further curb on potential heavy drinking.

In March a public meeting was held which led to a decision by the churchwardens to make the few last remaining rented pews in the church free. This was a measure partly necessitated by an increase in the congregations: a direct result of the Mission. Stephen hoped that 'where rich and poor mingle together, there will be greater reverence, check to misconduct and promotion of the congregational singing'. The issues of reverence in worship and congregational participation in the hymns, both dear to Stephen, were a key part of his High Church thinking. As far as conduct was concerned, he must have thought that the behaviour of the poor would be improved by sitting among the rich, which of course included his own family, rather than the other way round, unless he thought the rich would now behave more reverently in order to set an example to their poorer neighbours. The idea that hymn singing would benefit from the new arrangements may have been based on the assumption that people would be closer together, having conscientiously filled up the seats a row at a time, starting at the front and leaving no gaps. One doubts if the Victorians were actually any more eager to do this than their modern counterparts, at church or any other gathering.

CHAPTER 8 – HAWARDEN:
DREAMS DESTROYED, 1881–1884

'Very grave conversation [with SEG] on the way home.'
(Gladstone's Diary: 27 December 1881)

The Mission successfully accomplished, Stephen, never one to rest on his laurels, set about improving the Sunday schools. One of his ideas was to offer essay prizes to the teachers on the subject of what makes a good Sunday school teacher. This was the great era of prize giving: adults and children alike strove for success in contests in everything from growing the best brace of cucumbers or showing the best sample of honeycomb to playing the cornet and writing poems. However, the setting up of a working committee on the matter of the Sunday schools was probably a better idea than an essay competition.

Each year, Stephen seemed deliberately to increase his own workload, but at this point something happened that was beyond his control: his cousin and curate Albert Lyttleton, having been advised to winter abroad for the sake of his health, went off on temporary leave of absence to South Africa. His departure meant that Stephen was now alone in the Rectory with no one to share his burdens. Lyttleton did not in fact return. He was to find South Africa so congenial that he spent almost the whole of his working life there, in the diamond fields of Kimberley.

In the new year of 1881, perhaps missing his cousin, perhaps simply influenced by his example, Stephen also thought again of service abroad, and revived his idea of going out to the Oxford Mission in India. He had many long conversations with his father about his dreams of the mission field and interpreted, or rather, misinterpreted, his father's attitude, as being supportive. By the beginning of February he was writing to Harry, who since 1874 had himself been in India with the family firm: 'I feel the Indian plan will come off – at least I am bent upon it – and it will take great events to hold me back. And I am glad to feel the plan has been so much encouraged at home.' This positive optimism did not last long. Something happened between February and April which meant that, as he wrote to Herbert in that month: 'India is knocked on the head for me this year.' There is no evidence of any 'great events' having occurred which might have affected his plans, although a parish letter he wrote at the beginning of February about a return visit of two of the Mission preachers (in the event it was only one of them) indicates that by then the euphoria may have drained away. It seems most likely that a lack of family enthusiasm simply sapped his will to depart for the mission field: there would have been no one to encourage him. Optimism quickly turned to disenchantment, and in May, he wrote to Harry about his depression and sense of failure in his work in Hawarden.

He hid his state of mind well from his father, who with Catherine had spent Easter at the Rectory and who cheerfully enthused to Harry: 'Indeed it is a lively pleasure, were there no other, to witness the admirable way in which he bears the arduous charge of this parish.' Gladstone was no doubt seeing what he wanted to see, and even at such close quarters remained unaware of the strength of Stephen's longings. Stephen had learned that it was not always in his own best interests to confide in his father. Soon after Easter and, amazingly, without Gladstone's knowledge, he set about looking for a curate to fill his shoes while he was in the mission field. Sadly, this proved an insoluble problem, partly for financial reasons, and by

August he had given up the search and all his cherished ambitions had come to nothing. 'Ah – how I wish I could go to India. I have planned and watched and hoped, & everything seems to rise to hinder it,' he wrote to Harry. He went glumly off on holiday to Scotland, though still desperate to cling on to his hopes, as he also confided to Harry:

> Alas my coming here means my not going to India. It has been a severe disappointment to me in every way … it is not unlikely it may come off next year. Amongst other things (*entre nous*) I want to see the Oxford Mission, for I sometimes feel an attraction towards it, where I increasingly feel unadapted to Hawarden needs. But understand that this is all in the air, and it has only been breathed as the barest possibility to Father (who didn't take it in, I think) & Willy.

The final sentence must refer to his revived, rather than his original, plans to go out to India, since he had discussed those thoroughly with his father. But in any case the idea that Gladstone, even if he was now in his second term as Prime Minister, might not have 'taken in' anything concerning his son, was wishful thinking. His awareness of Stephen's wish was as great as his desire to crush it.

If his perceived failures in the parish had encouraged his desire to shake the dust of Hawarden from his heels and go out to India, the collapse of those plans only added to his despair. He was in a turmoil of emotions; and then another factor, entirely unforeseen, entered the mix, in the guise of Constance West. In November 1881, Constance, the nineteen-year-old daughter of Sir Algernon West, once private secretary to Gladstone, was invited with her mother to stay at Hawarden Castle. There she met Stephen, then nearly thirty-seven – virtually twice her age – and over four days, spent many hours in conversation with him, one suspects chiefly in a listening capacity. Stephen, depressed by the failure of his India scheme, lonely and anxious to please the parish and his parents by at last acquiring a wife, fell headlong in love. He knew nothing about Constance, except that she was reasonably physically attractive and a good listener, and in lieu of hard facts he created a complete fantasy figure, in a fantasy situation. In his mind she became the ideal clergyman's bride, and her parents the ideal sympathetic in-laws.

When she and her mother left Hawarden at the end of their visit, he poured out his feelings to his parents. Blinded by his passion, he thought they were pleased for him, and he wrote ecstatically to both his younger brothers. Although he knew Constance's mother was not disposed in his favour, and indeed actually disliked clergymen, and although he had no idea of Constance's feelings, if any, for him, he wrote confidently to Harry, describing the 'deep and sudden attachment' he found himself possessed of.

> She is good and beautiful ... I have some grounds perhaps of hope from feeling she was interested ... She is one who will be a fountain of beneficial light wherever she goes, & I can see would be an immense gain to Hawarden ... indeed I do not fear difficulties at all.

In his mind's eye he is seeing her ensconced in the Rectory, deeply committed to parish life and universally beloved. Even when Constance's parents insisted on his not seeing her for another year he remained confident, buoyed up by his own obsession.

Mary commented that, 'he is perfectly happy in the mere act of pouring out his love & almost indifferent now as to the future'. Mary may have resented the idea of Stephen's finding true love. She herself had been briefly wooed by the poet Alfred Tennyson's son, Hallam, in 1879, but rejected his proposal in favour of retaining her powerful unofficial post as her father's political PA and family organiser. Now she professed amusement at her brother's behaviour, and especially the necessity he felt, 'of telling all his nears and dears of this wonderful thing that has happened to him ... it was literal "love at first sight" & since that moment it has simply been headlong'. Perhaps there is also a trace of jealousy in her recording that far from having been selected for confidences because of her position as closest sibling, she was just one of 'thirty confidants'. This must surely be an exaggeration. It would have to mean her brother had told not only all his immediate family – eight people – but nearly two dozen others. Stephen had few friends. It is hard to imagine him, even in such a wildly excited state, confiding in his curates, churchwardens and lay helpers.

Mary did not herself take to Constance. She commented disparagingly on her to Catherine, describing her as 'cold and shallow' because she did not realise 'what it is to win the heart of one like Stephy'. This comment suggests sympathy for, even admiration of, her brother, but her description of Stephen's feelings when he had been forbidden to see his loved one is not very kind:

> And now here we are in Dismal Dumps. Stephy has gone back more to his normal state for a week. He talked of nothing else & read over & over again the letters on the subject, except when he was preparing children for Confirmation. Now he has for the present put it aside.

Keeping in his heart a great store of hope. Mama does not share in this hope, for evidently the girl showed coldness & inability to realise what a tremendous thing this was – I am still glad it took place, it will so much enlarge & soften Stephy's heart & experience. But oh it was curious to hear the old, old story, repeated with such naïveté & foolishness from his lips.

This verges on cattiness.

Catherine meanwhile showed motherly concern, spending hours walking to and fro between the Castle and the Rectory, or on the telephone, and, according to Mary, Gerty (as Willy's wife was generally known) got involved, and had a long talk with her brother-in-law. We don't know what line Gerty took, but his father, who himself had been disappointed in love in his youth, proved a sympathetic listener. Privately, however, he, like Mary, was somewhat amused by Stephen's plight, and did not share his son's hopes of a happy outcome, confiding to Harry in India:

> You have heard of the manner in which the Archer-God as he used to be called transfixed poor Stephy's heart without any sort of notice of what was coming. His character is so firmly balanced that we have no apprehension of any serious disturbance from this untoward incident. The dear fellow clings to the hope that the thing will come to pass. I do not think it will. But Mama believes that some other attachment will in due time be formed.

Stephen naturally felt otherwise and longed for the twelve months to pass before he was allowed to see Constance again.

The delay and disappointment strengthened his feelings of failure about his work in the parish. In June 1882, he poured out his heart to his father:

> It is now nearly ten years since I was appointed by Uncle Stephen to Hawarden. You will remember from the first I had strong doubts as to my fitness here, and I came, to some extent, 'on trial'... I do my work with an oppressed, almost crushed, rather than a free spirit.

He refers to 'inevitable worries', 'want of sympathy from the people', being 'kept at arm's length', and enjoying 'respect but not confidence.' Pointedly, he harks back to one of the reasons he gave for not wanting the job in the first place: 'The parish would now be far better served spiritually by one not so closely related to what may be called the "temporal power" or the ruling family of the place.' Sadly, he continued, 'it seems a moment for ... a married rector ... If I do not marry, something like a community life is to me a necessity'. This last comment suggests that his chief problem was simply loneliness. He was yearning for close companionship.

Now that he was doubting the possibility of marrying Constance, going out to join a mission community seemed the only bearable alternative to continuing to rattle about alone in the huge and, as he saw it, reproachful, Rectory. He told his father yet again that what he wanted was to join the Oxford Mission in Calcutta, describing it as the 'deep desire of my heart'. To make his argument more convincing, he added that he had received a 'hinted invitation' from the Bishop there. To sugar the pill, he volunteered the information that 'the Oxford Mission welcomes men who will only stay quite a limited period'. In other words, if his father would accept the idea of his going out to India, he,

Stephen, would guarantee that it would be for a short time only. He wrote to Herbert even more desperately: 'I have a strong conviction that I am not wanted here ... I am not trusted with the people's confidence ... I have always felt myself imposed rather than welcomed.' It was as if the worries surrounding his appointment in 1872 still haunted him. He told Herbert that he had kept Constance's bundle of letters. These letters are not extant, but can hardly have been encouraging. He seems to be hanging on to a 'slight possibility of marriage' even while at the same time thinking of leaving England for India. He was living in a confused world of opposing dreams, both of which were un- obtainable. Harry received a very similar letter, with the comment that Stephen doubted his parents' 'ability to judge impartially' their son's desire to leave the parish, and leave soon. It is clear how much he needed a close confidante, other than his parents: preferably, of course, a wife.

One of the reasons Stephen gave to both his brothers for his urgent desire to leave the country was that if he waited much longer, their parents would be too old to be abandoned, even temporarily. It looks as if what he really wanted was for his mother and father to tell him, unequivocally, that they wished him to go out to the Mission, perhaps even citing the Providence of God. Lacking such a directive, he wrote to his mother in anguished and convoluted terms about his undecided state, his lingering hopes over Constance, the possibility of leaving Hawarden, his desire to follow God's will, and the sense of responsibility he felt to his mother and father: 'In many ways there never was such a Home as I have had.' He does not want to perpetrate what might seem to them 'almost a cruel, ungrateful thing'. To an outsider, it may appear that neither parent deserved all this selfless consideration. In his childhood Catherine had certainly not been the conventional devoted mother, blind to any of her son's shortcomings; and she and Gladstone had dispatched him as soon as possible to a truly dreadful school. But like all his siblings, Stephen was in thrall to 'The Great People', as his Uncle Stephen had dubbed them.

Catherine and Gladstone conferred about how to help their son in this crisis, but it is obvious that their main aim was to keep him in Hawarden. Gladstone wrote to Stephen: 'This matter will be guided by a Divine hand ...' Unfortunately, the Divine guidance, as interpreted by his father, was not in the direction Stephen hoped for. The letter continued, purporting to put the ball in Stephen's court: '[you ought] not to be governed by a consideration of the effect of your decisions upon me, or even on your mother, whose claims are every way greater ... a real and great difficulty would lie in finding a successor to you'. Having made clear what he thought was God's will in the matter, and then indulged in a bit of moral blackmail, Gladstone witheringly suggested that in any case Stephen was quite unsuited to the Mission. He advised him to take counsel from persons in the Church who could really judge. With terrible finality, he closed by stating: 'I cannot attach weight to the Bishop's invitation.' Perhaps Stephen was unwise to have described the invitation as merely 'hinted'.

On 19 September, Stephen made the previously agreed and much longed-for visit to Constance. He was, rightly as it turned out, not sanguine about his chances, and by seven in the evening, in their second conversation of the day, Constance had made it very clear that she was not interested. Even then he didn't quite relinquish hope, thinking that at least the two families might draw closer together. But this was not to be, and Constance was shortly sent off to travel round the world. Stephen's brave but, as it soon turned out, not strictly honest, response was to announce that, 'I am personally disinclined to marriage.' He now even more deeply craved some other kind of support, and the Oxford Mission still seemed to be the only possible option, even though he wrote to Harry: 'Father's denunciation of my utter unfitness for India must be allowed weight.'

Thoroughly disheartened, in December he discussed with his father the prospect of applying for a vacant living in Llandaff, but nothing came of this idea. When change did come, in 1883, it was not in the form of Stephen moving out of the Hawarden Rectory, but of Willy moving in. Willy was also feeling the weight of parental interference, and with his wife, Gerty, moved out of the Castle where they had been living since their marriage in 1875. While their new house was being built – not far away – Willy and Gerty lived temporarily in the Rectory, an arrangement which seems to have worked well for them. Stephen found it led to some constraints on his parish work, but he was himself away from Hawarden from January to early March, attending on his ailing father in Cannes, with his mother and Mary. Gerty must have been delighted to get away from Catherine, whom Mary, not only in private but even in her hagiographical memoir *Catherine Gladstone,* admitted was not the easiest of mothers-in-law. Stephen's future experience was certainly to bear this out.

By August, Stephen, having given up thoughts of both Constance West and India, seemed to have settled for the inevitable. Willy and Gerty had left the Rectory for their new home, the Red House, and a new curate, who was to be in charge of the isolated daughter church at Sealand, was about to move in. Stephen mentioned this in a relaxed letter to

Harry, in which he also amusedly described a handsome new clock in the church, presented by the people, which 'is to inform the preacher of the lapse of time – he alone can see its face'. What Stephen did not tell Harry was that the clock had originally been intended as a personal token of the parishioners' thanks to him for his ten years' service. The parish magazine stated that 259 people, 'of all classes' had subscribed, but the Rector had wished it to be a gift not to him but the church. This discrepancy is interesting. Either Stephen was being modest in his letter to his brother, or he was concealing, consciously or unconsciously, his popularity, which did not fit with his own professed idea of his standing in the parish. Or it could be that to him, 259 people implied just a small proportion of his flock, confirming his view that he remained unwelcome in Hawarden. A far more significant piece of news in his letter to Harry, as events later turned out, was the pending arrival of one 'H. Drew, of Oxford and Cuddesdon, [who] comes as Deacon next month'.

It is apparent from this letter, and others written about the same time, that Stephen was becoming concerned about his mother's health, which might be an added factor in his abandoning thoughts of India. By now his parents were both in their seventies and he realised that, as he had feared would happen, he had effectively missed the moment when he could have gone abroad and left them without feeling guilty. The next year, by accepting from the bishop the appointment of Rural Dean of Mold, he tacitly committed himself to remaining at Hawarden at least for the next few years. Rural Dean is not an office particularly suited to one of Stephen's temperament, involving as it does co-chairing the deanery synod, calling and chairing meetings of the deanery chapter, acting as a communication channel between parishes and the bishop, and carrying out visitations on behalf of the archdeacon, all of which tasks demand organisational skills as well as time away from parish duties.

The only aspect of the job which might have tempted him was the pastoral care of the diocesan clergy, but in any case he would not have had much choice in the matter. The post of Rural Dean is a rotational one, and not much sought after. It involves regular travels round the diocese and – though this fact would not have influenced him – Stephen's Uncle Henry's death had been the direct result of one such trip undertaken when he had held the post. The role, shuffled among the various senior clergy of the diocese, is moreover cynically regarded by some junior clergy as a means of episcopal espionage. Although Stephen accepted the appointment, letters and diaries pay this part of his duties no attention, which suggests they were hardly onerous, and not among his first concerns.

Meanwhile, the magazine announcements suggested that the parish was pursuing its normal uneventful course – the current organist and choir master was leaving after four and a half years; the organ and chancel needed restoring; the church still lacked a proper vestry; Harry Drew was ordained deacon. But there were changes in the air: on the education front, a class was being held to help 'backward children' to enter the mainstream schools. On the social front, the Institute now had twenty-three lady members, two of whom were elected to its council. And in 1884 there began the most momentous change of all, both to Stephen's life and consequently to the parish as a whole.

CHAPTER 9 – HAWARDEN:
HAPPY FAMILIES, 1884–1886

'In the forenoon S came down to the Castle & conversed
with his mother and me dutifully desiring our consent
to his marriage with Miss A Wilson.'
(Gladstone's Diary: 20 December 1884)

Back in March 1883, Stephen placed in the parish magazine
the first of several pleas to his parishioners that they should
get married in their home church. Now, the parishioners
might be thinking of making the same request to their
Rector.

Late in 1884, on a visit to Liverpool to preach at Christ
Church, Hunter Street, Stephen stayed with a Doctor Wilson
and his family in Islington Square. In what at first appeared
to be a carbon copy of the affair of Constance West, he fell in
love at first sight with the Wilsons' not yet twenty-one-year-
old daughter Annie, whom he first saw sitting by the
morning room fire. Photographs of Annie in her later years
depict a woman with luxuriant hair, neatly piled up, a clear
gaze, a strong chin, and a mouth firmed-up by age and
experience. A family portrait of her children taken just after
the turn of the century, shows both her daughters as pretty
young girls. Since they look more like their mother than their
father, it is probably safe to assume that the young Annie's
looks, as well as her strength of character, were to Stephen a
major part of her attraction.

However that may be, at the end of his stay he went
back to Hawarden determined to return to Liverpool
forthwith, declare his feelings and ask Annie Wilson to
marry him. As usual, he confided in his family. Mary's
comment in her diary was not unlike her comments on his

130

passion for Constance: 'Stephy has been going it like a house on fire having only really known her during this one week.' His parents, whose consent he typically requested before making a move, commended 'reflection' while expressing 'unbounded confidence in him', as Gladstone recorded in his diary. He generously promised his son £10,000 if he married. Both parents certainly seem to have been of the opinion that Annie Wilson was a much better proposition than Constance West and they were also increasingly anxious to see their son married.

At the Liverpool end, things were not to be quite as easy as Stephen had assumed. When he arrived in Islington Square, he discovered that in the short interval between his visits, the Wilson family had moved, and he had no idea where to find them. Fortunately, an alert passing cab driver not only spotted the agitated suitor on the doorstep, but knew where the family had gone – to the nearby Abercromby Square. A relieved Stephen was ferried to the new address, and on arrival he promptly proposed. The proposal, though it must have been completely unexpected, was unhesitatingly accepted, both by Annie and her parents. They were delighted, although their prospective son-in-law was twice Annie's age, and, according to Sir Edward Hamilton, Gladstone's private secretary, of 'unprepossessing appearance'. No doubt it helped that their daughter would be marrying into, if not the aristocracy, one of the premier families in the land. Seven weeks later, Stephen and Annie were married, on 29 January 1885, at Christ Church in Hunter Street.

The marriage of the second son of the Prime Minister, himself a son of the city, to a local doctor's daughter, was a huge event in Liverpool. More than 6,000 people applied for tickets, six times the capacity of the church, and crush barriers had to be erected by the police to control the crowds, which began forming at 9 a.m., both outside and in the surrounding streets, two hours before the appointed time of the ceremony. Along the route which both the bride's and groom's parties would travel in open carriages, every window was jammed with people. The streets were decorated with flags and banners, and a red carpet was laid down under a specially erected awning between the church gates and the main door. All this reflected not only the popularity of Gladstone and Catherine, but also the affection in which Annie was held locally. Stephen had, if more by luck than judgement, chosen well: as the Rector's wife in Hawarden, Annie was quickly to become as loved and respected as she had been as a parishioner in Liverpool.

It was truly a family occasion. Harry, temporarily home from India, was best man, presenting Annie with a diamond ring, and Mary was one of the six bridesmaids. The *Liverpool Courier* described the church decorations and all the bridal finery, including the makers (Messrs Bolland and Sons of Chester) in extensive detail. It was all very grand, indeed so grand that some ladies in the congregation, accommodated in extra seating at the rear of the church, attempted to improve their view of proceedings by sitting on the backs of their chairs. These chairs then noisily collapsed: a cause of some apprehension among the discreetly placed detectives. The wedding breakfast was held at the Wilson family home in Abercromby Square, an impressive late-Georgian house with an ample-sized, long dining room overlooking the garden. The guest list, faithfully reproduced in the *Courier*, suggests that, large as it was, the room was more than full. There were Gladstones, Lyttletons, Wilsons, local worthies and several Hawarden curates, including Harry Drew. The Wilson descendants possess a family chronicle covering the time, which includes a memory of a relative, then eleven years old. She describes a horseshoe-shaped table on which were birds' nests made from hollowed out sponge cakes, covered with pistachio nuts and containing coloured eggs made from blancmange. That must have made for some messy eating.

Annie's going-away bonnet and muff were trimmed with humming birds, so there was quite an avifaunal theme (as Gladstone might have termed it.) After the reception the newly-weds were taken to Flint, which is today about an hour's journey away, and thence by a horse-drawn carriage, laid on especially for them, a few miles north-west to the village of Halkyn, near Holywell. Here they processed through specially erected triumphal arches to their honeymoon in Halkyn Castle, lent by the Duke of Westminster. The Castle was even grander than Hawarden, a huge castellated pile put up by the Duke some sixty years previously. Annie described it as 'so comfortable and nice' and the couple seems to have been well looked after: 'the servants very nice and the cooking good'. These sentiments of Annie's, unpretentious, undemanding and grateful, though not undignified, reflect her personality and her no-nonsense upbringing.

Stephen's parents were well satisfied with his choice of bride, showing no concern at all that he might have done better for himself socially. As Sir Edward Hamilton noted, having commented on the fact that 'it was not a great marriage for the son of a Prime Minister to contract': the Gladstones 'had not an ounce of false pride between them ... they have no worldliness'. They were almost certainly relieved that Stephen was now at last married and would stop wanting to leave Hawarden. Mary, who was already beginning to take an interest in the equally socially unconnected Harry Drew, had taken a liking to all the Wilsons and was only mildly satirical about Stephen's pre-marriage besotted state. She referred in her diary to his preaching a sermon she described as 'from the cupboard', presumably an old one, as he was too preoccupied to compose a new one, and commented on how he was 'writing to all his nears and dears'. Later Catherine was to become very critical of her daughter-in-law's household management, and the letter Annie wrote to her from the honeymoon suggests that the bride may have had a presentiment of this. After thanking her new mother-in-law for her 'beautiful & kind' letter, she expressed gratitude 'for all your good advice'. 'I hope', she continued, 'that this holiday will not only be a happy one; but a useful one in preparing me for the many duties which as you say are waiting for me at Hawarden.' Catherine's original letter has not, to my knowledge, survived. If we had it, it might be possible to guess at Annie's initial private reaction. At least she was forewarned of the high standards expected of her.

Stephen and Annie returned to Hawarden, having spent some time in Yorkshire and Lancashire, on February 17, Shrove Tuesday. The parish magazine recorded great preparations, including bunting and flags, and a procession with a band. Hawarden obviously didn't want to be outdone by Halkyn and in spite of dreadful weather there were large crowds. The Wilson Family Chronicles state that some enthusiasts even took the horses out of the harness and themselves dragged the carriage through the streets to the Rectory. Be that as it may, the welcome was certainly warm, unlike the weather, and Stephen was presented with an illuminated address, to which he replied that 'he didn't deserve such kindness and sympathy, but he hoped with the help of the lady he was bringing home with him, he might be able to show his gratitude by working more earnestly & sympathising more deeply with his people than he had done in the past'. In marrying, he was sure that he had made a popular move.

Mary's description of the homecoming in her diary was less sympathetic than that in the parish magazine:

> Day broke in utter gloom and snow and slush and fog. Up with Mama to rectory at 10.30 in lowest spirits, under the dripping flags etc. dawdled about for hours, and then got telegram announcing they had missed their train – this was really the last straw … However, after lunch we at last laughed … and cheered up as the snow ceased falling, and at 3 o'clock up the village they slowly drove, preceded by band … S replied [to the address with which he was presented] with great feeling and earnestness … Annie behaved gracefully.

Mary's tone seems a little detached, lofty, that of an older, more sophisticated sister-in-law. But she shared her parents' delight that her brother was, at last, happily married. The Gladstones generously gave five separate children's teas to celebrate, as well as a tea for the old people, at which Stephen and Annie went round shaking hands. In the evening there was a magic lantern show and two dances, at both of which the newly-weds made brief appearances. Annie apparently knew instinctively what was expected of her as the Rector's wife. Stephen's absurd prediction for Constance West – 'She is one who will be a fountain of beneficial light wherever she goes, & I can see would be an immense gain to Hawarden' – was to come true in Annie.

She and Stephen settled down quickly to the happy married life they were to enjoy for the next thirty-five years.

It can't always have been easy for her. Stephen continued to have bouts of ill health, particularly sick headaches resulting from eye-strain, and to suffer periods of depression, mainly caused, according to the tougher Annie, by his having too thin a skin. She bore six children, all of whom grew up devoted to her; she coped with the ageing and deman-ding Gladstone in-laws; and remained

Figure 14. Stephen and Annie at Hawarden. Reproduced courtesy of the Flintshire Record Office.

on good terms with all Stephen's siblings, even, for most of the time, Mary, who after Stephen's death described her as providing her brother with 'a bed of roses at home'. She managed to run the huge, money-consuming Rectory, if not with perfect efficiency, at least competently; and she was widely loved and respected in the parish.

This was no simple achievement: the parish was far flung, and extremely active, with Annie expected to show an interest in women's classes, mothers' meetings, the Girls' Friendly Society and many other associations, while not treading on her mother-in-law's toes. Then there were all the fund-raising bazaars with their months of preparatory working groups. Also, the parish was very diverse socially. At one extreme were the wealthy, though never flamboyant, Gladstones, in their family castle; at the other, people so numerous and so destitute that the very same magazine that described the newly-weds' return from their honeymoon printed a dinner recipe 'within the reach of the poorest of the poor'. Its main ingredients were onions, potatoes and bread. No wonder people flocked gratefully to the Rectory, and the Castle grounds, for the teas and other refreshments so frequently provided there.

On 6 December 1885 Stephen christened his firstborn, a daughter called Catherine after her grandmother. Mary recorded in her diary that her brother 'all but broke down in christening her and she stretched out her arms'. After such a long and lonely bachelorhood, this must have been a miraculous moment for Stephen. Less than twelve months later their first son was born, Albert Charles, and there followed four more children, Charles Andrew in 1888, Stephen Deiniol in 1891, Edith in 1895 and William Herbert in 1898. The simple pleasures that marriage and family life brought to Stephen are exemplified by this touching little vignette from a letter to Harry in January 1886: 'I made a big Snow man ... over 6 feet high; topped with an old beaver; lantern in one hand & staff in the other. Annie stood within the house as architect – I only executed; but it's really rather good.' (The snowman later fell over, but was restored.) A few weeks later he was urging Herbert: 'You must look out for a wife now! Every year lost is such a pity ... It would be an immense help in all ways & a good wife would help you to be economical.'

This advice was prompted not solely by his own experience, for in February 1886, Mary had married the curate Harry Drew. This match was even more surprising than Stephen's. Mary was not only heavily involved in the political scene but had a busy social life in London and frequently acted as her father's political hostess, a role which her mother Catherine had never much enjoyed. By now thirty-eight, Mary was nine years older and far more experienced than Harry Drew, who knew little of the world beyond Oxford (Keble College and Cuddesdon) and Hawarden, where he had arrived as deacon less than two years before.

Like Annie Wilson, he was not well connected, but in many ways he must have been a most desirable husband. As a boy his 'winning manner' and 'quiet strength' were already in evidence and as he grew older, people remarked frequently on his 'manly beauty' and modesty, preserved in spite of his many abilities. He was academically able, good at a wide variety of sports and known for his sense of fun. Harry had entered the priesthood relatively late, after the sudden and traumatic death of the son of Lord and Lady Manvers, a young man whom he was tutoring and accompanying on a trip to Europe. Harry's decision to go to Cuddesdon was life changing. The Vice-Principal, Charles Gore, took him under his wing, converted him from Toryism to Liberalism – thus making him potentially a more acceptable Gladstone son-in-law – and took him on a visit to Llanfairfechan, where Harry heard of a vacancy at Hawarden. According to the *New York Times* of 1 April 1910, Harry met Stephen while in Wales, and was personally invited by him to come to Hawarden. This may or may not be true. Whatever the circumstances, although, like Stephen, he had originally wanted an urban appointment, he applied for the Hawarden vacancy, was accepted, and met Mary.

Mary and Harry became engaged on Christmas Day, 1885. That night she 'sat up with Agnes and Helen talking it all over and trying to believe it was true'. Almost till the day of her wedding she wondered if she was doing the right thing in marrying the young curate, and she sought Stephen's advice on more than one occasion. As Stephen wrote to their brother Harry: 'I do not know whether you know that Mary's doubts have returned. I have had a long talk with her ... She will have to realize how very different will be the joys of her new & her past life.' Mary was not only loved, but in love, and Stephen may have feared that this was blinding her to the practical problems of adjustment which she would have to make. The positions of statesman's daughter and curate's wife were poles apart. She would of course still be a Gladstone daughter, and so there can hardly have been a question of her ever being short of money. But as a curate's wife she would be living in Hawarden all the year round, which would be very different from living for weeks at a time in London, enjoying political importance and a round of parties, plays and concerts, coming home to the Castle just for country holidays. Mary had always played a big part in parish life, but on her own terms, organising concerts and doing some teaching. Now, as a curate's wife, she would be far less in charge of her own time.

The Gladstones themselves, who might also have felt anxieties about the match, were quite sanguine. As in Stephen's case, and perhaps more surprisingly, considering Mary's key role in family life, they made no objections. It is significant, however, that it was decided that the newly married Drews would live in the Castle, conveniently on hand for looking after the now septuagenarian, if still very active, parents. Mary may well have had misgivings about this arrangement. She and her mother had never got on particularly well. Years before, she had, typically, grumbled to Herbert that Catherine was 'behaving like a naughty child' over some trivial detail concerning a carpet. Gladstone was probably completely unaware of the lack of harmony between his wife and his daughter. He and Mary had an excellent relationship, and he does not seem to have suffered from the idea that he would be losing a daughter, as, indeed, in a sense he was not.

Gladstone wrote to W. V. Harcourt, a close political ally, about his pleasure in the match: 'It [the marriage] is unadorned in the sense of worldly goods but promises the most solid happiness.' Following the parents' lead, local and London society responded generously, as Stephen told their brother Harry: 'I hear Mary's presents are pouring in on all quarters from all the friends and fashionables. It is a fine thing to see.' The engagement was short, like Stephen's, and on 2 February 1886, Mary and Harry Drew were married, by Stephen, at St Margaret's Westminster. Mary's doubts were now behind her: 'The great wonder was to feel it all so natural and to feel I was I when I thought I was going to be somebody else.' Aided by Helen, taking time off from her duties in Cambridge, she made all the arrangements herself, and very successfully, according to Agnes. If Stephen had reservations, he kept them to himself. But in the years to come the triangle of curate/brother-in law, rector and sister was to create tensions and even bitterness.

Mary and Harry returned from their honeymoon on 5 March to 'no lack of affectionate interest', as the parish magazine put it. The couple had specifically asked for no public demonstration, perhaps not wishing to compete with the extravagances which had greeted Annie and Stephen the previous year. Nonetheless, the church bells rang, flags were put out, and the orphanage children sang 'Home Sweet Home' as the horse-drawn carriage approached the Castle.

As so often, Gladstone family events were being publicly celebrated. They were the local royalty.

Harry Drew adapted easily to his new relationship not only with the 'Great People', with whom he was living, but also with Stephen, now his brother-in-law as well as his boss. The two couples were on friendly visiting terms, with Mary and Harry going to the Rectory for supper, although Stephen had 'one of his bad heads' the previous day, and Stephen and Annie going to the Castle for what Mary described as 'our first sort of being "at home."' It is not known for certain if the Drews had their own quarters. Catherine said they would live 'in a corner' but they seem to have eaten *en famille*, since visitors to the Castle commented on how Harry often missed meals or left them early to attend to parish business. Mary soon became pregnant, but, partly because she made little attempt to look after herself, sadly miscarried and was very seriously ill for several months, during which Harry nursed her devotedly. The happily married Gladstones senior must have rejoiced that three of their children were now enjoying the same matrimonial harmony as they themselves.

CHAPTER 10 – HAWARDEN:
CHANGES AND CHALLENGES, 1886–1890

'The Rector, ever ready for self sacrifice in things small & great.'
(Gladstone's Diary: 27 April 1886)

Stephen and Annie had a second child, a son, in October 1886. The family was growing, and so was the parish. A new coalmine, which opened in May 1886, brought welcome employment and encouraged people to come and live in the area. A much bigger influx of manual workers was imminent, caused by the arrival of the railway. Mindful of this, Stephen organised another Mission. As on the first occasion, he planned carefully. He asked a Rev. Robert Linklater, a vicar in Hornsey, to conduct it, and in September, Linklater came to Hawarden on a preliminary visit. The Bishop of St Asaph wrote a formal letter supporting the endeavour and Stephen put a letter of his own in the parish magazine, reminding readers of the success of the previous Mission, seven years earlier. Every aspect of the venture was carefully considered. He organised a series of cottage meetings, asking people to volunteer to make rooms available for them. He arranged for a trained lay evangelist with working-class origins, a Brother Webb, to talk to the navvies in their lunch hours and at evening meetings. Finally, he wrote to all the men building the Hawarden loop line, the Dee railway bridge and the railway line to Chester, telling them about all these activities, aimed at their 'spiritual good'.

The Mission duly took place between 28 January and 8 February 1887, concluding, as had the previous one, with a Eucharist at 4 a.m. in the parish church with 200 communicants. Throughout the twelve days, there had been large congregations and the whole operation was a great success. Keen to keep the experience fresh in people's minds, five days after it finished Stephen wrote a public letter which stated: 'I venture to hope that all of us, Dissenters as well as Church people, will have reason to bless God for many lessons taught us during the Mission.' Again, this illustrates his desire to work closely with the local Methodists. He himself was satisfied. There are no comments from Mary on this second Mission: she was away from Hawarden, convalescing from the illness following her miscarriage.

Outwardly, Stephen welcomed the changing dynamic of the parish caused by the sudden influx of large numbers – about 300 – of single working men. He did his best to make them feel welcome, writing to them about the 'great work for the good of the neighbourhood' on which they were engaged, and the parish's desire 'to stretch out the right hand of brotherly fellowship'. He tried hard to provide them with some kind of social and cultural life. Apart from the activities already on offer, which presumably they were eligible to join in with if they so desired, he arranged free weekly concerts especially for them in which they were encouraged to participate. To cater for their spiritual needs, following the Mission, he proposed permanently employing an evangelist with the specific task of ministering to the navvies, although this would put a strain on church finances. He hoped that at a later stage, some of the parishioners might take over the job, and he made sure that the parish letter which floated this idea was also seen by the local Methodists, because he 'did not like to leave them out'. This may have been simple tactfulness, or he may have hoped that they would be a possible source of volunteers, or even finance. The parish magazines of this period are silent both on how the navvies reacted to these opportunities laid on for them, and on the reactions of the Hawarden residents to the newcomers. There may have been an uneasy social mix.

Privately, Stephen himself, as he admitted in a letter to his brother Harry, was rather alarmed at the 'awful' nature of the railwaymen who came down from London for work. This is a little surprising when one considers how he had relished his early work in Lambeth among such deprived and often godless people. He had of course been much younger then. Furthermore, being conservative (with a small 'c') by nature, he did not altogether welcome the coming of the railway itself, fearing it would change the nature of the village. Both Gladstone, 'the People's William', and Catherine, were held in deep affection not only by their neighbours in Hawarden but also by vast numbers of the general public, and Stephen feared crowds flooding in at holiday time. This indeed happened one August Bank Holiday, when some 15,000 people arrived in the village on special trains, hoping for a glimpse of their hero.

There were other, ongoing worries. The problem with school funding was endemic and Stephen was losing patience. In May 1887, the debt arising from people not paying their subscriptions had risen to £60. Not for the first time, Stephen used the parish magazine to spell out the situation: if a School Board were to be set up, everyone would have to contribute, through the rates. On the other hand, if the voluntary system were to remain in place, subscriptions would have to rise anyway, as more school places were needed. So whatever happened, people would have to pay more.

By now, he himself had swung round to the view that the establishment of a Board was the preferable way forward. In his view, that would free up time, effort and money, which could be better spent on the Sunday schools.

A new Education Act in 1891 complicated matters. It supposedly made available government grants which would eliminate the need for elementary schools, including church schools, to charge, but as Stephen made clear in a letter to the parishioners, they would still have to 'work hard to earn the grant'. He made an earnest appeal for continued, and indeed, increased, financial support, on moral grounds, and took the opportunity to ask parents to do something about the continuing poor attendance at the day schools. An attendance committee of the Guardians which had been set up to tackle the problem had proved useless.

Stephen wanted to know the views of all his parishioners, including, significantly, the Nonconformists, who had their own school, to which Gladstone had contributed money for renovation in the 1860s. A public meeting was called, to decide the question of whether to build eight new board schools, which would increase the rates by twelve to eighteen pence in the pound, or to keep the voluntary system by raising an extra £100 a year. The meeting decided to retain the voluntary system, raise the subscriptions and increase the number of subscribers. To this end, representatives would be appointed to call on all householders. Unless he was somehow persuaded to share their optimism, Stephen must have felt like tearing his hair out.

Catherine had not helped the situation. Aware of the problem and over-anxious to assist her son, she stated publicly that the annual Flower Show in the Castle grounds ought to pay a contribution to the school funds, in the same way as did the Institute Festival. This suggestion appears to be reasonable, but it seems that Catherine was out of touch with village opinion. The idea caused much unpleasantness, and resulted in the temporary demise of the longstanding local Horticultural Society.

Fortunately, no clouds were cast over the forthcoming celebrations for Queen Victoria's Golden Jubilee, to be held in Hawarden on 21 June 1887, the date having been fixed to coincide with Gladstone's being down from London. Stephen and Annie gave a series of teas in the Hawarden coffee house for 1,600 children, 150 older Sunday school scholars, 130 teachers and 200 parents and friends, a mind-boggling total of eaters and drinkers. In the Castle grounds there were feasts for the 'aged people' and the children, marching with bands, games, demonstrations by the fire brigade, tours of the old medieval castle ruins, a gym display, sports and, of course, prizes. The jollifications culminated in a congratulatory telegram being sent to the Queen.

The spectacular generosity of Gladstone and Catherine on such occasions was appreciated by parishioners and Rector alike. Gladstone was in opposition from 1886 to 1892 and so marginally less busy politically, and although he and Catherine were both by now in their late seventies, they maintained their keen and active interest in parish matters great and small. Catherine gave a welcome £20 to establish some more cookery classes. More problematically for Stephen and Annie, she continued to maintain a high profile and regularly distribute prizes, just as she had done in the long years before Stephen was married. It is possible that Stephen asked her to do this, to relieve Annie of some of the burden, but it is more likely that Catherine did not wish to cede any of her influence or power to the younger woman. She had been jealous of Mary's closeness to Gladstone, and was probably equally jealous of Annie's closeness to

Figure 15. "Oh, Stevey, Stevey, that's a shocking bad move." Mr Gladstone at Hawarden: playing a game of backgammon with his son, the Rev. Stephen Gladstone. Drawn from life by Sydney P. Hall. © The British Library Board. All Rights Reserved, F60113-49/4211.220000/.

Stephen, or even of her popularity in Hawarden. Catherine could never bear to feel marginalised.

Harmonious relations were at least outwardly maintained. The Gladstones senior often dined at the Rectory, occasions which almost invariably ended with Stephen playing backgammon with his father while Catherine chatted to Annie about parish matters and household economy, a subject she herself had triumphantly mastered long ago. Catherine was economical and good with servants, who mostly stayed with her for years. Annie was still very young and inexperienced and Stephen would have been no help: he was hopeless with money. It is one of the

147

few areas in which his father failed to influence him. In 1866, Gladstone had actually commented, in a letter about the management of money: 'You know this has been the one subject on which you and I have always in a quiet way quarrelled.'

Neither mother-in-law nor sister-in-law had much of an opinion of Annie as a household manager. Mary on one occasion complained about a servant whom she dismissively described as having 'had a very poor training at the rectory'. Annie must have told her mother-in-law about problems with her housekeeper, who thwarted her attempts at economy, for Catherine passed the problem on to Gladstone. Ever generous, he offered to help with the household expenses, but Stephen, either out of pride or in defence of Annie, declined to accept. Meanwhile Catherine opposed the idea of dismissing the housekeeper.

There were tensions. In June 1888, Stephen described as 'difficult' a parental visit lasting eighteen days. Later that year, in response to a letter from Catherine containing criticism of Annie, he wrote back – after a caveat describing his love for and indebtedness to his mother – complaining of 'a spirit of prejudice & distrust on your part of our arrangements, and a want of fairness & of just judgment in anything which we do which, for any reason, goes against your ideas; & along with this a feeling of having been a good deal interfered with and embarrassed'. After this uncharacteristic outburst he excused himself on the grounds that he was overworked and, in a revival of his old anxieties and self-questioning, continued:

> I am extremely doubtful & have been so always more or less, but am so now, whether my continued residence here is either good for me or for the Parish; and on this

subject – after all that has been said by me and thought by me, I shall reserve my own independent judgment. It is a matter on which after all that has passed now for near 16 years I alone can fully judge.

A letter he wrote to Harry shortly after this has had a piece cut out of it. This is the only example of which I am aware of such a thing occurring, but speculation as to its contents, though tempting, would be idle. Meanwhile, ignorant of or ignoring any signs of strain, Gladstone extended his tree chopping activities to the Rectory grounds, cheerfully cutting down a copper beech.

At this time, Gladstone was also busy with his latest project, the founding of a library to provide a lasting home for his massive collection of books. He had already erected a corrugated iron building near the church to hold the volumes which he was gradually moving from his Temple of Peace. There were rumours of his intentions, both locally and nationally, and he wrote a letter to the parish magazine of December 1889, assuring people that his plans 'would not be without utility to the parish, though possibly not to the parish only'. A PS announced the only definite decision he had made: the proposed library would be named after the church: St Deiniol's. So began what was later to become one of the most stressful episodes in Stephen's life.

With the help of Annie, who was used to supporting him through troubled times, Stephen overcame his latest fit of despair, and the early 1890s were a briefly settled time. Family affairs were happy. In 1889 Stephen and his siblings had harmoniously marked the occasion of their parents' Golden Wedding, on 25 July, by building a new stone entrance porch on the Castle, replacing the rickety wooden original. (Public celebrations were deferred until August, since on the actual anniversary the Gladstones were in London.) Harry, permanently back from India and since 1890 married to Maud Rendell, was settled in their new home on the Wirral, Burton Manor, an easy distance from Hawarden. In March 1890, Stephen went to Cambridge to visit his sister Helen, now well established in her post of Vice-Principal of Newnham, which he described as 'her element'. Stephen was as proud of his sister as was their father.

Later in the year Stephen took his family on holidays to Barmouth on the Welsh coast and to France. There were now three children, all under five. Stephen revelled in his offspring, whom he described to his father in a letter as 'very well, & tremendously happy'. He went on: 'I never before had the privilege of seeing, from without, how extraordinarily happy human nature has the capacity to be.' The exact meaning of this statement is unclear, but what is clear is that Stephen and Annie were excellent parents. Mary, who must for years have been envying Annie and her brother their happy family life, now, at the age of forty-two, gave birth to a healthy daughter. The baby was christened Dorothy, by Stephen, but known to all as Dossie. She was doted on by her grandparents, whose home she shared.

Parish affairs too were going well. In May, moving with the times, Hawarden began to formulate plans to follow the example of nearby Mold and apply for government aid in building an intermediate school – offering education above the level of the compulsory elementary schools – and there was the usual generous offer of financial help from the Gladstones. The parish was flourishing under Stephen's care. The Institute membership had increased to over 3,000 and the new billiards table, installed after years of procrastination, was raking in much needed money. A series of discussions and papers with subjects ranging from the execution of Mary Queen of Scots to Socialism and Science attracted good audiences. In August 1890, Stephen and Annie hosted a gathering of over 200 church workers at a Rectory Garden Party.

In May 1891, a new gymnasium and an armoury room for the Volunteer Corps, built by public subscription, next to the Institute, were opened by Gladstone and Herbert, the latter being the driving force behind the enterprise. The gym was a project dear to Harry Drew's heart, but it was Stephen who had originally dreamed up the idea back in 1885, to provide for the needs of the young men in the parish. A Young Men's Society had then been set up, and now the gym provided them with the better facilities they needed.

In the winter of 1890–1891, Stephen himself had unsparingly completed a personal three month visitation of the entire Parish, that is, between 1,100 and 1,200 houses. People warmed to this display of interest and concern for their welfare.

Even when absent from Hawarden, Stephen kept the parish in mind, and his finger on the pulse. From Barmouth in August 1890, he wrote to his mother: 'The Mother's meeting, we think, had best be left a little longer: there were several little differences between some of the members, & time will soften them. Supposing Gerty [Willy's wife] would rather not entertain the Mothers this year at tea, would you do so, as we had them last year?' This letter underlines the significant place held by the whole Gladstone family in parish affairs. It is difficult to see how Stephen could have achieved so much without this supportive family network, even if he did find it oppressive at times.

He seems to have believed that his flock was as interested in his doings as he was in theirs. From France in

May 1891, he sent a letter-cum-travelogue to the parish magazine, rather as one might do to an interested family member. (Such letters were very common: Albert Lyttleton wrote frequent bulletins from South Africa.)

It was the spiritual well-being of the parish that was Stephen's paramount concern. A teetotaller and fanatical non-gambler himself, he was always concerned over the moral righteousness of his flock. In June of that same year, 1891, Mary wrote crossly, so crossly that punctuation went completely astray, to Herbert: 'Stephy came and put his foot down on raffling [at a Hawarden Women's Bazaar] and said if it was done it would bring a curse much too violent language I thought.' Herbert might have been reminded of the time when Harry won money on the Derby Lottery while at Eton and had been gently rebuked by their elder brother. Stephen was somewhat straight-laced and formal. Years later he was to express horror when he discovered that Willy's grown up children were in the habit, unrebuked, of calling their younger uncles by their Christian names. In 1919, he objected to an anecdote about their mother, which Mary wished to include in her biography, on the grounds that it was 'coarse'. It referred to a male friend saying he could not take Catherine with him as he was off to bed. Her brother's objection struck Mary as absurd.

At the beginning of July 1891, not long after the writing of that irritated letter from Mary about the raffle, tragedy struck the Gladstones. Willy, the oldest son and inheritor of the Hawarden Estate, died at the early age of fifty-one. It was not totally unexpected: he had been ill for some time with what was finally diagnosed as a brain tumour, had suffered a serious stroke and did not recover from a last-ditch operation. Gladstone himself was so devastated that his diary entry wrongly records Willy's age; Catherine hid away all photographs of her son; Stephen could not grasp how his own situation was affected.

His father recorded that he had a conversation with him 'on his position, which he had never dreamt of'. Stephen was now the eldest son and if Willy's son, another William (Will), now heir to Hawarden, did not himself have a son, it would be Stephen's sons who would inherit the estate. Although not as close to his older brother as he was to his two younger ones, Stephen had been very fond of Willy and he owed him a lot, both for his care of him when he was a child at school and, in later years, for his involvement in the parish. Willy had not only provided financial support, but contributed to the life of the community, particularly through the Glee Club and Choral Society which he had founded, and occasional organ playing. His death was deeply felt by the family and the parish, and created a shift in the family dynamic.

CHAPTER 11 – HAWARDEN:
FUTURE UNCERTAIN, 1890–1894

*'My opinion is that preferment is in the Providence of God
to be at some time your lot.'*
(Letter from Gladstone to Stephen: 8 April 1893)

With Willy's death, perhaps just by coincidence, the
solidarity between Stephen and his family over parish
matters seems to have begun to disintegrate. Herbert,
supported by Gladstone, Mary and Harry Drew, wanted to
build a new Institute, financed by a fete. The old building
was in need of repair and too small for the wealth of
activities it now housed. Stephen was opposed to the whole
idea. In a would-be clarifying letter to Herbert, which is
actually rather confused and not always legible, he set out
his reasons. He thought an extension of the present building
on the same site was all that was necessary; he objected to
the idea of money being raised other than by subscription;
and he felt that any new building would require the
payment of a heavy ground rent unacceptable to the
working men who would be the prime users of any new
facilities.

The one thing the letter was clear about was that he
would not join a guarantee fund, which he described as
being 'wholly out of the question'. Proceeding without his
approval, an executive committee was formed with Herbert
as chair, and a Great Fete was held in the Castle grounds in
August 1892. Posters advertised a spectacular range of
attractions: 'swordfeats', three military bands, flood lighting
of both the old ruined castle and of avenues through the
park, and the village itself, a display of the Golden Wedding
presents and a 'grand display of scientific, ornamental and

humorous swimming'. This must have been in the lake on which the family and local children are known to have skated. Large crowds came on thirty-two special trains, there was none of the feared 'intemperance' nor 'unruly conduct', and £1,271 was raised towards the rebuilding. Further fetes in 1894 and 1896 not only paid off the building debts but furnished both the new Institute and the Armoury, paid off the outstanding debt on the Gymnasium and made a surplus of £110 which was given to the schools.

The Institute Council asked Herbert, now president, to request Gladstone, the patron, to open the new Institute, but Gladstone, perhaps mindful of Stephen's views, was evasive, and agreed only to a low key ceremony. The Institute subscription was increased from four to eight shillings a year for labourers, but for that, they got not only a lending and reference library and a reading room, but also a lecture hall, billiards and games rooms, a private bath, with special times for ladies, and a chess and smoke room, with extended opening hours. Gladstone donated fifty-two of his own books, the works of Walter Scott, to the new Institute, and Isaac Pitman, the inventor of shorthand, gave over 2,000 volumes. Classes were held on subjects ranging from mining to freehand drawing, but not dancing, which some members had asked for. A special boys' games room was set up, but that was never much of a success, partly due, apparently, to the bad behaviour of its users.

New rules were drawn up, declaring that the Institute was 'for the social, moral and intellectual benefit of the people of Hawarden and in particular the artizan [sic] and labouring classes thereof'. Gladstone thought it would foster 'common intercourse among all the various classes that make a local community', but this is a somewhat ingenuous view. In reality, Herbert and the other members of the committee had deliberately set up a two-tier system, with 'simpler accommodation' for the working men.

All the ideas behind the extension of the Institute – except for the two-tier system – were close to Stephen's heart, and it is sad that he had not been at the centre of the scheme. He remained as a vice-president for a year or two but his name then disappears from the Institute minutes. He was now entering the most unsettled period he had experienced since his marriage. This latest attack of self-doubt was, as usual, brought on by pressure of work. He was *ex officio* chair of the local schools committee and in February of 1893 was seeking to resign, 'already overcome with pure business'. He was still trying to find a replacement in October, by which time he was becoming desperate. He asked in the parish magazine for a volunteer to replace him, someone who could 'master the laws in connection with education and keep a watchful, sympathetic and tactful eye on them all [the eight schools]'. The tone became almost threatening: 'This is what is imperatively required, if we wish to retain what we have got, and avoid a great and permanent increase of rates.' He sounds like a man at the end of his tether.

In March, he had heard of a vacancy in Boston, Lincolnshire. He had not been offered the living but it seems that Catherine might have been in correspondence about it with her daughter Agnes's husband Edward Wickham, recently appointed by Gladstone as Dean of Lincoln Cathedral. Stephen wrote to his mother:

> I have today through the Bishop of Lincoln been able to get a few facts about the finance of Boston ... If it is open, I am perfectly willing to visit the place for further enquiry, & then to consider with the advice of friends

whether I ought to go. The offer was never made to me; and so as you had to do with it, I write at once to ask you to act in this matter as you and Father think best. I feel very sure that a change here would at least do no harm, & might do great good. But I shall take no initiative in moving – at present at all events. I am certain that I am incapable of taking a higher post than an incumbent. That is a matter I should not ask advice upon. With the splendid money help I have from Father I think I might live at Boston: I should lose £300 or £400 a year but it would be cheaper by far than living here … Lincoln diocese is a most attractive one; and I should be thankful to get away from Wales, where I have long felt the Church revenues are not a satisfactory thing to live on.

This letter is absolutely typical of Stephen. He is not prepared to commit himself; he is dependent on the advice of others, especially his mother and father; he is completely unambitious for promotion; and while being aware of the importance of money, he is vague about financial practicalities. There is no mention of his wife or children in the letter, but he must surely have discussed the prospect of Boston with Annie. We know she was upset when they did finally leave Hawarden so it is hard to imagine her encouraging the Boston idea. Perhaps she knew Stephen so well that she realised nothing would come of it, as indeed was the case, and she simply sensibly avoided stating her views.

In 1893 and 1894, matters became immensely more fraught, and ever more complicated. What happened to Stephen in those years was, to an even greater extent than usual, almost entirely governed by the aims and activities of his father. Gladstone's intentions are the key to understanding events. Now in his mid-eighties, he was not only Prime Minister for the fourth time but also Leader of the House of Commons, in which latter role he had to stay late almost every night to write the daily report of the business of the House to send to the Queen. He had a small Commons majority, his cabinet was divided, and he was trying to steer his controversial Government of Ireland bill through Parliament. He was physically frail, increasingly deaf and suffering from poor eyesight and insomnia; and his trusted doctor, Andrew Clark, died in December 1893. Catherine was also old, weak and unwell. They both wanted to be sure that Stephen and perhaps even more, Mary, the only daughter permanently at home, would be close at hand in Hawarden for what was left of their lives. Their position was not entirely selfish. They both cared deeply for the parish and wanted what was best for it.

At the start of the years in question, not only was Stephen anxious to move away, but so also was Mary's husband, Harry Drew. He had now been in Hawarden for ten years, and for seven of those years, since marrying Mary in 1886, he had been living in the Castle. His daughter was now three years old and he was still not in a home of his own. By now, one imagines, he was tired of living with his overwhelming in-laws, and professionally, he was keen to gain wider experience. If Harry left Hawarden, he would take Mary, and the doted-on granddaughter Dossie, with him.

Gladstone had a plan for keeping both his son and his son-in-law in the parish. As a result of the arrangement originally made between Gladstone and Sir Stephen Glynne in 1865, Gerty, Willy's widow, was now technically the patron of the Hawarden living, until her son, another William (Will), came of age. However, Gladstone seems to

Figure 16. Some of the Gladstone family at Hawarden. Back row: Stephen (holding Deiny), Annie, Mary, Harry Drew, Herbert (with dog), Helen. Dossie is centre front. Reproduced courtesy of Flintshire Record Office.

159

have felt that the rectorship was in his gift. Genuinely in his gift was a new position, head of his proposed memorial Library, St Deiniol's, and the 'Clergy House', which was to provide accommodation for readers from beyond the parish. His plans for St Deiniol's, first envisaged in 1889, were now beginning to firm up: he would bequeath his personal library to provide opportunities for residential study and refreshment to Anglican clergy and other suitable scholars. If Stephen was determined to give up the rectorship, Gladstone thought he could keep him in Hawarden in charge of the Library and Clergy House. Then, the vacant rectorship could be offered to Harry Drew, thus keeping him, and importantly Mary, in the parish. To this end, Gladstone set out on a series of increasingly devious manoeuvres, most of them behind Stephen's back.

What happened in those years still rankled with both Stephen and Mary seventeen years later, when Harry Drew was dead and Stephen across the other side of the country in Barrowby, near Grantham, in Lincolnshire. Some of the complications were due to Stephen's indecisiveness, but most were caused by the actions of his father. Throughout 1893 and 1894, Gladstone, regardless of what the younger generation wanted, employed a variety of stratagems in order to achieve his overriding aim of keeping both Stephen and Harry Drew, and therefore Mary, in Hawarden. It is impossible to separate the issues of the Library and the rectorship, which Gladstone, with great cunning, first combined in his response to issues raised in a letter from Stephen in April 1893.

In this typically convoluted letter, Stephen told his father, not for the first time, that he wished to resign his living. He also noted that Harry Drew, too, felt in need of a change of scene:

> There is very much to be said in favour of Harry
> Drew's getting an independent sphere, and of having
> their responsible [*sic*] & own home too. His going
> would be a very sad break to me ... And how could
> you and my mother ever spare them – or at least Mary
> from Hawarden? Again, Mary seems very happy here.
> Harry should not have a big church ... the longer I stay
> here the less time I have for myself ... I am used so
> much on all sides – not alas! Spiritually ... Wife and
> children are all so absolutely happy and richly blessed
> here that it would seem wrong of me ... to seek a
> change.

He reminded his father of the Boston prospect three years
previously.

> I could not go with any enthusiasm to anything like an
> easy berth (eg canoning or the like), unless it were some
> quiet country living. I do not think a new Rector here
> would do well ... I should greatly like to have a year or
> two 'out of harness' – or with light or changed duties ...
> Annie approves of all I have said except S Thomas [in
> Toxteth].

He had briefly mentioned the Toxteth option as one
possibility, but it is hard to believe he thought seriously
about it. The confusion of the letter reflected his state of
mind, as did its attempt to cover a number of different if
connected issues: the desirability of Harry Drew moving
from Hawarden, his own and his parents' reaction to that
notion, and his indecisiveness about his own future.
Overall, he seems anxious to make his father realise that he
is keen to get away. However, it is also clear from what he
says about Harry's unfitness for a 'big' church, that he does
not want Harry Drew to be considered as a possible

successor as Rector of Hawarden, even if that might suit his parents, and maybe Mary, by keeping Harry and Mary in Hawarden.

Gladstone, ignoring all the comments on Harry and Mary, applied himself solely to Stephen's desire to leave the parish. He replied with a combination of flattery and moral blackmail:

> I have read your letter with deep interest. It raises you, if this be possible, still higher in my estimation. The idea of your severance from Hawarden rectory is from many points of view frightful. But I must admit there is great force in your reasons. Especially do I enter into and adopt your desire for some mental leisure and opportunity of refreshment and enlargement.

Stephen replied, trying to clarify his position: 'I certainly should greatly dislike "preferment." If I go from here it will distinctly be under a combination of conscientious feelings. (Not from any discontent or unhappiness ... I should greatly like to be free.') Gladstone played for time:

> What I think is this. We should hope, if you will have us, to come to you [from a holiday in Brighton], and at any rate to Hawarden, at Whitsuntide; when we can prosecute this subject in free conversation. In the meantime, pray understand I do not seek to be a party in propelling you to resign Hawarden. But if God guides you to that conclusion, and if you arrive at it, I shall feel assured that it is by his guidance.

God's Providence, again.

He now raised the question of the Hawarden or St Deiniol's Trust, that is, the Memorial Library project: 'Could not you perhaps undertake the quiet and cautious modelling of all this … In association I think we would get on, & you would have a full share of influence.' He offered him the paid post, at 'not less than £300 p.a.' of Head of Trust of the Library and Clergy House, taking practical overall charge of the Library, which was still temporarily housed in the corrugated iron shed, and of the – not yet built – adjacent hostel. It is not easy to tell whether or not this stipend would have been an inducement to Stephen. It is only about a tenth the annual worth of the rectorship, but as Rector, Stephen had to pay all his curates as well as himself out of that income, and maintain and staff the large Rectory. In any case, it would have been the nature of the project, offering to other hard-pressed clergy the respite he himself so desired, that would have appealed to him.

Some progress had been made in the several years since Gladstone had first decided to build the Library, and the 'House of Rest and Refreshment' where readers could live while they used it. Back in 1889 he had found the site near the church on which to erect an iron building for the books, and by now he had bought the nearby defunct grammar school (on the site of what is now 'Gladstone's Library') which could be adapted to serve as the hostel. On receipt of the letter, Stephen, who had for some years been discussing the project with his father, accepted the offered responsibility and agreed 'with great delight' to get the hostel up and running. Encouraged by his father's assurances: 'In association I think we would get on, & you would have a full share of influence' and 'We should have much Counsel & I think sweet Counsel upon it', Stephen, with Annie's help, worked until September of the following year supervising repairs to the old grammar school and furnishing it appropriately to provide living accommo-dation. The main buildings were converted into sitting rooms, studies, bedrooms and a common room, in time for the arrival of the first resident, a Rev. W. M. Wilkins, in Easter 1894.

This energetic effort is the more remarkable since at the end of May 1893, Stephen had fallen very seriously ill and been told not to work for twelve months. He and Annie and their then four children rented a house, with servants, in Colwyn Bay in North Wales while he recuperated from what was some kind of mental breakdown. He himself described it as 'a crisis in life' and said it meant 'my head was very sore and very easily tired'. Colwyn Bay had grown up rapidly since its origins in 1865, but it was still a quiet, restful seaside town, with a sweeping mountain backdrop and a wide, gently sloping, uncrowded beach. The pier would not be built for another eight years. It was, then, a beautiful and quiet place, ideal to convalesce in, if not, as Mary was quick to point out, cheap. He had to pay rent for the house they stayed in, and the servants' wages, as well as continuing to pay the salaries of the curates and the Rectory expenses back in Hawarden.

While Stephen was away recuperating, Harry Drew, in June 1893, publicly announced his desire to inhabit an 'independent sphere', the wish that Stephen had alerted his father to, back in April. Increasingly frustrated by living in the Castle, so closely under his father-in-law's eye, he resigned his curacy and, in January 1894, went to South Africa, without Mary but with her blessing, to a temporary posting at St Saviour, Claremont, six miles from Cape Town. He explained his actions, in the third person, in the parish magazine:

> Some months ago he felt that a change was desirable, and he intimated his resignation to the Rector to take place at

next Christmas … It is right to say that, when the Rector fell ill, Mr Drew was anxious not to press any of his own plans, but to be of any use he could in an emergency. The Rector however is obliged for some time to come to devolve a good deal of his work; and he had to find one who presumably would stay on permanently with him.

The magazine explained that this person was the Rev. Ulric Allen, who 'has been secured by the Rector as Assistant Curate for Hawarden. Mr Allen will relieve the Rector of much of his business and other work, and will act for him in his absence. He will begin his regular duties and his residence at Hawarden at the beginning of August.' Allen had for some years been in charge of St Bartholomew's Sealand, where he had been very popular, and 'The Rector hopes his parishioners in Sealand will not think this robbery and spoliation on his part, for we must remember that otherwise we should have lost Mr Allen altogether.' This comment refers to the fact that Allen had resigned from Sealand before, though not very long before, he was offered the curacy at Hawarden.

Allen had originally come to the area from an insalubrious urban parish in London, in the hope that the country air would be good for his ailing wife. Sadly, she had not recovered her health, had been ill throughout Allen's time at Sealand, and had finally died. This might have prompted in him a desire to move on, or maybe Stephen had already approached him with a request for help in Hawarden. It is not possible to know, as it is also not possible to know if there is a hint of pique in Harry Drew's explanation of why he had not been chosen as the person to assume Stephen's devolved workload. Harry may have simply been anxious to suggest that he had acted with total selflessness in the whole affair, most of the details of which remained deeply hidden away from the scrutiny of the readers of the parish magazine. As far as they were concerned, everything in the garden was literally lovely: Stephen had invited them all to visit the Rectory flower garden on Sunday afternoons. Mary, if not Harry, certainly resented Allen's position, and particularly the fact that Stephen had doubled his curate's salary. She was to remark huffily to her brother Harry, some months later in October 1894, in a letter severely critical of Stephen, his current work in the parish and his general attitude to his proposed resignation: 'Mr Allen is rector now.'

CHAPTER 12 – HAWARDEN:
THROUGH BITTER BETRAYAL TO TEMPORARY
CONTENTMENT, 1894–1895

'I dreaded seeming unfilial or hard.'
(Letter from Stephen to Herbert: 26 September 1894)

Stephen returned from Colwyn Bay to Hawarden in the middle of January 1894, under doctor's orders not to take up his parochial duties until the forthcoming Easter. Ulric Allen assumed much of the pastoral work, using Stephen's office in the Rectory, as well as being in charge of Ewloe, and a Rev. W. T. Williams was appointed to replace Harry Drew. In February, Stephen told his parishioners that he was writing them a letter. This promised letter, which might perhaps have contained his decision to resign, did not appear in the next or indeed any future issue of the parish magazine, and extensive searching has revealed no draft copy. It may never have been written, for some time in the early spring, Stephen decided he did not after all wish to resign the living. He would combine the rectorship with the charge of the Library. The hostel, in the converted old grammar school, had opened provisionally on 2 February. The public was told that the Library was not ready to be on show, but was available only to those residing at the hostel or by special permission from Gladstone.

At the time, Gladstone was far away in Biarritz, with Mary and Catherine, and answered Stephen's letter about remuneration for expenditure on the hostel with 'a few bewildering phrases'. In September, Harry Drew returned to England and soon after, Gladstone asked his youngest son Herbert to mediate in what Stephen later described with massive understatement as the 'Hostel misunderstanding'.

167

Stephen was outraged that his father had written offering him and Annie a piece of plate as thanks for all the work they had already done for St Deiniol's, a gesture he described as 'grotesque'. The reason for the inappropriate gesture is that the moment Harry Drew returned to England, Gladstone 'propose[d] to him a temporary charge of St Deiniol's', an offer which he formalised in October when he offered Harry Drew the temporary wardenship.

The facts lying behind these developments must be fascinating, but, alas, are almost impossible to retrieve at this distance. Some evidence can be found in Gladstone's diary and some in letters and other documents written seventeen years later, but by then memories were not always reliable. The first enigma concerns what happened when Stephen told his father in April 1893 that he wished to resign the rectorship. When Harry Drew, who finally did become Rector of Hawarden, died at the end of March, 1910, Mary, anxious to protect and enhance the reputation of her beloved husband, wrote a piece about him for the May issue of the parish magazine. In it, she stated that Harry had been pressed to accept the rectorship in 1893 and had refused, for two reasons: his innate dislike of the custom of 'family livings' and an 'irresistible longing to breathe a larger atmosphere'. This statement was to be expanded upon in her planned Memoir, in which she intended to present Harry's refusal of such a desirable position in a way that would show his character in the best possible light. She wrote to Stephen, now in Barrowby, suggesting that he might like to contribute to the Memoir, describing his own part in the affair. In her letter, she stressed that there had been intense pressure on Harry from both the Gladstone parents to accept the post of Rector. If her memory is correct and unbiased, then this is evidence of Gladstone's original two-pronged

168

plan: to keep Stephen in the parish in charge of setting up and then running St Deiniol's and to ensure that Harry also remained in Hawarden, in the Rectory.

When Stephen read his sister's letter, he was furious and wrote agitatedly back from Barrowby:

> I quite understand the greatness of your desire to have a worthy memoir [of Harry Drew] & I hope it will be realized. But in the case of all matter strictly confidential, all persons intimately concerned ought to be consulted before publication of such matters. If this matter of Harry's refusal in 1893 had been referred to me, I think I should have said, 'It is so intimately connected with private matters, that it is best left alone; but if any reference must be made to it, it is due to me that (1) my motives in the matter should be stated; and (2) it should be made clear that, that [*sic*] there being no vacancy, Harry was only sounded as to the appointment.' It cannot accurately be described (as in the May Mag) as a matter of offer and refusal. All this was previous to my illness. My motives were due to the family difficulties & unrest as they appeared to me at that time. Harry had given me notice of his resignation as Curate after 10 years of patient and admirable work. His departure I supposed would have involved yours also – at the time when Father and Mother were so aged. It was for this reason that I made known to my Father & to Harry my readiness to retire, feeling as I did that Harry was so worthy of the position. I have no doubt that you will see that my demand that (if you proceed with the matter) these circumstances should be made known to the writer of the memoir, is right & reasonable. I will send a few lines for the June mag. to put myself right there, but without entering into details.

Some of this hysterical outpouring accurately reflects what was discussed in letters at the time, and we cannot know what was said in face-to-face conversations, for example the one between Stephen and his father at Whitsun 1893. Still, Stephen seems to be quibbling here. If as he says he had offered to resign in Harry's favour, it is hard to see why he was annoyed at the suggestion that Harry had received the offer of his job. It may be that he was irritated by Harry's refusal to accept it. Further, he too had a reputation to keep up in Hawarden, and would not want the parish to think he had been keen to get away, even if he was. His own recollections are hardly reliable. 'Feeling as I did that Harry is so worthy of the position' does not by any stretch of the imagination mean the same as his statement to his father at the time: 'Harry should not have a big church.'

Mary had always felt that there was some injustice in the way her brother treated her husband, and she may have had some right on her side. Not only had Stephen implied that Harry was not ready for the rectorship of Hawarden – undoubtedly a big church – but he had also made it clear to his father that he did not want Harry's help with the Library: 'He is not the one I ought to try & get as my future Right hand man [at St Deiniol's]'. It was Ulric Allen, whom Stephen had headhunted from the daughter church of St Bartholomew's in Sealand and later described as 'a godsend', who was given that position, combining it with that of Stephen's unofficial pastoral deputy.

The vehemence of her brother's reaction to her letter of 1910, combined with her belief that he had always underestimated Harry's abilities, led to Mary's asking Stephen not to raise the question of what she described as the 'succession' again in the parish magazine. Stephen meanwhile had written to Herbert of that 'period of scheming and unrest' adding: 'It is only comparatively recently that I have felt able to tell you at all about Mary – at that time I could not open to anyone of the family. All my time at Hawarden this was one of the troubles – in one way or another – beginning with December 1872.' He is anxious that Herbert, and others, should understand his side of 'this rarely disinterred incident'. Feelingly, he wrote: 'If I could find words which would remove the incidence [*sic*] from my shoulders, I should be content.' He also wrote to Harry Gladstone, sounding him out on the wording of what he (Stephen) wanted printed in the parish magazine:

> In ref to an incident in 1893 in the last [Hawarden] mag. About Can[on] D[rew] & the Living of H[awarden] I should like to say that my readiness to retire at that time (ie just before my illness) from the Rectorship of H. was due to what I personally ... felt might be for this family conveniencies [*sic*] & with the blessing of [?] the Parishioners. I had no other wish to leave H[awarden].

In the archive there also exists a slightly different version of this:

> In reference to an incident of 1893 named in the last magazine, I should like to say that my readiness to retire from the Rectorship at that time, (that is, just before my illness) on the understanding that provisionally it was offered to & accepted by canon Drew, was due to what I conceived would then be for the family convenience & without loss to the parishioners. I had no other wish to leave Hawarden. S. E. G.

Stephen was deeply anxious that his case should be put as strongly as possible.

Mary also tried to enlist sibling support, even suggesting to Harry Gladstone that if Stephen put his side of things into the parish magazine: 'I think too it would rather disturb Gerty [the widow of Willy, Stephen's older brother, in her role as patron of the living.]' In the event, Stephen's response in the June magazine – 'A Word from the Rector of 1872–1904' – formed part of a general piece not only about Harry but also on several other Hawarden clergy who had recently died. This would hardly have appeased Mary.

Stephen seems inordinately concerned to make it clear firstly, that his illness had in no way affected any professed intention to leave Hawarden, and secondly that he was acting not on his own account but for the good of the family, aware that Harry Drew wanted to move away but that William and Catherine Gladstone wanted him, and Mary, to stay. Although Mary insisted to their brother Harry that there was no truth in this – 'I never knew it was for the convenience of the family' – something had certainly been going on. It was not just the parishioners who were kept in the dark about developments, so was Stephen himself. Gladstone's diary for 25 May 1893, stated 'Conversation with Sir A. Clark [six months before Clark died] on the situation in the family' and on 17 June, he again 'saw Sir A Clark & conversation on SEG and his rectory'. Like Stephen himself, we are not privy to the exact substance of these conversations, but it seems likely that if we were, we could understand Stephen's anger, still seething seventeen years later.

The second enigma also concerns Gladstone's plans for the rectorship. If he wanted Harry Drew to succeed Stephen as Rector in 1893, why did he write thus to his son when he knew he wished to resign: 'The whole idea of severing you from the charge let alone the House, is a wrench, and a rend;

and separates bone and marrow. It is moreover a very complex business; and the succession is most formidable.' If he had Harry Drew lined up, this makes no sense. The succession was not 'formidable', but on the contrary, was already satisfactorily fixed.

The final enigma concerns exactly who was understood, and by whom, to be in charge of the development of St Deiniol's. An insight into the 'period of scheming and unrest' to which Stephen referred comes from Mary. In August 1894, she scribbled to her father, explicitly stating that her husband was out of the room:

> A great deal of the trouble and anxiety of last year's discussions on proposals arose from the fact that everything was done, first in the form of hints & gradually of conditional & rather uncertain proposals through me ['for me to pass on to him' has been crossed out.] ... it gave him the feeling that it was mostly for my sake, & because he was my husband ... but you see it is very vague and indefinite, & if he was to turn his mind seriously towards it, he might afterwards find Stephy would really prefer not giving it up, or Stephy's wish to relinquish Hawarden might grow again in a manner that he would feel himself pledged to take up his work. I rather am inclined and advise that nothing should be said to Harry [Drew] until Stephy and you either are in a position to make him definite proposal, even though of a temporary nature – Stephy has had all the responsibility the anxiety the trouble of starting the Hostel in connection with the Library, it is quiet interest and delight to him, & I do not feel sure he would care to give it up yet, unless to some more permanent person who was obviously well cut out for the post. This letter is also for Mama.

Mary was obviously writing in a hurry here, but it is clear that Gladstone had involved her, behind the backs of both her husband and her brother, in his plans to offer St Deiniol's to Harry Drew. She was unhappy about her situation, not least because she felt some sympathy for Stephen, whom she described as 'dreadfully disappointed at giving up St Deiniol's'. Later, writing to Herbert, when Harry was in post at the Library, and busy on the catalogue, she went out of her way to say:

> All this is very delightful and happy, the only thorn being in the feeling of Stephy's not having been treated with fairness & consideration ... HN [Henry Neville, their brother Harry] told us what had happened between father & Stephy, & I have been pondering it, because it distresses me that Father has been wanting in justice.

In October 1893 Stephen and his father were discussing 'initiatory measures' but in January 1894, Gladstone recorded 'a little conversation with C[atherine] & Mary on the sore subject, and two subsequent 'nagging conversations', which were followed in February by, 'drive with Mary. Family conversation on the situation'. In view of Mary's later comments it seems probable, though not certain, that these conversations, again behind Stephen's back, were about St Deiniol's.

Further duplicity is suggested by Gladstone's diary entry of May 1893, stating that he had had conversations with Stephen, Harry and Mary. It was soon after this that Stephen fell ill, from overwork, according to his father, and later diary entries describe conversations, one with his son, in which he was 'hit but rallies fast' and one with Harry Drew, whom Gladstone described as 'admirable'. If in this conversation Harry had stated his desire to escape from

Hawarden, it is impossible to believe that Gladstone would have described him as 'admirable', so the discussion must have been about the St Deiniol's post. These conversations may mark the start of the whole sorry saga. When Gladstone hadn't got what he wanted from his original plan, with Stephen at St Deiniol's and Harry and Mary in the Rectory, he had immediately concocted Plan B, which entailed the exact opposite, but was from his point of view equally satisfactory: all his family remained in Hawarden. Indeed, in some ways it was an improvement on his original plan, because it involved Harry and Mary continuing to live in the Castle. It is possible that Gladstone's real aim was that neither Stephen nor Harry, but rather, Mary should be the one in charge of St Deiniol's. He trusted her, and as early as January 1894 she had said that the Library had been financially under her care. However that may be, by the end of the saga, Stephen, duped and totally outmanoeuvred, was no longer in charge of St Deiniol's, though he did retain the title of Head of the Trust and he was still Rector of Hawarden.

During this troubled period, in March of 1894, Gladstone had finally resigned as Prime Minister and been replaced by Lord Rosebery. Rosebery, a friend of the family who was aware of Stephen's unsettled state, offered him, in October of that year, the Deanery of Winchester. Rosebery had discussed the issue with Sir Edward Hamilton, who expressed reservations. He told Rosebery that Stephen had got 'quite average ability – indeed his father thinks it far above average – and he is a very strong Liberal – in fact he is a Dis-establisher' [in favour of the Welsh Church severing links with the State]. The latter two points were obviously seen as being in Stephen's favour, and Gladstone seems to have talked up his son and even overstated his own view of

175

Stephen's mental prowess. However, Hamilton was not convinced. He had a serious objection to Stephen's being offered the job, namely, astonishingly, the drawback of his personal appearance which Hamilton described as 'certainly not prepossessing', exactly the sentiment he had expressed at the time of Stephen's marriage. One can see why a lack of good looks might be relevant in the choice of a bridegroom, but it is less easy to see what it had to do with preferment in the church.

Gladstone had originally told his son about the Winchester vacancy some six months previously, when Stephen was still ill. As Prime Minister, he felt he could not offer the preferment to his own son, and, now he was out of office, he may, in recommending him to Rosebery, have exaggerated his view of Stephen's abilities to salve his own guilt about how he had handled the issue of St Deiniol's. But such a position was in any case the last thing Stephen wanted. By letter, he explained to his father that he wished to turn it down because what he really hoped for was not promotion, as indeed he had often said, but another parish appointment, and at that, a humbler one than Hawarden, or perhaps not a living, but a chaplaincy. He wrote at the same time to both his younger brothers, saying much the same thing, explaining how he wanted a post involving one-to-one pastoral work, and less 'official' work, which he had never enjoyed.

His health was also again a concern. Annie was worried about her husband's state of mind, writing anxiously from Colwyn Bay to Gerty:

> If Stephy is to come to Hawarden tomorrow, I do hope they will be careful what they say to him. His mind is made up and I do not think anything would make him

take the Deanery at this time, but it will be very easy to make him leave Hawarden, if they are too urgent, but the Deanery ought to be settled at once, for it is on his mind – he really has been quite different the last 3 days & is looking worried. I thought you might send Harry [Gladstone] a note asking him to be careful not to let the talks be too long.

Annie here seems to have fallen into the family habit of going behind Stephen's back. Probably she was desperate. Whatever was said in the various consultations, Stephen did not, surely wisely, accept Rosebery's offer when it finally came.

In the midst of all this uncertainty Stephen, having picked up the pieces after his illness, had, as he told his parishioners he hoped would happen, acquired new energy. He produced a fifty-two page pamphlet, illustrated with photographs taken by one of Annie's sisters, in which he not only gave a short history of the parish but also set down in detail all its current assets. The parish is indisputably flourishing: apart from the eight free day schools, there are thirteen Sunday schools, with fortnightly meetings for the teachers, seven mothers' meetings, a Girls' Friendly Society with six sub-branches, separate classes for men, women and young women, five branches of the children's missionary guild, and numerous church societies. Laypeople are fully involved, not only as bellringers and members of the large choir, but in positions of responsibility such as district visitors (nineteen) and Bible readers for the sick (eight). The Institute is doing well and the gymnasium attached to it is popular.

The pamphlet also contains information on curate turnover during Stephen's rectorship. In Hawarden itself,

Figure 17. Stephen and Annie with their three older children and Annie's parents and sister at Hawarden. Reproduced by kind permission of Sir William Gladstone.

only three out of ten were there for less than three years, and the average time for a curate's stay in the parish was about six years. This suggests, contrary to what some critics, including Mary, came to believe, that most of his curates were happy with his leadership. The pamphlet reminded its readers of their Rector's availability: daily for a set hour in his study, at any time in the Rectory, or in the church after services, or by arrangement. This open door policy reflected Stephen's love of personal contact, as opposed to administrative duties, but if even a small proportion of parishioners took advantage of these opportunities, it is hard to see how he fitted in the necessary office work.

The pamphlet ends with 'Hawarden Aims and Principles', which shows that Stephen has kept firmly to the path on which he was set by Robert Gregory in Lambeth a quarter of a century before, and has learned from his own early mistakes. All children were to be taught steadfast and full fidelity, and everyone should support the parish schools; Dissenters should be tolerated and honoured for their beliefs; the aged, weak and helpless must be looked after. In church, worship should be simple, with people kneeling for prayers, and making proper preparation for Holy Communion, for which adequate time and silence should be set aside. There is to be no 'fear or favour' and, writes Stephen firmly: 'My pew' is a fiction. The abolition of pew rent was one of his personal triumphs. The tone of the pamphlet, which is a reflection of Stephen's public face, is strongly upbeat, in total contrast to his frequently reiterated personal comments on the parish and his work in it. It is almost certainly a truer reflection of the reality of the situation than that found in his letters. The comment on the Institute, however, hides Stephen's deep concerns about what he called 'the anti-religious element' which was now creeping in. One Barnett, whom he described to Herbert, with uncharacteristic uncharitableness, as 'a man of no seriousness at all, & of little brains I should guess', seems to have become very influential. He was the treasurer and frequently also acted as chair of council meetings.

A photograph dating from about 1895 shows Stephen in the Rectory garden, hosting the annual summer tea party for the inmates of the Hawarden Union Workhouse. There are sixty to seventy people, ranging from the very old to several young children. All are clothed in their Sunday best, though few are smiling, perhaps due to the length of time they had to hold their positions in these early days of photography. The picture stands as a record of Stephen's sense of philanthropy, propriety and sense of duty to all his parishioners, regardless of 'fear or favour'.

In May, Ulric Allen had left the parish and gone up to Tydd St Mary's in Lincolnshire. Stephen could now manage without his support. Over the last two years he had weathered serious illness, a crisis of confidence in his own abilities, and a severe disappointment over St Deiniol's. He was fifty years old. Annie must have hoped that the family was set for a period of stability, even contentment. She was to be disappointed.

CHAPTER 13 – HAWARDEN:
PERSONAL AND POLITICAL CRISES, 1895–1900

'I received a very peremptory note from Mama
this evening… I shall be glad to know if you judge that
[the action she complained of] was wrong.'
(Letter from Stephen to his father: 17 August 1896)

If Stephen had accepted Rosebery's 1894 offer, there would have been one big advantage: he would have escaped the jurisdiction of the Welsh Church, with which he was by now set on a collision course over the issue of Disestablishment. The Welsh Church, an arm of the Established Church of England, enjoyed many financial and legal privileges denied to other Christian denominations in Wales. The call for Disestablishment was part of a wider anti-English movement. In 1889 when Queen Victoria visited Wales, Thomas Gee, a Calvinistic Methodist who owned a publishing business and produced a bi-weekly Welsh language newspaper, had suggested that the Welsh people should not turn out to express loyalty to the 'head' of an 'alien church'. Three years later, Liberal candidates in the General Election had made a big issue of Disestablishment. The issue was still contentious.

Traditionally, the Established Church could claim the payment of annual tithes, that is, a tenth of each person's income (since 1836 in the form of a rent charge on land) whether or not that person was actually a member of the local Anglican Communion. There were considerable numbers of Nonconformists in Wales, and for some time there had been unrest among them, arising from the not unreasonable view that the advantages enjoyed by the Established Church were unfair. Among other perceived injustices, Nonconformists were perforce supporting both their own places of worship and also their local Anglican churches. In many places, they were effectively subsidising schools that were teaching specifically Anglican doctrine. Stephen, on good terms with the Methodists in Hawarden, felt an instinctive sympathy with the Nonconformist demands for the removal of these injustices. He supported the Disestablishment of the Welsh Church and this view brought him into direct conflict with official Welsh Church views.

Unrest over tithes was already on Hawarden's doorstep, in Denbighshire, which neighboured Flint and so was uncomfortably close. The trouble was originally ignited by the campaigning Thomas Gee. His newspaper supported the Nonconformist farm labourers in their anti-tithe campaign and deliberately stirred up rebellion, leading to the so-called 'Tithe Wars'. In the years 1886–1890 there had been running battles between farm labourers and the local police, resulting in eighty-four people being injured, including thirty-five police officers. Eventually, a troop of lancers was called in to relieve the police of their duty to protect the tithe collectors. There exists a photograph which shows several ranks of armed cavalrymen, headed by two figures, one of whom appears to be a drum major, advancing purposefully across the Denbighshire countryside.

In 1891, perhaps because of fears of further trouble, the rent charges (still popularly thought of as tithes) were transferred to the better-off landowners, but there was still considerable opposition to the system and to the whole idea of an Established Church.

In the Hawarden parish there were no less than eight Nonconformist places of worship. Ever since his slip-up of 1874, when he had had to repair the damage caused by his statement that their religion was 'in vain', Stephen had been anxious to remain on good terms with his Nonconformist colleagues. He had consulted them, particularly, on the future of local education, which was at least as delicate a matter as was that of tithes. Disestablishment of the Welsh Church would threaten the system of church (voluntary) control over the schools. Currently, in Hawarden, by popular demand, the schools – apart from one Methodist establishment – were still under church control, but local education was increasingly vulnerable to takeover by the state. For years, Hawarden had been avoiding the need to set up a School Board, choosing to continue to build and fund its own schools by subscription. Stephen himself had become increasingly disillusioned with the idea of voluntary aided schools, with all the accompanying hassle over collecting the necessary money, and he was still chair of the local school managers, in spite of all his efforts to relinquish the post. He may have thought that Disestablishment would force Hawarden to set up a Board, and so free him from years of time-consuming trouble. This could have been a strong contributory factor in his support for the Disestablishment of the Welsh Church.

Unsurprisingly, Stephen's own Bishop, A. G. Edwards, the English Bishop of St Asaph, and John Owen, another Englishman, who was to be appointed Bishop of the Welsh See of St David's in 1897, were totally opposed to the idea of Disestablishment, which would cut off their financial and other support from the state. Owen had made a distinction at the diocesan conference of October 1889 between those who 'honestly pursued the policy [of Disestablishment]' and those who 'unscrupulously promoted ... tithe agitation', but he remained firmly anti-Disestablishment. Stephen, as Sir Edward Hamilton had noted to Rosebery a few years earlier, was well known to be in favour. (The Welsh Church was eventually to be disestablished in 1920 on the logical grounds that the majority of the Welsh people were Nonconformists.)

As early as April 1893 there appeared as a supplement to the Hawarden parish magazine 'A Dialogue between Two Churchmen', subtitled 'Is Disestablishment and Disendowment in Wales a Righteous and Just Thing; or Wrong and Unjust?' Fairly obviously the work of Stephen himself, it purports to be an even-handed discussion between two churchmen, A and B, written with the laudable aim of replacing wild allegations and emotive language with sober, balanced, well-argued points of view. Speaker A is against Disestablishment and the closely linked issue of Disendowment, which would involve the Church in giving up its ancient endowments – another source of its income – as well as its tithes; Speaker B, who clearly represents Stephen, is in favour of both concepts.

Speaker A's main arguments are, firstly, that to renounce endowments would dishonour the original bestowers, and that, secondly, 'the Church's privileges are open to all. It is not her fault if all do not use them'. These arguments are countered by Speaker B with the point that the original endowments were made on the assumption that the Established Church would remain in perpetuity 'the spiritual mother of all the citizens', which is indisputably no longer the case. Speaker B thinks that it is worth losing 'our privileged heritage' in order to be free from the State, self-supporting and correspondingly strong. Speaker A does not have a convincing response to this view and Speaker B concludes triumphantly with a quotation from a speech of Gladstone of 30 March 1868: 'The Church establishment regarded in its theory, and in its aim, is beautiful and attractive. Yet what is it but an appropriation of public property, an appropriation of the fruits of labour and of skill to certain purposes?' There are two things to be said about this quotation. Firstly, the printers have seemingly made an error, swapping the labelling of the last two speeches in the discussion, which then ends amicably with a joint statement of agreement to differ. Secondly, and rather more seriously, the use of the quotation from Gladstone is somewhat disingenuous, since it is about the Disestablishment of the church not in Wales but in Ireland, and Gladstone was actually not in favour of Welsh Disestablishment. It is one of the very few major issues on which Stephen was not at one with his father.

Two years later, in the April 1895 edition of the parish magazine, Stephen made his position even clearer, writing a long article putting forward his reasons for actively supporting the parliamentary bill to disestablish the church. In it he boldly states that he can have nothing to do with the organisation which had been set up to protect Establishment, 'the so-called Church Defence Society'; nor (he respectfully adds) with the Archbishop of Canterbury's new scheme for the same purpose. He believes the case for Disestablishment has been 'amply made out' and that 'the Church's claim to exist as the State Church cannot be fairly sustained', indeed 'involves political injustice'. Radically, he declares that any poverty resulting from Disestablishment is to be welcomed: 'A poor church is much more likely to do God's work, than a richer Church in possession of Endowments.' Finally, he urges the Churchmen themselves to face the matter 'with something wiser and better than a mere position of resistance'. His footnote accepted sole responsibility for the views expressed, and made it clear that he did not wish to bring the subject 'into the pulpit'. Unfortunately for Stephen, the *Manchester Guardian* picked up on the article, thus giving his views a much wider airing than intended. Even as late as 1913, he was writing to *The Times* clarifying his position on the issue.

The unhappy situation of being at odds with both his own bishop and the bishop of the neighbouring see over such a crucial issue renewed Stephen's restlessness over his Hawarden living, but sadly, this public stating of his views effectively put a stop to any chance of his receiving another church appointment in Wales. Presumably aware of this, in a letter to Herbert in May in which he refers obliquely to his unhappiness with the current state of the Welsh Church, he floated various ideas including applying for a vacancy in an English diocese, or in Scotland, or perhaps in the colonies. He does not take this last idea seriously, as it 'would not be well suited to the Parents' great ages'. Considering that he first mentioned this as a problem when thinking of India in June 1882, the wonder is that at this stage, missionary work even crossed his mind. Other possibilities mooted are an institution chaplaincy, even a prison – anything, it seems – rather than an incumbency. Never very practical as far as financial matters are concerned, he does not seem to have considered that he would hardly be able to support his family on the stipend of a prison chaplain, though it had occurred to him that 'I must have something before resigning.'

Much of this letter is in fantasy land, not least because 'Annie … I need hardly say is not at all favourable to [my] resignation.' He wanted the contents of the letter to be passed on to Gerty and Harry Gladstone, 'to avoid rigmarole and multiplied statements'. But there was rigmarole, indeed, not least about Harry Drew and, once more, St Deiniol's Library. He wrote:

I feel more and more incapable of in any way being a party to asking Harry to give up – even for a time, his clerical vocation. Were he a real Theologian, he could slip nicely into the Library permanently: but he is of course not this … nevertheless, many things would forbid my resignation on that ground mainly.

Apart from making it clear once again that he did not have a high opinion of Harry's abilities, this was, even by Stephen's standards, an obscure statement, and one not obviously connected with his views on his own future.

As two years previously, various issues and personalities were entangled and the whole Gladstone family was involved, including, particularly and inevitably, Harry Drew. The Library catalogue having been now completed, Harry of his own accord decided that he would prefer an incumbency to being Warden of St Deiniol's for the rest of his life. In May 1896, he escaped briefly to Egypt and the Holy Land, ostensibly to escort Albert Lyttleton, who was on furlough from South Africa, on his way home. It gave him a breathing space: after Christmas 1896, he resigned the wardenship. The previous March, surprisingly, there had been a thought that Stephen might now take it on, if he had proper support. In the event, Gladstone appointed the Rev. G. C. Joyce, who was sub-warden of St Michael's College, Aberdare and indisputably, unlike Harry Drew, a 'real theologian'.

Mary hinted to her brother Harry that her husband Harry might now be prepared to take over the rectorship of Hawarden, if Stephen did actually, this time round, resign. She also made it clear that Harry Drew would want to have, if not Hawarden itself, a living nearby, for the sake of her elderly parents. This might have been Mary's own idea rather than her husband's, but it must have occurred to him that things would be very difficult for Mary if she was living a long way from the Castle, dividing herself between husband, child and parish duties on the one hand and her parents on the other. The prospect of nearby Buckley seemed ideal, but there was a problem. The current incumbent, the Rev. William Dampier, who had been there for over ten years, had up until then expressed no desire to leave.

This might have seemed an insuperable difficulty to some people, but not to Gladstone. In January 1897, he wrote to the Bishop of Asaph saying: 'I believe that our neighbour, Mr Dampier of Buckley, has appealed to your Lordship to remove him on some early opportunity from Buckley to a less rough and laborious country living. I need hardly say that this was not done upon instigation from us.' Just in case the Bishop did not pick up on his meaning, he went on to recommend Harry Drew as a worthy successor, adding that 'it would be a matter of great importance to us, to my wife in particular, that such employment should be so near as not to remove our daughter, his wife, beyond the circle of constant domestic intercourse'. This interference by her father put Mary in an awkward position. It threatened to be a re-run of the events of 1893, and she would again be caught in the middle. Stephen had not, or not yet, resigned. If he did, then Harry would be offered, and this time would accept, the living of Hawarden. In that case, Buckley would not be needed, and Dampier forced out for nothing.

In February she wrote to her father: 'Gerty [as patron of the living] has begged me not to move at present in the Buckley matter, on account of Stephy's wishes (as far as she can understand them.') This last phrase is telling. No one, least of all himself, knew if Stephen was on the point of resigning Hawarden or not. He even applied for some kind of junior post, a 'conductship', at Eton at about this time, and toyed with the idea of a living in St Albans. Gladstone had written enquiring on his behalf about the possibility of his joining the Scottish church and had made it clear to his son that if Stephen was so uncertain about staying in Hawarden, then he should, for everyone's sake, resign. He seems to have been losing patience with all the shilly-shallying. Also, from the point of view of Gladstone and Catherine, it would be better if Harry succeeded Stephen, and so took Mary from the Castle to live in the Hawarden Rectory, walking distance away, than if he succeeded Dampier and took her to live in Buckley, two miles down the road.

At the end of 1896, Stephen had an 'interview' – his word – with his father about his future. Stephen thought it was quite a friendly conversation, but a week later they met again and, as he wrote to his brother Harry:

> for nearly half an hour I think he fell upon me for irrational action & the like with all his force of words …
> I must say throughout that I felt so coldly used by him on this subject, that I always dread any talk about it with him: and I am by no means anxious for more.

Nonetheless, a few days later there was more, when Gladstone and Catherine dined at the Rectory and it seemed to Stephen as if his father was saying, 'Hawarden or very likely nothing'. Gladstone was thinking more clearly than was his son. He must have realised that Stephen had no real idea about what he wanted to do if he resigned, and the uncertainties must have been putting an intolerable strain on Annie, coping not only with an unhappy husband but with five children, all under ten.

Stephen was frustrated that his father neither understood him nor seemed aware of what on this occasion

189

he chose to describe in a letter to his brother Harry as the lasting debilitating effects of his illness, nor the extent of his workload: 'in fact he [Gladstone] knows nothing of the burdens of the parish'. At the same time as he was grumbling about his father's lack of sympathy for him, he himself was showing a marked lack of concern over Mary and Harry Drew. All this time, he had apparently been naïvely assuming that they were unaware of his uncertainties, in spite of the fact that he must have realised that his future and theirs were likely to be bound up together. When he found out that they had known about his doubts all along, he made it clear that he didn't want Harry's plans 'to be shaped by mine'. Back in 1893, indeed, they hadn't been, but things were different now, with Gladstone and Catherine much older and far more dependent.

If Stephen felt misunderstood and frustrated, he can't have been the only one. Not only Harry and Mary Drew, but all his siblings, and Gerty, would be affected by any decision he made. As Mary wrote to Herbert: 'The uncertainties of the last 2 years must be as unwholesome for him as for everybody else concerned.' The frailty of the elderly parents meant that if Harry, and therefore Mary, went to Buckley, someone else would have to take Mary's place as chief carer in the Castle. Until Stephen made up his mind, Harry could not be sure if he would be Vicar of Buckley, Rector of Hawarden, or neither. Mary herself must have been desperate to know where she would be living for the foreseeable future: in the Buckley Vicarage, in the Rectory in Hawarden, or still in the Castle.

In the end what happened was that Stephen, yet again, decided to stay on as Rector of Hawarden, and, Dampier having been shifted to Nailstone, in Leicestershire, Harry Drew was ordained as Vicar of Buckley on 30 May 1897.

Figure 18. Stephen, Annie, William and some of the younger generation outside Hawarden Castle. Reproduced courtesy of Flintshire Record Office.

Mary feelingly commented: 'No words can express the relief of Buckley being settled so we are no longer dependent on the windings of Stephy's path.' On this occasion, one sympathises with her. Mary and Harry were happy, and so, in a way, was Stephen who at least had made a decision. Annie and the children, who loved Hawarden, were relieved. Gladstone and Catherine did not suffer, because Helen gave up her post at Newnham, not altogether willingly, to take Mary's place in the Castle.

Helen was the family member who came off worst, writing to her father:

> Dearest father: It seems as if the time has now come when I ought to take my share regularly of home duties – so I have now given notice to leave Newnham at Christmas if they can arrange with my successor … You will not think I have done this lightly or easily – although I shall be so glad to do what I can at home. I can only thank you & others at home for making it possible that I should be here for 19 and a half years. I shall be grateful if you will keep this entirely private, excepting with Mary.

Helen had not been very close to her mother in childhood, if we are to believe Mary, who in her old age was to describe to Herbert the endless rows that Helen, and Agnes, had had with Catherine. Furthermore, her mother had been disapproving of Helen's decision to pursue a career in the first place. It was not an easy relationship and Helen was making a sacrifice.

Elsewhere, happiness prevailed. In July that year, Hawarden celebrated Queen Victoria's Diamond Jubilee, with the usual festivities in the Castle grounds. By now there were so many schoolchildren to be marshalled into parades and sports that the parish schools had to be colour coded, Hawarden itself sporting light blue. As well as tea, there were medals, buns and oranges, and, excitingly, 'fire balloons'.

Local life proceeded on an even keel. Albert Lyttleton returned, as he intended, to South Africa, and a new church was planned for Shotton. Annie was pregnant again. There was an air of normality, even permanence. Then, on 19 May 1898, the almost unimaginable happened: Gladstone died.

He had been on holiday in Cannes, suffering from agonising facial neuralgia, and on his return home to Hawarden, via Bournemouth, had been diagnosed with mouth cancer. Stubborn to the end, he took a long time to die. The family was in limbo, unable to make any plans for the immediate future, and divided among themselves about what details to divulge to the Press.

Finally, at five in the morning on Ascension Day, he gave up the struggle. All the family was at his bedside, with Stephen reading the prayers and his father's favourite hymns. Reputedly, Gladstone's last word was 'Amen'. The body was laid out in his beloved Temple of Peace, where the local people came to pay their respects. Stephen wanted him to be buried in Hawarden, next to Willy, although he admitted that the number of pilgrims 'might present mountains of difficulty'. Meanwhile, Parliament offered a state funeral, which Herbert accepted. However, Gladstone had been such an important figure in Hawarden that his coffin was first taken to the parish church, where Stephen conducted a service of Holy Communion for the family and the people of the village. It was a funeral in all but name. The remains were then taken to nearby Broughton Hall station and, in a train pulled by the engine appropriately named 'Gladstone', conveyed via Willesden to Westminster, where it lay in state for two days in Westminster Hall. More than 250,000 mourners filed past. Gladstone may not always have been the easiest of people to deal with at close quarters, but the nation revered him.

The funeral took place in Westminster Abbey on 28 May. It was a solemn and awe-inspiring occasion, with the Abbey packed with mourners. Thousands more gathered outside. Stephen, as the eldest son, was chief mourner. Newsreel footage exists of the funeral procession approaching the Abbey. Silent, black and white and jerky, it is eerily poignant, showing Stephen, wearing his canonicals, top hat in hand, walking, very upright and alone, behind the horse-drawn hearse. His younger brothers and his own sons, with his nephew Will, follow in a small group. The bells tolled and there was music from an orchestra, the organ and 100 male singers. Catherine, a frail figure in deep black mourning, was supported as she entered the Abbey by Mary and Harry Drew, with their daughter Dossie. The Prince of Wales, who had been a close friend of Willy, and his son, the Duke of York, acted as pall bearers, in spite of Queen Victoria's disapproval. The Prince kissed Catherine's hand. Stephen and Herbert stood by their mother as the family gathered round the grave in the north transept for the committal. The coffin was lowered into its tomb, fittingly opposite the statue of Gladstone's great political rival, Disraeli.

Stephen now had to adjust to living without the constant monitoring presence of his father. There was also the question of how best to preserve, and indeed protect, his father's memory. A few months previously, Stephen had received from him the 'declaration', in which Gladstone stated that: 'At no period of my life have I been guilty of the act which is known as that of infidelity to the marriage bed.'

Whether or not to make this statement public, later became a matter for much heart searching. Stephen, while very much aware that he had been specially selected to receive the declaration, decided to share the implied responsibility with his brothers Harry and Herbert.

Gladstone had not been without critics, and there would be those who wanted posthumously to destroy his reputation by suggesting that his work with 'fallen women' was far from pure and disinterested. In 1908, in a letter to Herbert marked 'Private', Stephen admitted that there were 'suspicions' about Gladstone, while at the same time rather naïvely denying that 'Father's habits and aims directly exposed him ... to [such] suspicions.'

It was not until after Stephen's death that it fell to Herbert and Harry to see off the first serious threat to their father's reputation, made in 1927 by the journalist Captain Peter Emmanuel Wright. In his book *Portraits and Criticisms*, Wright had bizarrely accused Gladstone of keeping a 'seraglio' which included – a ludicrous idea – Lillie Langtry, friend of the Prince of Wales. (The latter, being a friend of Willy, was something of a protégé of Gladstone, which explains why Lillie and Gladstone, then seventy-two years old, were on visiting terms.) Harry, by now Viscount Gladstone, called Wright a liar and Wright sued. Interestingly, counsel for the brothers advised them against using the 'declaration' as evidence, since to the legal mind its wording, which is certainly oddly precise, raised too many questions. Even so, Wright lost the case.

Less spectacularly than in the Wright case, all the siblings would for years to come be exercised about what to do about their father's legacy: his diary, his letters and his personally written hymns and Eucharistic prayers. There was no problem with the public writings. They gave the political papers to the British Museum and, in 1906, were deterred only by a distinct lack of public interest from publishing the speeches. It was a different matter with the private writings.

All the brothers read the diary and were impressed all over again by their father's energy and abilities. At first there was no question of publishing it. Stephen wrote to Harry, in 1906: 'I am of your mind & feel very sure he would have shrunk from the very idea of publication.' Privacy was the key issue here. John Morley, colleague of Gladstone and an ex Liberal MP, was chosen to write the authorised biography in 1902–1903, and was given access to both letters and diary. The brothers marked up the letters, making clear what he was and was not allowed to use. Morley was the soul of discretion, even going so far as to pronounce that 'Nobody ever had fewer secrets, nobody ever lived and wrought in fuller sunlight [than Gladstone]'. He was not told about the 'declaration', although some years later, in that private 1908 letter to Herbert, Stephen urged that 'the very intimate and sacred confidence of the position of a biographer' meant that he should know all. Yet Stephen in particular was worried about privacy. Decades before, he had even been anxious about readers in St Deiniol's Library seeing Gladstone's personal annotations on his books. In the end it was decided to lodge both the diary and the private letters with the Archbishop of Canterbury.

Their father's hymns and even more so the personally composed set of Eucharistic prayers presented a smaller, but more contentious, issue. Stephen favoured the 'lapse of a generation (say 25 years)' before the prayers and hymns were published. Mary, enthusiastically backed by their cousin Lucy Cavendish, was keen for the prayers to be published, but Stephen and his brothers balked at this idea, feeling there would be no market for them. Agnes agreed with them and felt Mary was trying, as she often did, to manipulate the rest of them. She wrote to Herbert saying: 'I am afraid Mary was and is disappointed, but it must be said that she takes up, & makes up, for her own & special pleading, too many matters which she has not been concerned with & which she does not know much about.' (This comment could equally appropriately have been made by Stephen many times over the years.)

Figure 19. Catherine Gladstone. Reproduced courtesy of the Flintshire Record Office.

There was less dissension about Mary's projected book on their mother, *Catherine Gladstone*, which she finally let her siblings read when it was finished. Stephen, while generally content, regretted there was too little 'dwelling on the home life'. According to Mary herself, this was at least partly because these years were full of unhappiness and discord, caused by the constant rows between Catherine and both Agnes and Helen which, she claimed, she had been sensible enough to keep out of.

In 1898, all these questions of publication lay in the future. Stephen had to deal with the more immediate concern of his mother. After her husband's death, Catherine, bereft of the dearest object of her affectionate care, became even more frail, particularly in mind. She began by demanding back various pieces of porcelain which she and Gladstone had given to Stephen when he first went to live in the Rectory, an irritating if minor domestic problem. A much greater worry was that she began behaving embarrassingly in church. After some kind of 'demonstration' by their mother, Stephen told Mary that they should stop Catherine attending the popular services, because she was making an exhibition of herself. Mary was still closely involved with her mother's care, despite the move to Buckley, generously spending a lot of time at the Castle helping Helen out. We don't know if Catherine's attendances at church were curtailed. If so, it would have been a sad moment for her. Apart from changing the habits of a long lifetime, it would also have increased her feelings of isolation. In spite of having two daughters on hand, Catherine, bereaved and lonely, was becoming demanding in her desire for company, and in September 1898, without success, asked Gerty to come and live with her in the Castle.

On 5 October 1899, Catherine was fit enough to cut the first sod for the St Deiniol's Library building, the most tangible part of her husband's legacy to his country, but this was her last appearance in public. By May 1900, she was declining steeply. She summoned Stephen to her one evening and he spent two hours calming her down. 'She was really out of her mind all the time & hated almost everybody', he reported sadly to his brother Harry. Catherine died on 14 June, mourned by not just the family but thousands of Hawarden people who had benefited from her kindness and generosity over seven decades, and came to pay their respects to the body. Three days later, she was buried next to her husband in Westminster Abbey. *The Times* death notice, an obituary in all but name, spread over two columns, in those days, approximately forty-eight column inches.

Catherine's death marked the end of an era for the family. Among other things, it increased the uneasiness that had always lurked in the relationship between Mary and Stephen. The latter had for some reason made a point of telling his brother Harry that he thought Helen managed their mother in her final decline better than did Mary. Now, in the immediate aftermath of her death, the latent ill feeling soon manifested itself, with Stephen angry because Mary, in searching for some lost letters, virtually accused Annie of hiding them: 'At Mary's urgency Annie had to pull every single thing out of her box & it greatly upset her, as it happened that Mary ... had searched for them in her room the night before, & apparently found and moved them.' It is impossible to know what this confused outrage is all about, but it did not bode well for the future. Subsequently, the bad feeling between brother and sister was to become even stronger.

CHAPTER 14 – HAWARDEN:
THE ENDGAME, 1900–1904

*'It is a very serious business leaving Hawarden, but I feel
it is determined by my circumstances, though I do not
say it is the ideal thing to go.'*
(Letter from Stephen to Herbert: 16 March 1904)

During the period between his parents' deaths, Stephen
worked conscientiously at his parish duties, making, in the
winter of 1898–1899, his regular visitation of 1,000 homes.
Even if this did provide opportunities for the one-to-one
ministry which he liked best, it must have been an extremely
tiring exercise. He managed to shed one burden, finally
resigning as the chair of the school managers in February
1899. He spelled out his reasons in the parish magazine:

> For 26 years and over I have acted as Chairman of School
> Managers of the eight Hawarden Parish schools. In
> consequence of the severe strain which now falls
> necessarily on the office, I feel compelled to resign it.
> That strain now exceeds what I am able to bear. It has
> rapidly grown of late years and from several causes.

He expatiated on the causes, all involving time-consuming
red tape:

> The correspondence involved with the Education
> Department, with the inspectors, with the teachers; the
> incessant business which every day turns up to be done;
> the anxiety involved in the management of Elementary
> Education, a matter which has now become so costly and
> so complicated, [that it] has assumed proportions which
> are beyond me.

Finally, he reminded them: 'You will remember I desired to resign 5 years ago.' His resignation by no means signalled a loss of interest in education. He was to speak courageously about his own pragmatic views over who should be in control of it at the St Asaph Diocesan Conferences in the autumn of both 1903 and 1905. Meanwhile, at local level, in August 1900 he announced plans to build a new infants' school at Queensferry as a memorial to his mother and a gift to the parish. It seemed as if at last, with the parental pressure off, he was reconciled to living out his days in Hawarden. He and Annie went on holiday to Switzerland in early 1901, and from Lausanne he wrote a letter to the parish magazine, as was his wont when absent, which firmly stated: 'Hawarden after all is home.' The parish continued to flourish and expand. The St Deiniol's Library building, designed by John Douglas, for which Catherine had lifted the first sod in October 1899, was progressing, and it opened on 14 October 1902. The planned new church, St Ethelwold's, was opened in Shotton, with financial aid from Herbert and Harry Gladstone, and Stephen planned a mission there; Albert and Charles, Stephen's two eldest boys, joined the Hawarden church choir.

All the Gladstone siblings were much occupied in discussions about memorials in the church to their parents. The Burne-Jones west window, depicting the nativity, and intended as a tribute to the lives of both parents, was erected soon after Gladstone's death in 1898. The statuesque calm of the scene belies the sibling rivalry and ill feeling which attended its genesis. In May 1896, Stephen wrote to Harry complaining about Mary 'for never having given me any hint of her west window plan, but still more for having several times named it to Mama before she was authorized to do so by others who would be parties to it'. Burne-Jones

Figure 20. St Deiniol's Library. Reproduced courtesy of the Flintshire Record Office.

was a close friend of Mary and, as so often, it seems that she had taken a lead in family affairs in what Stephen, at least, considered a high-handed manner: 'I thought, among other things, that it indicated an exaggerated idea of her own position with regard to the parents in matters that affected all of us.'

The memorial in the specially built chapel on the north side of the chancel came later, in 1906, and was less problematic. Harry took sole charge, commissioning and paying for the monument himself. The chapel, perfectly in keeping with the rest of the church, was built by John Douglas, the architect chosen for the Library, and the memorial was the work of Sir William Richmond, who had been responsible for the interior decoration of St Paul's Cathedral. Massive and luxuriant, the monument fills almost the entire space of the chapel and visitors (3,620 in 1907–1908 and 4,993 the following year) had, and have, to squeeze awkwardly round it. It took three years to make, and two and a half days to transfer it from the station. It represents Gladstone and Catherine lying side by side in the Boat of Life, surrounded by symbols representing Gladstone's love of Homer, the Bible, and Dante's *Divine Comedy*. One panel quotes words of Gladstone, another pays tribute to Catherine. On the chapel wall, stained glass windows with the figures of prophets and famous good women underline both the prophetic nature of Gladstone's statesmanship and the noble qualities of Catherine. Stephen, oddly, seems not to have been consulted about any aspect of the scheme, and was not present at the unveiling, performed by Harry himself. Perhaps he disapproved.

Amidst all the protracted business of memorialisation, the brothers and sisters continued with their own lives. Helen, resuming her career in education, had accepted the post of Warden of the University Women's Settlement in Southwark. In the same month, September 1901, Herbert became engaged to the much younger Dorothy (Dolly) Paget. Mary and Harry Drew were enjoying a popular and successful time in Buckley, where they were involved in a huge restoration programme, thanks in no small part to money donated by Harry Gladstone. Stephen's cousin, Albert Lyttleton, returned from South Africa for good, went to Southwark for a while to work with the poor there, and then returned to Hawarden, where he had held his first curacy.

The only discordant note was the continuance of the second Boer War in South Africa, which had broken out in 1899. Several members of the local Volunteer Corps went off to fight. Stephen turned down a request from a parishioner that the church bells be rung to celebrate every British victory, reminding him of the hundreds of men 'dying every week of wounds and disease'. He insisted that he would have the bells rung only when peace was declared. Meanwhile, he invited subscriptions for a memorial cross in the churchyard. It was erected in December 1901, and carries the names of six men from the parish. The war finally ended in May 1902. The next year, in June 1903, the Rev. R. C. Allen, a promising young man, came to Hawarden to be ordained deacon.

All seemed settled. Then in the winter of 1903, Stephen decided, for the last time, that he would resign the rectorship. He later told Harry that he: 'left Hawarden chiefly because it was too big for me: its Rector must be everywhere, & be in personal touch at all points ... I could not compass the new developments along the River.' This is undeniable. He had always set great store by knowing everyone in the parish personally and being involved with as many activities as possible. He must have realised that as more industry arrived in the area and the village consequently went on growing it would be quite impossible for him to continue with his annual visitation of every home. What is slightly more questionable is the second reason he gave for leaving: 'I knew Mama's great desire to see them [Mary and Harry Drew] at Hawarden some day.' He adds that this was why he almost resigned in 1895, which seems more likely. But if when Catherine, and indeed Gladstone, were both still alive in 1895, he had decided not to resign to make way for Harry, why did he do so now, when both parents were dead? A pious filial desire to honour Catherine's memory seems to be the only possible reason, because it was certainly not a good time for Harry Drew to give up Buckley.

The circumstances surrounding Stephen's final resignation are as difficult to disentangle as those which had surrounded his various earlier abortive attempts. As with his letter to his brother, his public announcement suggests that he was going for the good of the parish. He wrote in the magazine of December 1903:

> It is with the utmost concern that the Rector has now to say to his parishioners that he will be leaving Hawarden in the earlier part of next summer. It will then be 32 years since he received the appointment to the Parish of Hawarden at the hands of Sir Stephen Glynne. After much reflection, and much experience, he has come to the final conclusion that, taking everything into consideration, the parish would be better for a change. He need scarcely say what a severe wrench this involves to him and his. But he hopes and believes that good will come of it.

The use of the word 'wrench' is interesting, echoing as it does his father's comment of ten years previously. It was certainly the right word to describe Annie's feelings. She hated the idea of leaving Hawarden. The parish also wanted Stephen to stay, and considered getting up a petition to persuade him to change his mind. The church was about to re-open after an extensive restoration. His parishioners, who were almost certainly unaware of his many previous plans to leave, must have found it very difficult to see why he wanted to go.

The dismay caused by his announcement was so strong that the following month, January 1904, Stephen felt the need to respond:

> The Rector has to thank a great many friends for their most kind and indulgent letters, over a hundred of which he received in the first week of December. His heart's desire is that all that is good (and there is so much) in the whole parish of Hawarden shall meet with better help than he now could give. It is for this reason that he feels that his time to leave has arrived, not because of discouragement, or failing health, or for the sake of any other place or work preferred. No place or people could ever be the same to him after these long years. He earnestly hopes to be allowed to do his utmost to serve the parish till the summer; and he trusts that his parishioners will do their utmost to persevere now, and so to make the change well when it comes.

He has gone out of his way to list all the possible reasons he might have had for leaving, only to dismiss them. His comment on his health is somewhat doubtful, especially when one recalls his outburst to Harry in 1896 about his father's lack of concern for the ongoing effects of his mental breakdown, let alone his chronic physical weaknesses, not improved with the years. However, he was probably telling the truth when he denied discouragement, since by now he was less beset by doubts than at any time in his incumbency. What was indisputably true was that he was not planning to leave for 'any other place or work'. It seemed, and still seems, an extraordinary decision.

Mary was angry, on various counts. Firstly, Stephen had publicly referred to 'family arrangements' when talking about his resignation. This had upset Harry Drew, because his Buckley parishioners had jumped to the not unnatural conclusion that he was planning behind their backs to leave them for Hawarden. Harry himself, always sensitive to any idea that he owed his promotion to having married Mary Gladstone, had mixed feelings about what he and Mary both assumed would be the offer of Hawarden from Gerty (on behalf of the underage Will). Mary was loath to push Harry into accepting what she carefully described as 'the arrangement'.

She was also angry, in advance, about Annie's possible reaction to any hesitancy by herself and Harry: 'I could see for instance that Annie looks upon hesitation on H's part as not exactly humbug, but a sort of *de rigueur* courtesy.' She was angry, too, on Annie's behalf. She felt genuinely sorry for her sister-in-law, as is clear from her vivid description to Harry Gladstone of a scene in the Rectory:

> Our little new curate [Rev. R. C. Allen, ordained priest in June] was having tea at the rectory this afternoon, when Albert [Lyttleton] marched in waving the *Hawarden Magazine* 'Why, why why that's what everyone's saying, Stephy might have said less or more.' Stephy was out, & all this flung at poor Annie's face – she did not answer

and Albert went on 'I know why, but nobody else does –
I know because he has been resigning the last 20 years'.

Annie must have been very upset by this incident, feeling
that she should defend Stephen while at the same time
sharing the same puzzlement, and dismay. Mary had 'a
fearfully benumbing talk' with her sister-in-law and told
Harry Gladstone: 'I do feel broken hearted for her & for Cath
[the oldest daughter] tho she says all the elder children feel it
equally – the only thing that makes us laugh through tears,
was that little William [now six] has been extremely busy in
the nursery, packing up.' Assuming Annie had managed to
shield the children from their father's recurring doubts and
insecurity over the years, they must have taken it for granted
that Hawarden was their permanent home.

Yet another reason for Mary's anger was that she felt
that Stephen was not being honest about his reasons for
leaving. According to her he was 'glad to have Hawarden off
his back at the moment of such serious crisis'. She told
Herbert that the parish income was at its poorest and the
clerical staff feeble, that all the church property was in a run-
down state and the condition of the eight schools was
'pitiable'. Most of this is wild exaggeration, but the last
comment was to some extent true, though the situation was
not entirely Stephen's fault. The 1902 Education Act had
been opposed by the Welsh local authorities, who had then
threatened to confiscate all the church schools. This led to
great confusion over who was responsible for the upkeep of
school property. The buildings had been neglected, parents
were withdrawing their children because of unhealthy
conditions and jerry-built premises, and in particular there
had been complaints over Stephen's efficiency, or rather lack
of it, over the condition of the school at Shotton. Mary found

Figure 21. Stephen and Annie's children. Reproduced courtesy of the Flintshire Record Office.

it hard to forgive Stephen for what she saw as the poisoned chalice he was handing to Harry in the form of the poor state of the schools. She later came to believe that her husband's early death resulted from his struggles to cope with the problems caused, or at least passed on by, her brother.

Despite Mary's anger, and Harry's reluctance to leave Buckley, in July 1904 the parish magazine carried the announcement that Harry Drew had accepted the Rectory of Hawarden. Stephen and his family were to leave in August and the parish was without a Rector until Harry was inducted on 31 December. Even then, he and Mary stayed on at Buckley until 15 January, 1905. The explanation for the delay was partly red tape, but also Harry's reluctance to leave, and it does seem as if Mary was far keener on going to Hawarden than was her husband. Paradoxically, another reason for the delay was reluctance on her part to take over the Hawarden Rectory. If she had been angry at the way in which Stephen handled his resignation, she was even angrier at his attitude over the Rectory itself. The row between brother and sister continued long after Stephen had left the parish and taken up his new and final appointment.

Stephen himself was frustrated by the delay in the announcement of his successor, writing to Gerty as early as April 1904 'to impress upon her the great importance of the new Rector taking up the work in September'. He believed 'All sorts of troubles will arise if it is not to be so', thinking that the curates might start leaving because of the uncertainty. Furthermore, he was, as Agnes's husband Edward Wickham had told Mary, 'irritated by HD not jumping at Hawarden'. Sensing Harry's reluctance to leave Buckley, Stephen made it clear that 'now he had chosen it he must come to it the very 1st possible day'.

Meanwhile, the rituals of his own leave-taking continued. These drove Mary frantic with fury. She wrote to Herbert in August 1904:

> The 9 months of strain & gathering emotion & final blaze of glory, enhanced by cups of tea to the whole parish, has brought the autocracy to a climax which has been hard to bear, & if HD hadn't the temper & gentleness & perseverance of an Angel, then there must have been great reactions. I don't want to add anything to Stephy's pain in leaving Hawarden, so I keep silence now tho' my heart is hot within me but in 2 or 3 months, I shall have to speak out because he ought to know the truth.

She was sickened by the – as she thought – hypocritical exchange of expressions of mutual love and regard between Stephen and his parishioners which appeared in successive parish magazines. In her view, her brother's regime had been unacceptably autocratic, and she offered as evidence the fact that he had had a total of thirty-two assistant clergy in as many years. This is not the picture painted in Stephen's 1894 pamphlet and it is almost certainly coloured by Mary's view that Stephen had never appreciated the talents of her husband, Harry Drew.

In Stephen's 'Farewell', printed in the parish magazine of August 1904, there was, unsurprisingly, no sign of this supposed autocracy or of any other problem, for example that of past family interference. On the contrary, Stephen referred to 'the great days that we have seen' and the 'true example given to us [himself and Annie] by Mr and Mrs Gladstone', and he went out of his way to thank his 'faithful assistant clergy'. His past and present curates subscribed to have his portrait painted, he and Annie held two farewell

'At Homes' and the family was given a touchingly affectionate send-off.

As soon as Harry Drew had been officially appointed, Stephen invited him and Mary to 'go over the rectory and grounds with him'. The occasion seems to have been less than successful. In Mary's words: 'It was dreadful going over it with S & A. Like pulling out all their teeth, as Annie said, poor little Willie gazing at Harry as if he wanted to kill him'. She and Harry 'came home literally with our hearts in our boots'. The underlying problem was that the Rectory, which had been a sensible size for a married man with four sons and two daughters, was ridiculously large for a man and his wife with just one daughter. Six bedrooms at least would be surplus to requirements. Moreover, Stephen had not maintained either the house or the grounds adequately, perhaps because he could not afford to, perhaps because of his general unworldliness, and Mary felt that she and Harry could not afford either to restore it, or subsequently to live there. But that was not all.

Stephen had inherited the Rectory from their uncle, Henry Glynne, and at considerable expense had bought from Henry's daughters some furniture which he now insisted he wanted to take away with him. He also announced that he wished to be paid for various fixtures and fittings which he would have to leave behind, including library shelving, grates and marble mantelpieces. There were rules governing what happened to fixtures when rectories changed hands, as there were rules on 'dilapidations'. The 1871 Ecclesiastical Dilapidations Act had attempted to clarify the vexed question of dilapidations, by stating that the previous incumbent, in this case Stephen, was responsible for the costs of any necessary repairs to the property incurred by the successor, in this case Harry Drew, but there remained many grey areas. Stephen had certainly neglected to maintain the fabric of the Rectory. Some pipes and part of the roof collapsed in the terrible weather just before the Drews moved in, and the drains in particular were in a very bad state. Mary, and to a lesser extent Harry, felt Stephen was evading his responsibilities concerning the dilapidations and being greedy in his demands over the fixtures and fittings.

Both Harry Gladstone and Herbert were called upon by Mary to resolve the situation. Harry Gladstone tried not to get involved, writing directly to Harry Drew in August 1904:

> I think a 3 or 4 cornered conversation is a mistake, and I am sure Mary has written a good many things to me and others which she may regret. This question of Rectory fixtures is a family business matter between you and S[tephen] made more difficult by your relationship and friendship. The more help and advice Mary gives you the better but I hope she will leave you alone to conduct the correspondence ... There must and will be give and take in this matter.

In the same month, Mary wrote to Herbert:

> The last few weeks I have longed quite dreadfully for you to come and throw oil not on the flames but on the water, or rather our wounds – there is nobody like you in soothing & smoothing family misunderstandings & we have had a cruel time lately Stephy, unwittingly, I suppose making our path more difficult and painful at every turn.

In September, Harry Drew asked Harry Gladstone to meet him at the Rectory and 'go quietly over it with me'. Mary thought the answer to the financial difficulties was to use some of the money from the publication of Morley's biography of their father, which had been published in 1903. She wrote to Herbert again to enlist his support, stressing what sacrifices Harry Drew had made for the Gladstone family, and even suggesting that he, Herbert, would understand, because he too had made sacrifices. She waxed eloquently:

> Stephy's resignation again has forced him [Harry Drew] into a position from which he has always quietly shrunk, the family make it virtually impossible for him to refuse it & if the family, for the sake of sentiment & memories hold on to a house which will bleed its inhabitants very severely, it doesn't seem to me unnatural to have had hopes the family would pay something for the indulgence of that sentiment.

(Years later, she was still reminding Herbert that it was: 'a tremendous thing and demand of HD to give up for practically 12 years the sacredness of married life in our own home'.)

Herbert, who didn't agree that money from the biography should be used in this way, was appalled by her attitude:

> Frankly I don't follow your main argument which does not seem to hang together. I see no analogy between my position & HD's and really it is not accurate to say either that 'the family forced him' into the Rectory, or that 'the family' as such was responsible for seeing to the Rectory finances. HD could not escape from surroundings involved in the fact of your being Father's daughter any more than through life I have been able to escape from the mingled advantages of being his son.

He made it clear to Mary that it was Gerty who was the patron of the living and she had not consulted him on Buckley or Hawarden, adding that 'the Rectory is a temporal matter assoc. with Will [son of Willy and Gerty] & the estate'. Warming to his theme, he went on:

> HD's sacrifice was the loss of opportunity independently to work out his career so long as he was at Hawarden. As against this was the immense advantage of being closely daily associated with Father – not a temporal adversity. On the money side your residence at Hawarden [in the Castle] involved but little loss.

Herbert absolutely refused to take Mary's side against Stephen, as did their brother Harry. Eventually, Mary, stating 'how deeply I feel the sacred privilege of going to Hawarden … guarding and guiding this inheritance that Stephy has guarded and guided these 32 years', admitted that she found both house and grounds beautiful. She finally stated to Harry Gladstone, in a letter also signed by her husband, that if all else fails 'we shall start life in the Rectory with all the love that its associations and memories bring with them & trust that a way will be made clear for those that come after'.

CHAPTER 15 – BARROWBY: A NEW LIFE AND A POTENTIAL HAWARDEN, 1904–1906

'We ought to be happy here.'
(Letter from Stephen to Herbert: 25 March 1905)

Stephen, having finally made his decision to leave Hawarden and squared it with his conscience, looked resolutely to his own future. In the same magazine that announced the institution of Harry Drew as their new Rector, Stephen told the parish that he had accepted the Duke of Devonshire's offer of the rectorship of Barrowby, near the small market town of Grantham in Lincolnshire, from the end of January 1905. According to Stephen, 'this benefice [was] offered entirely unsought'. This may be true, but the following factors suggest that the odds were stacked very much in his favour: the Duke was a Gladstone family friend; Lucy Cavendish, Catherine Gladstone's niece and so Stephen's cousin, was the widow of the Duke's brother (Lord Frederick Cavendish, murdered in Phoenix Park, Dublin in May, 1882); Stephen's brother-in-law, Edward Wickham had been, since 1894, Dean of Lincoln Cathedral; and the Bishop of Lincoln was Edward King, Stephen's Principal at Cuddesdon.

All these circumstances, combined with the fact that Stephen was free to accept the post immediately, combined to lead to the offer. The vacancy was indeed fortuitous, arising from the unexpected death of the incumbent, the Rev. G. Rubie. Stephen needed employment, and Barrowby was exactly the kind of living which for years he had been saying he was looking for: a small, undemanding rural parish. For a man of sixty, temporarily unemployed, with indifferent health and deteriorating eyesight, it must have

216

seemed like a blessing from Heaven. Without a doubt, Gladstone would have ascribed the turn of events to the Providence of God.

Barrowby is a very pleasant, compact little village, set on a low hill, approached by high-hedged country roads. Stephen's church, All Saints, is an attractive ironstone and limestone building, smaller than Hawarden but in much the same early English and Perpendicular Gothic styles. It has a nave, two arcades, a chancel and a tower, topped by a spire with a ring of six bells. This was famous, attracting bell ringers from all over the local area. When Stephen arrived, the fabric of the building was in basically good condition, having been extensively restored between 1852 and 1870, with the spire repaired in 1879 and the roof redone ten years later. The inside of the church was, if a little neglected, potentially beautiful and of historical interest. Its most striking feature was a fourteenth-century font in Decorated style with an unusual hollowed-out base containing a carving of the devil. There was also some superb stained glass, partly fourteenth century, partly new, donated by Canon Welby (the Rev. G. Rubie's predecessor) or paid for by subscription. Sadly, one of the windows commemorates three of Welby's young children, Katherine Augusta, Edith Jane and Augusta Maria. Katherine Augusta lived for only two months in 1848. Her older sister Edith Jane died just under ten years later, in January 1858, aged ten, in the same month as the namesake Augusta Maria, only six. Stephen, seeing this window daily, would surely have thanked God constantly for his own six children, fit and well.

On a more cheerful note, he would have been pleased to find a small vestry, the lack of which facility he had lamented in Hawarden. It contained a chest for the church's valuable old silver, a Communion cup and patten. The walls are adorned with three watercolours of Faith, Hope and Charity, and a window looks out onto the pretty, tree-filled churchyard. Approached through a handsome lychgate – a gift from Welby to celebrate his Golden Wedding in 1899 – the churchyard slopes gently down to the fields beyond and has an extensive view over the lovely Vale of Belvoir, with Lincoln Cathedral just visible on the horizon. It must have seemed to Stephen and Annie, when they first stood there and looked at the panorama before them, that they were back in Hawarden, looking out across the plains of the Dee to the Wirral beyond. The similarity is uncanny.

The Rectory, now privately owned, was large, and compared more than favourably with the Rectory in Hawarden. Dating from 1588, it had originally consisted of two parlours, a hall, a kitchin [*sic* in a 1727 account], a back kitchin [*sic*], cellars and a pantry, one upper room over the great parlour and another above the kitchen. Over the years it was enlarged, and in the early nineteenth century was very attractively stuccoed and gothicised, probably by Welby's predecessor-but-one, James Stuart Menteith. Although it needed a lot of internal work, its potential as a family home and centre for parish entertaining was obvious. Stephen later described it as 'a wonderful house'. Its vast seventeen-acre grounds, in which the older Gladstone boys laid out a golf course, are now partly built over, but in Stephen's day they stretched as far as the churchyard. It was a longer walk from Rectory to church than Stephen had in Hawarden, but not by much.

This apparent paradise, Stephen's cherished ideal, the small undemanding rural parish, had one snag: it was socially circumscribed and very set in its ways. It was also far from the family's friends and relations, except for the Wickhams, just over thirty miles away. This does not seem to have unduly worried Stephen, however, and Barrowby, even in his day, had good transport links.

When the Gladstone family arrived in 1905, the village, which consisted of just a few streets and a village green, was little changed since the living had been described by John Marius Wilson in his Imperial Gazetteer of 1870–72, as: 'a parish with 3 hamlets ... Acres 4,462, real property £7,969. Population 862. Houses 187. The property is divided among a few. The living is a rectory ... value £1,200 [relatively wealthy, if not by Hawarden standards] ... The church is good.' The population was still roughly the same in 1911 when Stephen left, notwithstanding the fact that in 1905 the *Hawarden Parish Magazine* had described it as 'about 900' (less than a tenth the size of Hawarden.) Doing its best to give its readers an idea of what their former Rector could expect, the magazine had imparted the additional information that Barrowby was 'almost entirely agricultural, with a certain artisan element'.

The 'artisan element' consisted mainly of warehousemen, ironstone workers, railwaymen and engineers, some of them employed in very humble capacities, such as 'boiler smith's helper' as one man described himself in the 1911 census. These men would have worked for Richard Hornsby & Sons, a big agricultural engine and machinery manufacturers in Grantham, or on the Great Northern, London and North Western Joint Railway: the line from King's Cross to Edinburgh ran through Grantham station.

Most of the land was still owned, as Wilson described, by just a few families, including the Devonshires and the Welbys, of whom the retired Rector, Canon Welby, was a prominent member. The industrial workers, together with the farm labourers, gardeners and grooms employed on the local magnates' estates and at a local riding school, formed the majority of the population. These people were poor. Many, though not all, had large numbers of children. The 1911 census shows one farm labourer and his wife as having had eleven, one of whom had died, but nine were still living at home, ranging in age from twenty-six to two years old. It was common practice to take in lodgers to make ends meet. Two or three generations often lived together to save money, and a high proportion of wives took menial jobs to supplement the family's income. For the same reason, many boys only just in their teens went out to work as yardboys.

In the 1911 census, only one person described themselves as living off the parish, but many people must have relied on the various charities administered by the church, which doled out money and coal to those in need. Welby personally helped out many families who slipped through the official net. It was a close community, where everyone knew everybody else's business, and open-mindedness was in relatively short supply. Very limited education was partly responsible for their narrow outlook. From the way in which they filled in the census forms, it can be deduced that many fathers were not only in ill-paid, physically demanding and repetitive jobs but also that they were barely literate, and had difficulty both in reading the form and writing down the information required. There is much impatient scratching-out and some corrections in red, made by the official in charge.

It would be wrong, however, to suggest that Stephen was leaving a prosperous and well-educated Hawarden for a village whose inhabitants were at the bottom of the social heap. Although the population was small, at least two families of moderate means had produced schoolteacher daughters. A number of householders, mainly widows or widowers, described themselves as being of 'private means', there were several well-to-do tradespeople, such as maltsters and milkmen, shopkeepers, and a handful of professional men such as bank clerks, a surveyor of taxes and a retired army captain. These people, unlike the majority of the population, had servants, sometimes several of them. The army captain had five. One Anne Downing, a widow, had a maid, a cook/housekeeper and a house parlourmaid. Welby had four servants, including a butler, and Stephen and Annie themselves had six, including a Martha Elizabeth Edwards who was born in Hawarden and, it seems likely, had moved with them when they left.

There was, then, as at Hawarden, a social mix, and the parish registers suggest that Stephen's flock consisted of a cross section of society, albeit dominated by animal husbandmen. There were sheep, pig and cow farmers, each of the two latter groups having their own substantial clubs. In 1909, the Pig Club had seventy-five members, owning between them 109 pigs. The secretary of this Club had been in office since 1833, evidence of a backward looking society which did not encourage change. The Pig and Cow Clubs met regularly in the two pubs, the White Swan, still in existence, and the now defunct Marquis of Granby.

Apart from the public houses, the most prominent building in Barrowby was the Reading Room, a smaller version of the Hawarden Institute, a 'substantial building of brick, stone and slate' built in 1901, on land granted to Canon Welby by the Duke of Devonshire and paid for by Welby himself. The conveyancing document specified that it was to be open to all the inhabitants of Barrowby as a public room. This prescription was followed by the stern announcement that it was to be used for '(a) reading, (b) quiet and sedentary games, (c) mothers' meetings and (d) such other quiet meetings as might be approved by the committee, excluding altogether all political and controversial matters'. The committee was to consist of the rector, the churchwardens and the rural dean, so the church control was absolute.

The village boasted several shops, including a baker's, grocer's and butcher's, a post office, a Methodist chapel and one small elementary school. This had been erected in 1880, and served 190 children, boys and girls of all ages, who, unbelievably, were taught all together by a Mr Potter, the headmaster, in the single classroom. A Miss Yolland was appointed in April 1906 to teach the infants, but the age groups must have been divided, at most, by just a curtain. Canon Welby was responsible for the existence of the school as well as the reading room; he was a great benefactor in the Gladstone mould.

Barrowby was, in effect, Hawarden, scaled down and returned to a past era, before the creep of industrialisation had changed its character; that is, the Hawarden of 1872, when Stephen had embarked on his first rectorship.

Six years before Stephen arrived, the Rev. Canon Welby, who perhaps coincidentally was the brother of the Reginald Earle Welby who was Gladstone's right hand at the Treasury in the 1880s, had resigned after fifty years as Rector. This situation closely reflected that in Hawarden, where Henry Glynne had been the incumbent for nearly forty years before Stephen took over. When Welby's successor, the Rev. G. Rubie, suddenly and unexpectedly died in office, a curate, a Rev. A. H. Morris, was hastily recruited to be in charge of the parish. Morris had moved from Walsall in Staffordshire in 1903, and was attached to St Hugh's mission church in Sturton by Stow, in the Lincoln Diocese, nine miles north west of the city. He held the fort at Barrowby for three months, during which time he quickly became immensely popular with the church people, who flocked to his services and enjoyed his participation in their sporting activities. (There were cricket and football clubs.) The *Grantham Journal* described as 'wonderful the hold he had gained on the people' in so short a time.

On 5 March, just over a month after Stephen's arrival, Morris was presented in a packed schoolroom with an address signed by 'practically the whole of the inhabitants of the village'. He was praised for having 'entered into their joys and sorrows', a description of his attitude which seems to have been something more than the expected eulogising of a departing curate. Bitterness clearly lurked behind the stated regret that 'his services could not have been retained'. The parishioners and possibly Morris himself had clearly hoped that he would be offered the living. The Duke of Devonshire, the patron, had pointedly been made aware of 'the local desire of Mr Morris' and had himself written to Stephen about it. At all events, when Stephen was appointed, Morris resigned, or was possibly pushed out, and went back to the Mission in Sturton by Stow, where he remained for another two years. *Crockford's Clerical Dictionary* records no mention of his months at Barrowby. There does seem to have been some kind of conspiracy, quite possibly without Stephen's own knowledge or consent, to have Gladstone's son installed as Rector of Barrowby. It is all rather reminiscent of the events leading up to Harry Drew's installation at Buckley.

In the brief interval between leaving Hawarden and going to Lincolnshire, Stephen and Annie undertook a whistle-stop tour of old haunts. First they took the children, aged from nineteen to seven years old, to Penmaenmawr, one of the Gladstone family's favourite small North Wales seaside towns, for a holiday. Then they went to Lambeth, Stephen's old stamping ground, where they lodged in the vicarage while he took charge of St Mary's for a few weeks. The south London church presented the greatest possible contrast to the incumbency he was now bound for, and represented what might have been Stephen's life if his Uncle Henry had not suddenly died all those years ago, wrenching him from what he believed was his true calling, ministry to the urban poor. It seems that Lambeth remained always close to his heart, and it can be no coincidence that some years later, one of his curates, Raymond Allen, moved on to work there.

After Lambeth, the family travelled north to stay with Annie's family in Liverpool. No doubt Annie poured out to her mother her unhappiness at leaving Hawarden, a grief she had struggled to hide from Stephen. Finally, they went to Rome, where Stephen could show his family the sights he had enjoyed as a young man nearly forty years earlier.

Stephen was instituted to the rectorship of Barrowby at Lincoln Cathedral, in February 1905. He may have been partly aware of the situation with Mr Morris, or at least of the latent dissatisfaction. Having referred, in a letter to his brother Harry, to a reassuring communication from the Bishop on this issue, he confessed that he was worried at the thought of local hostility: 'So we must hope for the best. I doubt not that Annie will soon make herself felt in a way that will surprise many of them! But it is said that Lincolnshire people take a summer & winter before they lose a prejudice.' This comment suggests that neither the Bishop, nor anyone else, had told him how instantly the parish had taken to Morris. 'I do not now think', Stephen's letter continued, 'that the position of things is critical, but it certainly is unpleasant, & we must be very wise and wary'.

He must have thought back to his appointment at Hawarden thirty-three years earlier. Hostility then had been mainly theological, caused by anxiety over his High Church views. Recently, the Bishop of Lincoln had expressed the opinion that in his diocese, 'we are free from any serious [ritualistic] troubles', but even so, Stephen knew that a High Churchman would have to tread carefully. He was still feeling the need to be 'wise and wary' when he wrote to his brother again at the end of March: 'I am having a series of disagreeable little ebullitions here – showing there is fire under smoke ... it [this Parish] is under ways and rules & ideas of 50 or 60 years ago, & the Lincolnshire folk are very slow & obstinate.' He was also aware of some continuing personal hostility. Even in Hawarden, there had been a measure of resentment over the Glynne family's stranglehold on the living and the influence that the Gladstones had in parish affairs. In Barrowby, the problem of the not universally welcome Gladstone influence was inextricably combined with the feelings of resentment over the treatment of Morris.

One of the first difficulties to be overcome was purely practical. When Stephen and his family arrived in the parish, they had to find somewhere to stay. The Rectory needed a lot of work before it was fit for a family of eight to move in and: 'There is no lodging at all to be had: we began with the Grantham hotel, and this will give us time to look round.' Mary even generously offered to have the children to stay in Hawarden to ease the problem. The *Grantham Journal* for 18 February announced that it understood 'the reverend gentleman is anxious to obtain a home in the village, as a temporary residence, if he can possibly do so'. The family could not move into the Rectory until late March, and there was still 'no kitchen for weeks – & lots of men at work'.

Canon Welby had offered to put them up for a few days, but he was currently in bad odour locally, presumably having supported Stephen's candidature over that of Mr Morris. It is noticeable that Welby took no part in the fulsome farewell to Morris, though he was normally prominent on such parish occasions. As Stephen put it, 'he [Welby] has so put his poor foot in it that he has displeased all'. For that reason the Canon's offer was not taken up. Welby was hurt by their refusal 'and is going away for a few days. However that will all come right'.

Stephen was correct in this prophecy. Welby, recently widowed, remained in the village, in the White House in Casthorpe Road, throughout Stephen's rectorship, regaining any lost popularity, active in the parish until he was well over ninety, stepping in when Stephen was absent, and giving of his considerable wealth and spare time to the church. This situation might have threatened to duplicate the one in Hawarden, with Welby in the role of the dominating Gladstone father figure, but this did not happen, perhaps partly because Stephen was now in his experienced sixties, rather than his naïve twenties.

The empty curate's post was easily filled. The *Hawarden Parish Magazine* for February reported: 'The Rev. Raymond Allen who has worked well among us since he came in 1903 goes to Barrowby, as assistant curate, at Easter.' Presumably Stephen was responsible for this move, and Allen's presence must have been a great support. There is, incidentally, no connection between this Mr Allen and the Mr Ulric Allen who was at Hawarden in the 1890s. That Mr Allen moved on to Wisbech in Cambridgeshire, whence he paid at least ten visits to Barrowby to preach or talk, and thence to Oakham, Rutland, as vicar, before he disappears from the record, probably to retirement, in 1914.

At first, Stephen found it hard, as he had expected, to adjust to his new, much smaller parish, writing forlornly to Herbert soon after his arrival: 'I am still Rector, which is a little compensation.' He would have been forcibly reminded of the contrast with Hawarden when he and Annie went up to London in March 1905, to be presented with his portrait. As well as family members, Hawarden curates both past and current, who had paid for it to be painted, attended the ceremony. Stephen was hoarse from laryngitis, but still replied at length to the presentation address. He must have felt nostalgic. After being in charge of a mother church and six daughter churches, with a staff of curates to match, Stephen now had one small church, with just one curate to help him. Over a year later, in April 1906, he was to write to Harry even more glumly: 'I should thankfully leave this barren place where I can look to no practical good.'

His low mood, so reminiscent of those he experienced at Hawarden, was due partly to illness, and partly to irritating, unfounded rumours that he was a wealthy man. These rumours were probably spread by people who harboured resentment at his having been, as they saw it, foisted upon them by the combined wealth and power of the Duke of Devonshire and the Gladstone family. He was so depressed that he even briefly flirted with the idea of escaping to another living if anything should 'come my way', while admitting that this was an unlikely contingency. Annie must have been in despair at the thought of yet another period of unrest, and perhaps even another upheaval. But, as she knew well, Stephen was self-deprecating by nature and should not always be taken at his word. Their son Charles always maintained that his father was happier in Barrowby than he had ever known him in Hawarden, more at peace with himself.

There was lot of work to be done in the new parish. In May of Stephen's first year, the *Grantham Journal* printed a very cross letter from a man who had 'journeyed some miles' to hear the new Rector preach. On sitting down, the man and his two friends had been asked to move from the pew they had selected because it belonged to a young woman. 'I scarcely think it can be the wish of the Rector or churchwardens that strangers should be treated as we were', he wrote. This letter is interesting on two counts. Firstly, it shows us one of Stephen's widely recognised strengths: preaching. Records suggest that he regularly attracted large congregations. Secondly, it presents a perfect example of the 'ways and rules & ideas of 50 or 60 years ago' which he had complained of to Harry. The practice of pew rent described in the letter had been abolished by him in Hawarden in 1880, more than twenty years earlier. He was having to start all over again.

He began carefully, employing tact, just as he had done in Hawarden. At his first Easter Vestry Meeting, when he was voted into the chair because Welby – still chair after taking over on the death of Rubie – was ill, Stephen was careful to pay 'a tribute of praise to the late Rev. G. Rubie'. He did not mention the usurped Mr Morris, but then, Morris had not been there long enough to chair a vestry meeting. Stephen took the opportunity to express 'his great wish to do anything he could for the good of the parish'. This humility, which came naturally to him, stood him in good stead, and he also exercised much needed patience and tolerance. The Preachers' Book, which lists every service in the church during Stephen's incumbency, with the name of the preacher and the subject of the sermon, records that on 19 November 1905, Mr Morris preached at one service and Stephen at the other. This may have been a gesture of reconciliation and at the very least, would have raised Stephen's stock with his parishioners.

By the spring of 1906, he was beginning to settle down. Gradually he was earning the respect and trust of the people, as he began quietly to mould All Saints' Barrowby into a replica of St Deiniol's Hawarden. One of his priorities was, as might be expected, to raise the profile of the church music. He had already arranged for the choir to have new cassocks and surplices, and the Easter Vestry of 1906 now agreed to an increase in the organist's salary, a sign that the choir was becoming more important. Services were fully choral, and on special occasions the choir performed anthems by contemporary popular composers such as Maunder and Bartlett.

Music already had an important role in village life. Off and on, there was a band, the viability of which was the subject of many touchy letters in the *Grantham Journal* over the years. More respected was Barrowby's permanent team of bellringers. Bellringing had become an immensely popular pastime in England since the improvements in bell tuning made by John William Taylor in the 1860s. The village may also have had a team of handbell ringers. In the church vestry there is an old set of handbells, possible testimony to the existence of such a team. Before and during Stephen's time, handbell competitions were widespread throughout the country.

There was also non-competitive music on a more domestic scale. Mr Potter, the headmaster, who doubled as organist, often played the piano (another gift of Canon Welby) for entertainments in the Reading Room, as did one of his sons. The Potters had seven surviving children, and if only some of those still living at home had inherited their father's talents, they must have provided a solid core of

229

musical ability. A Glee Club was to be formed a few years after Stephen's arrival. The new Rector's family added to the local musical resources. Stephen's older daughter Catherine was a competent violinist and pianist, and all the children sang.

In July 1906, the Barrowby old folks were presented with a new and unexpected source of music: at a tea at the Rectory for the older parishioners, Stephen played his guests music on a phonograph, which 'much pleased them and puzzled some' as the *Grantham Journal* put it. If the family was amused, or dismayed, by this lack of sophistication, they hid their feelings well. They were becoming fully co-opted into Barrowby life. In that same July, at a Sale of Work – 'work' which resulted from hours of sewing meetings held by Annie at the Rectory – Annie herself ran a Plain Clothes and General Stall, Catherine was in charge of refreshments, and Edith and Willie, aged respectively eleven and eight and no doubt with their mother's guidance, were in charge of a Sweets and Toys Stall. The older boys were away at Eton, or they too would surely have been usefully deployed. Stephen's belief that Annie 'will soon make herself felt in a way that will surprise many of them', was fully justified.

To her and the children attached much of the credit for Stephen's growing acceptance. They had all loved Hawarden, but for Stephen's sake, readily made their contribution to Barrowby. Catherine helped to teach in the Sunday school and the siblings all clubbed together to buy a new ewer for the font. Annie, whom Stephen said had been practically worshipped in Hawarden, soon became confident enough in her place in Barrowby society to introduce new ideas, notably starting up a Girls' Friendly Society, which met twice a week, on Sundays and Fridays. There is a photograph of her with twelve of its members, all solemnly

Figure 22. Annie with the Barrowby Girls' Friendly Society. Reproduced by kind permission of Mrs Eileen de Ville.

staring at the camera, uniformly smartly dressed in huge hats, long-sleeved, high-necked blouses, tight-waisted skirts and laced-up boots. A formidable crew, good advertisements for the Society's aims to encourage 'respectable' girls in purity of life, dutifulness to parents and faithfulness to employers. Annie, in a smartly trimmed jacket, stands at one end of the back row, smiling with slightly grim satisfaction as she surveys her girls.

Stephen was now over sixty and content to lead a quiet life, but Annie was still in her early forties. She must have missed the stimulating variety of Hawarden life, but remained devoted to her husband's interests, encouraging him in his plans and boosting his confidence.

CHAPTER 16 – BARROWBY:
OUTER STRENGTH, PRIVATE FRAILTY, 1906–1911

'I have to look for the coming time when I shall
give up B[arrowby.]'
(Letter from Stephen to Harry Gladstone: 1 August 1907)

Stephen now began to turn the church itself into a building more reminiscent of St Deiniol's, Hawarden, and more in sympathy with his own High Church ethos. At the Easter Vestry Meeting of 1906, he had announced that he was putting in an application for permission to restore the choir seats, replace the old screen, and lengthen and slightly raise the Holy Table. Several of these ideas, and a few others which he put into the actual application, must have secured general approval. Some choir seats had been removed when the new organ – a very fine-looking instrument – was installed back in 1870, and had never been replaced. Repositioning these seats, taking up part of the chancel floor to allow that to happen, and paving the floor with black and white marble, was uncontroversial work, as was colouring the dirty chancel walls. Moving the screen back to its traditional place in the east end, however, was a gesture which could have been viewed by some as overtly High Church.

The screen, which is in handsome Perpendicular style, had become 'fearfully mangled and reduced', was lacking its original figures, had been moved around the church several times and was currently languishing at the west end. Some of its wood had even been used to repair pews. When Stephen had it moved back to its original position before the chancel, the altar rail was brought forward, the carved, hexagonal wooden pulpit lowered by a few inches and the

233

altar, or Holy Table, lengthened and slightly raised. These changes, emphasising the High Church insistence on the centrality of the ritual of Holy Communion, might have caused some anxiety. Stephen, perhaps to stave off possible criticism, met the cost of all this work (about £120) himself, also contributing new hangings, cushions, kneelers and reading desks and a new white altar cloth. A combination of public subscription and private donation would have been more usual, and indeed the clerk who drew up the necessary documents – there was endless red tape involved - assumed this was so and had to make the necessary corrections.

A week-long Dedication, from 31 October to 7 November, was held to mark the restoration of the screen and the re-opening of the chancel. There were special services, including not only the normal Sunday afternoon ones for children but one specially for women, at 3 p.m. on the Thursday afternoon. The Diocesan Guild of Ringers came to ring the bells on the Saturday, and the Lord Bishop of Grantham preached at Sunday Evensong, which was followed by another peal of bells, this time by the Barrowby ringers themselves. There was also some kind of event on the Friday evening, but an accidentally discovered flier, very professionally printed, has frustratingly got a large tear through the middle, so there is no way of knowing what that involved. Maybe it was a service especially for the men, who would otherwise be the only group not specifically catered for.

It was not only the church building that benefited from Stephen's exertions. There are some signs that at this time, in spite of the combined efforts of Canon Welby and Mr Potter, the general quality of life in the village had been deteriorating. That November in 1906, there were complaints that the Feast Week was now 'an almost forgotten festival'.

The schoolchildren's concert was no longer held, and the band, in one of its periodic declines, failed to give a dance, to which 'a good many were looking forward'. Between them, Stephen and Annie encouraged the revival of many of these traditions. In February 1907, the schoolchildren, flushed with successes in needlework and penmanship competitions at the Grantham Industrial Exhibition, gave a concert. In May, Annie's Girls' Friendly Society put on an entertainment, joined by Catherine, Edith and Willie, who all dressed up in Welsh and Irish costumes, to play, sing and perform dramatic dialogues. Stephen also took part, though he did not go so far as to dress up. From the evidence of newspaper reports and extant programmes, it would seem that Stephen and his immediate family took a bigger part in church entertainments in Barrowby than they had done in Hawarden. This presumably reflects the variation in the size of the two parishes, and the corresponding difference in the depths of their talent pools, as well as the fact that the children were growing up.

In the same month as the Girls' Friendly Society entertainment, the Feast was revived, with a parade headed by the temporarily revived band, and a dinner for the 114 men of their Friendly Society, to which the teetotal Stephen, in a popular move, contributed beer. In July there was a Sunday school treat, complete with a march from the church to the Rectory grounds, swings and seesaws, a 'sumptuous' tea, games, races, prizes – of course – and buns and packets of sweets to take home: Hawarden recreated in Barrowby. Stephen and Annie also gave another party for the old people that month, and in November they had a large party indoors at the Rectory for the men of the choir, the bellringers and the church officers, with wives invited 'for 8.00 p.m.' These events, which were to be repeated annually,

235

may to our eyes seem trivial, but they were of great importance to the community, and were recorded not only in the monthly *Barrowby Parish News*, started up by Stephen in imitation of its Hawarden predecessor (and of which unfortunately only two numbers are now extant), but also in the *Grantham Journal*.

The energy shown by the Rector and his wife is the more praiseworthy because Stephen was never really well. His health did not improve as much as he might have hoped with the lifting of the burdens of Hawarden, and in Barrowby he continued to suffer from terrible headaches and worsening eyesight. The left eye, the only functioning one, was now failing. He went for treatment, including an operation, to an eye surgeon in Wiesbaden in February and again in October 1908, leaving the curate Raymond Allen in charge.

Wiesbaden, a historic spa town on the Rhine in south west Germany, was in the early years of the century relatively small and undeveloped. Given that Stephen was there to undergo uncomfortable, if not painful, treatment, it was a pleasant place to be, with a large English-speaking church, St Augustine of Canterbury, interesting old buildings, several concert halls and a museum, markets and attractive surrounding countryside, including acres of vineyards. Barrowby must have seemed a long way away, but as was his wont in Hawarden, Stephen did not forget his parish duties and responsibilities when he was away.

In between his enforced absences, he encouraged the holding of a meeting in May at which Raymond Allen gave a talk on Christianity and Socialism, shortly to be a topic at the Fifth Lambeth Conference. This was not the first time such a meeting had been held on a topic of public interest. As early as December 1905, Ulric Allen had come to give a talk on old age pensions. Social issues were close to Stephen's heart, and the people responded. There was plenty of discussion after Raymond Allen's talk and a date was fixed for a further meeting. A pattern of instructive talks, such as those at the Hawarden Institute, was established.

Also occupying Stephen's time between Wiesbaden visits, much less seriously but symptomatic of everyday irritations, was the matter of the tumbledown shed. This shed, with brick walls and a tiled roof, was in the middle of a field on the Rectory Farm, and had been a source of frustration to Stephen since his arrival. It was of no use to the tenant and was in constant need of repair and maintenance, the costs of which were born by the Rector. In the summer of 1908, Stephen finally lost patience and applied for permission from his patron the Duke of Devonshire to have it knocked down. With unwonted financial canniness, he pointed out that the sale of the materials would pay for the costs of the demolition process. Permission was duly granted in July. Stephen's thank you letter was written from the Red House in Hawarden. He was staying there, although by then Gerty and her children had moved to the Castle, while he helped with the church services in the absence of Harry Drew. Mary and Dossie were in the Rectory, but maybe Mary had not invited her brother to stay with them. Not too much should be read into this, since the next month, Mary and Harry were to invite Stephen and Annie to stay with them in their home.

The following year, in February, rested after his time in Wiesbaden, a reinvigorated Stephen was telling funny stories at an entertainment put on by Annie's 'girls'. In May, more importantly, he turned his attention to the village school. He had always been involved, taking classes in Scripture and visiting assemblies, but now he felt something more positive was needed. Compared with Hawarden, with its separate elementary schools for girls and boys and its intermediate school, Barrowby was educationally poorly provided for, with the authorities regularly asking for improvements.

Mr Potter was a popular head and Canon Welby had done much to maintain the fabric of the school building and playground, but Stephen, with his extensive experience, had a wider vision. A medical inspection in February had found that the children were well nourished, clean and well clothed, which suggests that the parents were doing their part. They and their children deserved better, and in May, Stephen called a meeting to discuss enlarging the classroom, which had been overcrowded for years, and further improving the playground. The parishioners responded to his enthusiasm and a building fund was set up. In August, the inevitable Sale of Work was held to raise funds. The Sale was opened by Agnes, coming over from the Lincoln Deanery, and in June the work began. A new classroom was built on to the existing one, the old wooden floor was replaced by tiles, and ventilators were installed. Regular dances, at least one of which was organised by Annie, were held to raise money for the project, with the main room and the new classroom being thrown into one for the purpose. The school log book for 18 April 1910, proudly records: 'The Reverend Stephen Gladstone brought in the Duke of Rutland, Lord Gladstone [Stephen's brother Harry] and another gentleman to inspect the improvements in the school premises.' The school still exists, next to the church – a simple one storey stone building with mullioned windows and a prettily tiled roof complete with a small bell tower.

At that time, Stephen was also intent on the further embellishment of the church. In March 1909, he applied for permission to erect a small statue of the Virgin and Child, the so-called Emblem of All Saints, three feet high, with niche and canopy, above the front porch. He commissioned A. G. Walker, who was responsible for the figures of Aristotle, St Augustine and Dante, all heroes of his father, at St Deiniol's Library. He estimated that the carving would cost £30 to £40 and instigated a general appeal to the parish. In fact, the final cost was £66, but the statue was worth it, being to this day a significant addition to the appearance of the porch. It depicts a lifelike Mary, calm and collected, eyes closed in contemplation, holding up a believable Christ child whose head rests on her right shoulder. Stephen was also responsible for commissioning a small

Figure 23. Stephen at Barrowby. Reproduced by kind permission of Mrs Eileen de Ville.

coloured figure of the Good Shepherd – a red-robed Christ holding a lamb – inside the church on the south wall, which was dedicated by the Bishop of Lincoln at the same time as the 'Emblem', at a special festival in November.

Barrowby must have felt that their new Rector was putting them on the map, and publicly he was clearly making a success of these final years of his ministry. However, personally things were not good. An oculist in Lausanne in January 1909, who could sadly offer him no help, ordered him to read for no more than ten minutes a day, and at New Year 1910, although he conducted the services, his youngest child, Willie, read the lessons, probably because his father could no longer see well enough to do so: he had reached the stage when he could not even recognise his parishioners in the street.

Perhaps for comfort, he retreated into the past. Somehow he struggled to reread his mother's and father's letters to him, and wrote to his brothers appreciatively, if illegibly, of the support he realised his parents had given him. The whole family was exercised over the possible publication of Gladstone's letters. The siblings, as ever, were far from unanimous. Harry and Stephen felt that publication would have been against their father's wishes; Mary, as was her wont, disagreed. She was also at cross-purposes with Stephen over developments at St Deiniol's, of which he remained Head of Trust. Stephen, who was still plagued by Mary's accusations over the reasons for his resignation from Hawarden and the state of the Hawarden Rectory, wrote to Harry Gladstone: 'You and H[erbert] will handle this most wisely. I may be thought prejudiced; but accuracy is a thing she is very far from.' Oddly, although many acrimonious letters were exchanged and Mary grumbled for years to the two younger brothers about Stephen's faults, she and Harry Drew invited Stephen and Annie to stay with them in the Hawarden Rectory in August 1908, and the visit was so successful that the next year they offered them the Rectory for a holiday in May and June.

As early as August 1907, Stephen had begun to think about his final retirement. Rather surprisingly, he wrote to Harry that the parish 'can only be retained by someone whose heart is in it'. The implication of his own indifference is not supported by any evidence. Either he was suffering from yet another bout of depression or, more likely, he was aware of his own growing physical frailty. He continued: 'I shall be 65 in 18 months & I do not seriously think I can now take up any fresh work.' He went on to refer to his recurring headaches.

At intervals, Rosebery offered him an honorary canonry at Lincoln, but he turned it down three times. He was feeling old and tired. In 1910, he and Annie began seriously planning his retirement. Typically, he wrote to Harry Gladstone: 'I am feverishly anxious to keep this entirely secret now, as if it came out it must hasten my resignation.' Since Mary was still insistent on keeping alive the unhappy disagreements and awkwardnesses which had marked his departure from Hawarden, this desire to conceal his intentions is perhaps understandable.

That year, 1910, was a year of endings and change. Herbert had taken up his new post of Governor General of South Africa. The curate Raymond Allen left Barrowby for Lambeth. Annie's mother died. Deiny (Stephen Deiniol), Stephen and Annie's third son, decided against following the family tradition of going up to Oxford. Agnes's husband Edward Wickham died in April while still in office as Dean of Lincoln, and a dumb peal – with muffled bells – was rung on the Barrowby bells and a memorial service held. (He had occasionally preached there.) Agnes and her children went to live in London. Headmaster Mr Potter retired, and he and his wife decided to emigrate to Canada, where his brother farmed and whence their son had recently emigrated. It is

241

certain that it was from them that Deiny, having decided against Oxford, caught his enthusiasm for farming in Canada, since he was to follow them out there when the Potters finally left Barrowby, much feted, the next August.

Stephen, who had suffered another bout of illness in the previous May, finally announced his decision to retire on 7 August 1911. Raymond Allen, who preached his final sermon on Easter Day 1910, had not been replaced, and this meant an added pastoral burden for Stephen, who also had to conduct almost every one of the four weekly services – three on Sunday and one on Wednesday – himself. Canon Welby, who, judging by his deteriorating signature in the Preachers' Book, had become increasingly frail, could no longer be called upon, and other occasional preachers seem to have faded from the scene. Barrowby was a small parish, and the authorities may have felt that one incumbent should be able to manage easily on his own, but Stephen had high standards for himself which he knew he could no longer reach. When he had been away having treatment in Wiesbaden in October 1908, his curate, Allen, had cut out the midweek service to ease the workload. This is something Stephen himself would never have contemplated.

Faced with his increasing blindness and continuing fragile health, he felt he could no longer go on. His letter in the *Barrowby Parish News* said, with typical humility: 'it is my hope and prayer … that whoever comes here as Rector may be able to do much which I have not been able to do'. Mirroring the situation in Hawarden nearly ten years earlier, his resignation came as a surprise, and not a welcome one. The *Grantham Journal* for October quoted his resignation letter in full, commenting: 'Expressions of regret are heard on all sides from Nonconformists and Churchmen alike, as the broad-mindedness of the rector has earned him the respect of all parties.' Right from the start of his rectorship, when he had preached at a mission church in Grantham where many Nonconformists were present, Stephen had been on excellent terms with the local Methodists. Together with tact and patient determination, tolerance was one of the many qualities, developed in Hawarden, which Stephen brought with him into Lincolnshire.

Much of what Annie and Stephen did at Barrowby was modelled on what they had achieved at Hawarden, and was marked by the unfailing warmth and generosity which had been so characteristic of the Gladstone parents, William and Catherine. Annie and Stephen were renowned for their 'sumptuous teas' and donations of plum puddings and 'nice pieces of beef' to the poor at Christmas. At the frequent parties in the Rectory, they and Catherine, their eldest child, 'did everything in their power to amuse the visitors'. They inaugurated, and accompanied, trips to Skegness for the older Sunday school children who had outgrown the treat of tea in the Rectory garden, and Stephen procured a magic lantern and operator to amuse the younger ones.

He was always alert to the needs of others: he would regularly send his carriage round for any old person too frail otherwise to make it to the Rectory for the annual old folks' party. He was both relied on and respected. He became a trustee of the constantly folding and reforming local band, and a patron of the Gardening Society, which was revived in 1909 after eight or nine years in abeyance, a recreation in miniature of the Hawarden Horticultural Society. Stephen was also elected treasurer of the Friendly Society, which represented a noted mark of confidence in his financial acumen, somewhat misplaced, as it happened. At some stage he lost two of the railway certificates purchased by the

Society and had to ask Harry how to avoid the club suffering as a result.

In those final years, Stephen's sons provided him with endless delight. Albert, Charles and Deiny all followed in his footsteps and went to Eton. Albert and Charles were champion rowers – Albert was to win a gold medal in the 1908 Olympics – and he was very proud of them, announcing their successes at Henley Rowing Week in the *Parish News*. Following family tradition, Albert went up to Christ Church in 1905, followed by Charles, who was by far the most academic of the brothers. He read History and French, spent time in France and Germany to improve his language skills, kept up his rowing, joined the Artillery and planned to return to Eton to teach. Willie followed his older brothers to Eton in January 1911, just before Deiny left, and Edith, the younger daughter, went happily to a school in Mill Hill.

Albert was the only one of the children who gave even minor cause for concern. He expressed a wish to follow his father into the church, but also flirted with the idea of a business career like his Uncle Harry. His parents were worried that 'He is very young for his years. We all find him sadly uncommunicative, and he takes in things slowly … his feelings are very deep but take time to reach.' This sounds uncannily like Gladstone's description of the young Stephen. But unlike his father, who believed 'if a boy is at all shaped for the Church work, he should be encouraged towards it', Stephen said that: 'I do not wish to put the slightest pressure on him. He must choose freely for himself.' A similar attitude is apparent in his support for Deiny's colonial farming ambitions, so far removed from anything the family had previously been involved in. Albert was finally to opt for a business career in India under his uncle's tutelage. By

December 1910 he was in Calcutta, where he joined the Light Horse. The children were nearly all grown up and living independent lives and Stephen, if not Annie, was now approaching old age. It was time for him to retire.

There was a farewell party for the family at the Rectory and over a third of the population of the village (350 people) were there. Annie was given a brass letter scale and Stephen was presented with a silver salver and an address:

> Dear Rector and Mrs Gladstone, – We the underscribed residents of the village, respectfully beg to convey to Mrs Gladstone and yourself the regret we all feel that you have found it necessary to resign your work among us. The seven years during which we have had the privilege of your ministrations have endeared yourself and family to us all, and we feel the loss will not be easily replaced.

Stephen was surprised and touched. His farewell letter, characteristically, spoke of: 'much which I have not been able to do' and 'my many failures and faults', but he must have been popular. Two years after he left, he wrote to Harry Gladstone, saying he and Annie had been back for a visit and 'In the 2 days we made 127 calls: the people were wonderfully hearty.' He added that 'things are far from happy here', suggesting that the people had not taken his successor, the Rev. Charles Codrington Nation, to their hearts. What Stephen did not know was that Nation's arrival in 1911, unlike his own in the difficult circumstances of 1905, had been celebrated with a peal of bells. This implied optimism had perhaps been misplaced.

CHAPTER 17 – MANLEY HALL:
A DRAWING-DOWN OF BLINDS, 1911–1920

'I always like to see what you think
before doing anything big.'
(Letter from Stephen to Harry Gladstone: 25 October 1913)

As soon as they began to think about retirement, long before it was officially announced, Stephen and Annie started looking for a suitable house, and enlisted Harry Gladstone's help in their search. Naturally enough, they wanted to be within reach of Eton, where Willie was at school and Charles was now on the staff. They also wanted to be not too far from London, for reasons unspecified but probably connected more with past associations than a desire to be at the heart of social and cultural life. Interestingly, they did not even consider returning to Hawarden, where Will, Stephen's nephew, who had come of age and entered into his inheritance in 1906, was now living in the Castle with his mother Gerty and sisters Evelyn and Constance. Stephen wanted both Helen and the now widowed Agnes to go back to Hawarden, but although Helen did return, Agnes preferred London, as, eventually, did Mary.

This disinclination of the sisters to return to their childhood home again raises questions about how happy their childhood had actually been there. Mary certainly remembered friction between their mother and Helen and Agnes. In Stephen's case, the avoidance of the place where he had spent not only his childhood but the greater part of his working life is more understandable. Even though he was still fondly remembered in the parish, his own memories were soured both by the anxieties and depression he had experienced, and by the continuing fuss Mary had made about the state in which she maintained he had left the Rectory, and indeed, the parish as a whole, when he resigned.

Annie and Stephen had no plans to downsize. Stephen told Harry: 'We must have a real house which can take our furniture and with a minimum of 17 rooms. (This rectory has 22!)' Deiny was in Canada, Albert was now in India and Charles was teaching at Eton. Why a retired Rector with a wife and just two children living at home, albeit with two more there in the school holidays, should need such a large house, is a mystery, until one remembers that Stephen had lived in large houses, with the necessary staff of servants, almost all his life. Furthermore, he probably found it hard to envisage a life where he would not be constantly throwing large parties for church workers and holding annual Sunday School Sports in his grounds.

He and Annie finally settled on an attractive, well-proportioned, good sized property, though one admittedly smaller than the Barrowby Rectory, in Holby, about five miles north of the village of Frodsham. Frodsham is about twelve miles north-east of Chester and only about sixteen miles from Hawarden. The name of the house was Manley Hall. Harry, whom Stephen relied on throughout his life to deal with his financial affairs, negotiated the price: £5,300. This was probably a bargain, since not only did it have a large walled garden, but it was set in twenty-five acres of wooded grounds.

Agnes, who was sad to hear that her brother was giving up Barrowby, had heard that Manley Hall was a 'poor house', but Stephen and Annie modernised it, installing electricity, extending the dining room, making a billiard room and adding on a small chapel. They also transformed an old field into a tennis court, planted a rose garden,

247

constructed a sunken rockery, put in flowering shrubs and cut down some trees. Like father, like son. The problem of its comparative remoteness was easily solved. Stephen, though by nature a very conservative man, was moving with the times. The archive contains several torn out pages, in very small print, of advertisements for motor cars. One imagines Annie, or possibly Catherine, reading out the details to him – he couldn't possibly have read them for himself. Perhaps he dithered over what model to buy, for in the end, Harry gave them his own old car.

Before they took up residence in Manley Hall, Stephen, Annie and Catherine went to India to visit Albert, and while he was there, Stephen eventually realised his dream of seeing the Oxford Mission in Calcutta. It seems to have disappointed him somewhat. In his thirties, he must have imagined himself as a pioneer, boldly taking the Gospel into the heathen countryside. Whatever it was like then, by now the Mission was rather less inspiring. He praised its work, but felt it was not reaching out to the 'uneducated masses'.

Albert found the travellers a flat in Alipore, on the outskirts of Calcutta, and organised a horse for Catherine to ride and a carriage for family use. He stayed with or near them throughout their four month stay in the country. Stephen reported to Herbert that his son was happy and had made a lot of nice friends among the English community. He himself felt 'more and more a sense of the wonderfulness of India & its people'. They were in Calcutta during the visit of George V and Queen Mary, who were in India for the Coronation Durbah in Delhi in 1911. The celebrations which marked the queen and king/emperor's visit to Calcutta were a mere shadow of the five-day extravaganza in Delhi, a resplendently exotic demonstration of Imperial power. Nevertheless, Stephen and his family attended and enjoyed various impressive events in Calcutta, including a dance at the Viceroy's.

Stephen formed a low opinion of the Viceroy, Charles Hardinge and his wife, a view which was apparently shared by the people of Calcutta, possibly because Hardinge was known to be about to transfer the capital to New Delhi. No doubt Stephen was comparing the Hardinges unfavourably with Herbert and Dolly, in South Africa. He was extremely proud of Herbert's Governor Generalship and while in Barrowby had written accounts of his brother's doings in its *Parish News*.

The family left Calcutta, with its grand Raj architecture and huge central public space, the Maidan, to see the real India of small native villages, travelling through the strikingly varied scenery of rural West Bengal. The only thing we know about their itinerary was that it was probably curtailed because Annie got ill. Their final destination was Bombay, another city of elegant Raj buildings and ancient temples, whence in February they sailed for England. On the boat home Stephen wrote a long letter to Harry in which he gave a character sketch of Albert, much in the manner of his father's character sketches, in his diary, of his children:

> [Albert] is patient, judicial, free from prejudice, unimpulsive, absolutely straight, independent, resourceful, & blessed with an unruffled temper, & with a power of learning facts & acquiring knowledge on all sorts of subjects – wise and careful in his reasons and conclusions. He is so very like what Willy [their older brother] was, but he is more painstaking, & though not at all brilliant, moving on to what is far better – the wisdom of experience.

Stephen was nothing if not a proud father.

Back in England, he and Annie settled in to life at Manley Hall. He had no pension and was keen to emphasise that they had 'not a penny to spare all our married life'. However, he had inherited money from his father, which was invested, under Harry's close supervision, and he does not seem to have had any money worries, except for those incurred by his visits to Wiesbaden for treatment.

We know from his will that as well as the Hall, he owned two cottages which he rented out, and he employed a gardener, cook and various indoor and outdoor servants. Annie, who as he said 'wonderfully adapts herself to all circumstance which may turn up', was as steadfast a help to him in retirement as she had been while he was in full-time church work. Stephen wrote contentedly to Herbert just before Christmas 1912, to say: 'By degrees I think I may fall in with little bits of useful work in neighbouring and/or poor churches, as well as here in garden [sic] & the woodchopping horse.' This letter is almost illegible and the last part has clearly been dictated. His eyesight was deteriorating once again.

In late February 1912, he had been back in Wiesbaden with Annie and their daughters, having effective if expensive treatment. His sight had become, if briefly, better than ever before. Mary was also there, seeking relief for her neuritis in the spas. She wrote to Herbert describing how Stephen was enjoying long tramps with the girls in the surrounding countryside and going to concerts in the various concert halls. Brother and sister seem at last to have buried the hatchet and in the following years Mary paid many visits to Manley Hall.

Mary's attitude not just to Stephen but also to her other siblings and her mother is not easy to fathom. In 1919, she would comment to Herbert, whom she professed to believe was the only brother always on her side, that Catherine's mother-love never failed her, 'specially with her sons'. There had always been jealousy between Mary and Catherine, not least over their relative importance to Gladstone, but Mary's biography of her mother, in its final form, is a panegyric. Publicly, she was equally uncritical of all her brothers and sisters, while believing that they all 'had licence to criticize each other behind their backs'. She herself certainly used this licence freely when writing family letters, particularly with regard to Stephen. By nature she was an organiser, which explains and excuses her exasperation with her impractical and procrastinating brother, but it neither explains nor excuses her frequently expressed anger. With time she mellowed. Her own daughter Dossie married in 1912, the year Mary and Stephen were both in Wiesbaden. Dossie and her husband Francis (Paddy) Parish, who like Mary's husband, Harry Drew, was sadly to die young, provided her with a steady flow of grandchildren. For a while Mary had no home of her own and moved from one relative to another, several times going out to Herbert and Dorothy in South Africa. She spent time visiting both Helen, after she returned to live in Hawarden, and Agnes, who was living in London. Finally she bought a house in the Boltons in south west London, within easy reach of Agnes.

Stephen and his family were also in London in June 1913, when Edith, the younger daughter, was presented at court, like her sister Catherine before her. All four boys, Albert and Deiny being briefly back in England, went with their father to a Court Levée at Buckingham Palace, 'bedizened in hired baggery', except for Charles, who was wearing 'Uncle Harry's old Court Dress'. Stephen wrote jokingly about the occasion to Herbert, saying he was doing it all for the sake of the children, but he seems to have enjoyed it thoroughly on his own account. Deiny had by now decided against spending his life farming in Canada, which worried his father, who 'as a rule [was] against changes in life'. This is not a surprising comment coming from one who spent about thirty years wondering whether or not to leave his position in Hawarden. Harry arranged for Deiny to be taken into the family firm in India, as he also did with Albert, causing Stephen to worry, unnecessarily, in case he should disappoint his uncle.

Apart from this small area of concern, 1913 was a good year for Stephen and his family, but the happiness was not to last: it was to be the final year of peace, and war broke out in August 1914. Charles, their second son, known as Charlie, joined the Royal Flying Corps, and Albert and Deiny, the first and third sons, both out in India, joined the Gurkhas. Willie, the youngest, was still at Eton. With hindsight, it is obvious that the family would have been incredibly fortunate not to lose some of its young men in the cataclysm.

The first casualty was Stephen's nephew, Will, his older brother Willy's son. Will had left for the front in March 1915, a second lieutenant in the 3rd Battalion Royal Welch Fusiliers. By the next month he was in the trenches near Laventie and on 12 April he was shot dead while trying to locate a German sniper. Will was still under thirty. In his short life he had become a popular figure as 'the young squire of Hawarden', served as Lord Lieutenant of Flint and been returned to Parliament, at a by-election in 1911, as Liberal MP for Kilmarnock Burghs. Gerty was desperate to have Will's body repatriated, a course of action almost unheard of, but Harry used his connections with the Prime Minister and by special permission of King George V, he – Harry – travelled to France to bring the body home. Will was buried next to his father in Hawarden churchyard. His death must have come as a terrible blow to Stephen, bringing back the memory of Willy's own death, and forcibly reminding him of the fact that he had three sons in the army and a fourth impatient to join.

Only weeks after Will's death, Charlie, who had left for France with the expeditionary force in August 1914 and was attached to the Royal Flying Corps as an observer, was reported missing in action. Stephen endured an agonising time trying to find out what had happened. He and Annie had heard nothing from Charlie since 23 April 1915, and they had to wait two weeks to get any information from the War Office. 'They seem heartless, but are no doubt run to death by enquirers', wrote Stephen to Harry on 7 May, doing his best to show Christian charity. He had heard unofficially that Charlie's plane had developed engine trouble, and that he and his pilot Captain Crosbie were now German POWs. This proved to be the case, and their son was not to return home until the end of 1918. Stephen and Annie gained some comfort from being told by a colleague of Charlie, a Captain Freeman, that 'he was a universal favourite and a first rate observer'.

Catherine, the older daughter, who had been in India when war broke out, had meanwhile taken up nursing duties at Liverpool Royal Infirmary. Both Albert and Deiny were seeing action. Deiny had some hurdles to overcome at first and was 'most unhappy, almost unhinged' about the initial refusal of the military to let him see active service. He had a theory that this refusal was connected with the recent death of his cousin Will, or that the authorities had somehow mixed him up with his brother Albert. Stephen wrote to both Harry and Herbert to see if they could help and Herbert eventually cleared Deiny's path. Both sons distinguished themselves in their respective military careers, with Deiny being awarded the MC in the spring of 1917.

Stephen was hugely proud of them, which may explain why he himself took on the role of local recruitment officer in Holby. It is not easy now to imagine a man of God actively encouraging young men to go and fight and kill, but in those years, patriotic feelings, especially for the son of a former leading British statesman, would have overcome all others. Furthermore, the church authorities had promoted the conflict as a Holy War. Even so, Stephen and Annie could not bear the idea of their youngest, Willie, going off to fight, and with reason: five of his Eton fagmasters had already been killed in action. Willie told his parents he wanted to leave Eton by Christmas 1916 and Stephen hoped his headmaster would dissuade him. He wrote desperately to Herbert: 'The war must be over by the time Wm. strikes 19.'

In spite of his parents' wishes, Willie, inspired by the example of his older brothers, applied in November 1916 for a commission in the Coldstream Guards. By February the next year, he was in training at Windsor. Stephen accepted the inevitable and, true to form, wrote proudly to Harry of his son's achievements: already he was in charge of fifty-four men. At the end of December Willie was posted to France, where the following March, 1918, in a raid on enemy lines, he was conspicuously successful, taking twelve prisoners and capturing a machine gun. He succumbed to 'German Flu' at some point, but recovered and in July was home on leave for just over a week.

Like most men on leave from the front, he was reluctant to talk about what conditions were like there, and Stephen and Annie did not press him. With Albert and Deiny serving with the Gurkhas, the former in the Dardanelles and the latter on the Tigris, and Charlie in a POW camp, they must have been happy just to have their youngest son safely home with them again. By the end of August Willie was back in the front-line. Stephen wrote to Harry passing on the news of an occasion when Willie's major, just in front of him, and his servant, just behind, were both wounded in an attack in which a man close by was killed. Willie survived unscathed and received an MC, but his parents' relief and pride would have been severely tempered by the realisation that he might not be so fortunate next time. Of the 4,852 Old Etonians fighting on the front-line, 1,157 were killed.

On 4 October 1918, Harry, who by chance had seen his nephew setting off back to France at Victoria Station, received a terse telegram from Manley Hall: 'Dearest William killed on 27th.' Later, Stephen filled in the details. His youngest son had died instantly after being shot in the head during hard hand-to-hand fighting amidst deafening machine gun fire. He had just been promoted to captain. His body was buried in a small cemetery, Sanders Keep, near the battlefield. Less than two months later, on 11 November, the armistice was signed. In the archive there is a Glee Club programme dated 8 October, 1918, on which a fellow officer has scribbled a poignant note about Willie's popularity and his bravery in death. That must have meant a lot to Stephen and Annie.

After the war was over, they were able to visit Willie's grave, but meanwhile, they had other worries to cope with, concerning Charlie's physical and psychological health. At first, things had gone comparatively well for Charlie. After his capture he had been moved to an officers' camp, an *offiziergefangenenlager*, in Stralsund, a remote place on an island in a sound of the Baltic Sea. Letters in both directions took weeks to arrive and often turned up all at once, but at least he could keep in touch. Parcels were also allowed and he was able to ask for books in German, various scholarly works and the occasional novel. Eton sent him works of history. He wrote that he was 'fairly free', had some good company, was well and happy and being well treated, even if there was only one meal a day and a bread ration. Soon he began studying Russian.

Then in May 1917, he was moved to Mecklenburg in North Germany, and conditions deteriorated. He was luckier than those many prisoners who suffered severe physical punishments, were despatched to the Russian front or sent to work in mines, but the camp was dirty, the food bad and the treatment rough. His health declined, he lost his appetite and 'all power of study' and lost two stone in weight. Luckily, after about twelve months there, with repatriation in sight he was moved to a camp in Holland where 'all changed'. There was no more barbed wire or armed sentries and he was much better treated. There was even a possibility of a visit from his father. Occasionally, in special circumstances, such visits to POW camps were allowed, though there is no evidence to suggest such a visit to Charlie took place.

By September 1918, he was looking forward to going home and by the time the Armistice was signed he was in a Red Cross Hospital in The Hague. By early December he was back at Manley Hall, but in a very weak state physically and mentally. Stephen and Annie became accustomed to his 'ups and downs' and there was more than one 'sad collapse'. The doctors, faced with 'something probably of a new malady', didn't know how to treat him, and he became increasingly frustrated by being told that he was run down and needed rest. 'He wants to know what is the matter', wrote Stephen to Harry, voicing the frustration which all the family must have been feeling. Still, the doctors turned out to be at least partly right and by March 1919, Charlie had recovered and was well enough to return to his teaching post at Eton later in the year.

With their worries about Charlie at an end, Annie and Stephen began to make plans to try and find Willie's grave. There had been prayers at Manley Hall in the little oratory chapel beloved by Willie, and a memorial service in the local church, but these were of limited comfort. As Stephen told Herbert, 'the loss remains unspeakable to us'. In late May or early June 1919, armed with a map prepared by Deiny and accompanied by Albert, they managed to find the small Sanders Keep military cemetery, at Graincourt-les-Havrincourt, on a rising plateau seven miles south-west of Cambrai, to see for themselves their son's grave.

At this date, military cemeteries looked little like they do today, with their serried ranks of neat white memorial headstones on manicured lawns, studded with lovingly tended beds of roses. Stephen, Annie and Albert passed through an entrance in a simple picket fence to be confronted with rows of graves in bare earth, each marked with nothing but a small wooden cross bearing the dead soldier's name and rank. Rather than the sense of calm orderliness which is the predominant impression of Sanders Keep now, they would have experienced simple desolation. There was no towering cross on the horizon to command the gaze, just a view across fields to the hills beyond. The pathos of the scene is unbearable. The father, sixty-five years old and half blind, the mother and the older brother kneel to pray at the grave of a gentle twenty-year-old. Universally loved and respected, Willie had been planning to follow his father's footsteps into the church.

In All Saints Church, Barrowby, there is a Service Roll which lists all those young men connected with the parish, 162 of them, who went to fight in the war. All four of the Gladstone sons are listed. Willie's death is not recorded on the war memorial there: he was not a Barrowby parishioner at the time of his death. But he would have been both remembered and mourned.

After he had visited Willie's grave, Stephen made what was to be his final visit to Wiesbaden. During the war his treatments there were obviously suspended, and his sight had grown worse again. He had finally given up acting as honorary curate at St John the Evangelist, Manley, and had been grateful to hand over his work on his father's letters and papers to Herbert. Apart from his virtual blindness, as he grew older he was in surprisingly good shape physically, for a man who had suffered all his life from poor health. He was scarred by the death of Willie, but his religious belief was strong enough for him to not to suffer a crisis of faith. Although two of his sons were far away, in India, Charlie was within easy reach at Eton, and at home he had the company and comfort of his wife and two daughters. There was every reason to think that he would live on well into his eighties, as had both his parents.

In April 1920, he and Annie went on holiday to Colwyn Bay, one of their favourite coastal haunts in North Wales. On their return home to Manley Hall, Stephen developed flu, but nothing prepared Annie for the sudden heart attack he suffered on 23 April, just nineteen days after his seventy-sixth birthday. Annie quickly summoned Harry, and they were both at his bedside when he died. His body was brought to Hawarden for burial in a corner of the churchyard. Harry's wife, Maud, planted forget-me-nots round the grave. Mary wrote most movingly to Herbert, in

South Africa, about the burial service, commenting warmly on Annie: 'Only think if he had married some ordinary woman.'

In August Mary went up to Manley Hall to stay with Annie, who remained there till her death in 1931, filling the house with the family children each holiday time. The local people still recall memories of Albert, Annie and Catherine, and Annie became a prominent local figure, much involved with the emerging Girl Guide movement. The annual staff dance, to which every staff member could bring one guest, remains in living memory. Catherine lived there until her death in 1947, having allowed the army to take over the Hall in the Second World War.

Annie erected a cross over Stephen's grave, adding to the inscription the name of their son William. It is symptomatic of the lack of interest in Stephen that the grave was for years neglected and the inscription has become almost indecipherable. Charles said of his father that 'he was a very simple man'. An old schoolfriend remembered him as 'always the same, gentle, kind; but determined in every question of right and wrong, persevering & full of the industry which he inherited from [his] father'.

Like many of the children of powerful, influential fathers, Stephen inevitably lived in Gladstone's shadow and it was not in his nature to rebel. His reverence for his father almost certainly caused his lack of self-confidence and inability to make a decision. On the other hand, the qualities he inherited from him, in particular a strong sense of duty to man and God, gave meaning to his life and brought him both respect and love. When Stephen left Hawarden in 1904, Harry Drew, setting any personal grievances aside, wrote (to A. G. Edwards, Bishop of St Asaph) of his brother-in-law's professional abilities, and the way in which Stephen had set an example of how to work out as a parish priest the standards set at Cuddesdon. This was high praise.

Herbert wrote a long tribute to his brother, covering both his professional and personal qualities, which Harry, then the official family recorder, reproduced in *The Hawarden Events Book*. It begins with the unequivocal, if partial, statement: 'From boyhood to death his was a spotless life.' Herbert praised the way in which though 'not gifted with the highest intellectual qualities' he had triumphed over his physical problems by sheer force of will. Tactfully glossing over Stephen's refusal of preferment as the result of his 'views on Church organisation which he considered inconsistent with positions of high responsibility' he is full of praise for his brother's devotion to the responsibilities of the life of a parish priest, his preaching skills, his organisational abilities and his training of his assistant clergy. Mary might have questioned the truth of the two latter assertions, though she would have agreed with Herbert's description of Stephen's being 'stern and even austere in matters of principle and duty'. On the other hand, Herbert remembered his sense of fun, pleasure in domestic affairs, love of music, walking and travelling, and delight in the sea and mountains. He recalled how in his sixtieth year, incredibly, Stephen walked sixty-three miles in one day, from Hawarden to Bangor and then Flint to Hawarden, presumably, though Herbert does not say so, taking a rest on a train journey between the two laps. The tribute ends with a comment on the happiness of his marriage and the pleasure he took in his children.

Stephen was undoubtedly a family man. Herbert had no doubt that: 'His devotion to Mr Gladstone was absolute' and whatever passing irritation he felt with both his parents, he loved and revered them, valuing their support and in his turn supporting them in the frailties of old age. Herbert, writing to Mary in 1904, had referred to 'the mingled advantages of being [Gladstone's] son'. Stephen would have appreciated and understood, all too well, this description of their inheritance. Like all sons of famous fathers, he had demons to fight: high expectations, fear of failure, problems of asserting his own identity. But he learned to cope. He had a deep affection for his siblings, particularly for his brothers, keeping in close touch with Harry and Herbert throughout his life. His relationship with Mary, complicated by her marriage to Harry Drew, recovered during Mary's long widowhood and as they grew older they became closer than they had ever been before. His own marriage was deeply happy and his children were a constant source of pride and joy. Charles's comparatively swift recovery from the horrors of life as a prisoner of war testifies to the loving strength of his home. The appalling early death of Willie was made more bearable by the support which Deiny and Albert gave their parents in the finding and visiting of their brother's grave. In 1919, Mary had noted 'how utterly devoted to one another' were her brother's family. It is an apt description.

A combination of natural fortitude and faith also played their part in healing the wounds of war, and apart from his care for his family, the main motivating force of Stephen's life was of course his religious faith. This was originally inherited from his parents, but he found his own ways to put it into practice. Through all his personal trials, he never failed in his determination to do his utmost to serve the physical, mental and spiritual needs of his people. In a world of increasing scepticism, indifference to organised religion, and rapidly escalating social change, he kept the faith. A simple faith, but nonetheless sustaining, and above all, communicable. A reluctant Rector he may have been, and a

Rector more than once faced with reluctant parishioners, but in his quiet way, he made his mark, and his name lives on.

AFTERWORD

This book set out to examine both the personal – Stephen Gladstone's relationship with his father, and the institutional – his relationship with the Established Church.

To take the second of these themes first: for the student of Victorian life and thought, the state of the Established Church is a central area of interest. Statistics and official pronouncements are not difficult to come by, but of equal value is knowledge of the reality for the priest on the ground. It is important to establish how typical was the experience of Stephen Gladstone, who though briefly an urban priest, was essentially a country Rector, in spite of the increasing urbanisation of Hawarden in the 1900s.

The experience of two urban priests, Robert Gregory and Charles Lowder, both High Churchmen, have already been referred to, in Chapters 4 and 5. The former skilfully navigated the choppy waters of church politics and provided Stephen with the template for his own ministry; the latter, less experienced, was physically intimidated for his beliefs and practices.

Thanks to Owen Chadwick's *The Victorian Church*, we know something of several country priests with whom we can directly compare Stephen's experiences. In general, in rural parishes there seems to have been less trouble over Ritualism than in the cities and large towns, and, as at Hawarden, tact on the part of the incumbent usually led to trust and acceptance on the part of the parishioners. However, this was not the case with John Sharp, incumbent of Horbury in Yorkshire from 1834 to 1899. When he joined the Oxford Movement, he introduced a surpliced choir in his church and got rid of the pews. These actions involved him in a lawsuit, which he paid for only by selling most of the vicarage furniture. (Less controversially, he built two churches and helped to found a House of Mercy for reclaiming penitent women.)

James Skinner, who had been at the centre of the ritualist troubles at St Barnabas', accepted the vicarage of Newland near Malvern, Worcestershire, in 1861. His experiences were more typical, and more like Stephen's. Skinner gradually introduced Ritualist practices (including more frequent celebrations of Communion), encouraged church music and built a bigger church. Like Stephen, he suffered from poor health, which forced his resignation in 1877.

George Bayldon, Vicar of Cowling, also in Yorkshire, between 1850 and 1894, was an oddball. Like Stephen, he was a teetotaller and friendly with the local Nonconformists. He built up his church from almost nothing. Then, in his later years, he moved away from the parish and simply turned up on Sundays in case anyone came to church. This is about as far removed from Stephen's practice as it is possible to imagine.

J. C. Atkinson, Vicar of Danby in the heart of the Cleveland Moors from 1847 to 1900, was different again, a throwback to the country scholar-parson of the eighteenth century. He claimed that 'not much changed' in his over fifty years at Danby. His book, *Forty Years in a Moorland Parish*, is mainly about such topics as local folklore, manners and customs and places of antiquarian interest. He summed up: The changes are less striking, and lend themselves less to description than the permanent stability of not a few of the habits and usages of the Dale dwellers.' He describes the appalling decrepitude of the church and the school when he first arrived in the parish, but otherwise there is no mention at all of his church or his ministry.

Afterword

We have to turn to the Rev. Francis Kilvert – bearing in mind the editorial tampering with his diary – for the best available comparative model with Stephen. Kilvert was born in 1840, just four years before Stephen, and was active in the years 1864 to 1879. Their ministries thus overlapped for over a decade. Like Stephen, Kilvert, the sixth child of a country Rector, came from a large, god-fearing family, but unlike Stephen, Kilvert was spared the experience of both preparatory and public schools, and went up to Oxford after being privately educated by an uncle. After ordination, which followed, not unusually, immediately on his graduation, he worked in the same part of the country as Stephen, in various rural parishes in or bordering Wales, including two spells in his father's parish, Langley Burrell, just north of Chippenham in Wiltshire. His ministry was practised in churches in various states of decay, with tiny congregations, as unlike Hawarden as possible. His parish responsibilities were mainly concerned with visiting the poor, sick and lonely, and few administrative demands were laid upon him.

Unlike Stephen's father, William Gladstone, Kilvert's father was content to let his son choose his own path in the church. In the very same year that Stephen was forced to take on the rectorship of Hawarden – 1872 – Kilvert simply stated clearly, on being approached with the offer, that he did not want to be Vicar of Clyro in Radnorshire, where he was currently a curate. Although Kilvert, unlike Stephen, had no formal training for the priesthood, he did have eleven years of experience behind him before he took on the responsibility of a living. Another relevant difference is that although, like Stephen, Kilvert did not marry until late in life, indeed, just before his death, he never lacked for close and supportive companionship, of both sexes.

No comparison of the two men's experience would be complete without an examination of their respective doctrinal leanings. It is extraordinarily difficult to find out the affiliation of nineteenth-century Anglican clergy, except through an interpretation of their deeds and words, and after the growth of the Oxford Movement, it was often in their interests to downplay their personal beliefs. Kilvert is clearly hostile to Anglo-Catholicism, writing a vivid and derogatory account of a mass at St Barnabas in Oxford, with its endless processions involving banners, incense bearers, thurifers, acolytes and priests in extravagant robes. But he does seem to have had High rather than Low Church leanings, on one occasion (in Lent, 1870) speaking 'very seriously' to his congregation about coming to Holy Communion and regretting the small number of communicants. That same year he himself took the sacrament five times in four days.

He records with a mixture of horror and amusement various examples of the shortcomings of Low Churchmanship: 'The clergyman [at Monkton Wyld in August 1871] ... gabbled the prayers. The singing drawled and droned by a weak surpliced Choir. No sermon. Imitation Mass, the clergyman going about the chancel, to and fro like a puppet on wires.' That was a first-hand experience. Other more extreme examples are presented second or third hand, and relate to the previous fifty years. The Vicar of Fordington, who discovered that his predecessor had celebrated Holy Communion only three times a year, was asked by a group of women to pay them for taking Communion; a male communicant, on receiving the cup, 'touched his forelock' and said 'Here's your good health, Sir', and another declared 'Here's the good health of our Lord Jesus Christ.' An even funnier, or perhaps more disturbing, story recalls a visit by the Archdeacon of Sarum to a small upland parish where, in answer to his questioning about the frequency of Holy Communion, a bewildered clerk finally blurted out: 'Aw, we do never have he. We've got no tackling.'

These stories put Stephen's wrestling with the fallout from the Ritualist movement into perspective. Kilvert was aware of the issues, but seems to have maintained a more detached view. Unlike Stephen's Lambeth, Hawarden and even Barrowby, Kilvert's Wiltshire and Radnorshire were remote from central church influence. He recorded, in October 1874, that his bishop (of Malmesbury) 'took the much raised questions of the Ornaments Rubric and the Rubric directing the position of the Celebrant' and commented on 'the present pending questions and difficulties', but there does not seem to have been any pressure to admit to any kind of stance.

The Bishop was also, like the Welsh bishops, fearful of future Disestablishment, and Kilvert seems to have shared his view. In this he was also unlike Stephen, as he was on the whole issue of Dissenters and their grievances. Far from sharing Stephen's sympathy, in May 1876 he was sneering at their proclamation, at a meeting in Chippenham, of 'the intolerable monopoly of the Church, the social disadvantages of Dissenters, the arrogance of the Church and Clergy and the usual rigmarole'.

The question which arises is whether Kilvert or Stephen was the more typical in their response to the issues facing the Church of their time. The differences in temperament and social position clearly play a part. Kilvert was a less complex man than Stephen, and his ministry was conducted in comparative obscurity. In those troubled times, these assets were luxuries compared with the lot of a constantly self-questioning, self-doubting man inevitably in the spotlight of attention as the son of a famous father. Most clergy probably found a middle way between Stephen Gladstone's dogged determination to preserve his own spiritual integrity and Francis Kilvert's more pragmatic approach. Future research may prove this conclusion to be wrong. The historian must be grateful for those first-hand records which have come down to us. The insight afforded us into the mind of Stephen Gladstone is a unique and precious gift.

To return to the personal theme: it was his father, William Gladstone, who in more than one sense, created Stephen. He passed on to him, through both nature and nurture, many of his own qualities. Some of these were beneficial to Stephen: a strong sense of duty to God; an earnest desire to improve the lot of his fellow men; an ability to work intensively for long hours. Others were less positive. Most obviously, the father's habit of constant self-examination, as practised by the son, led to paralysing bouts of indecision and self-doubt.

Gladstone's desire to have a finger in every pie also stunted his son's development. It was as if his father could never quite believe that his son had grown up. He wanted to influence his every thought, his every action. His overwhelming paternal care could be stultifying in its effects. Furthermore, the father could not, or would not, distinguish between his son's best interests and his own. This failing led to frustration, unhappiness and even despair for his son.

Stephen Gladstone was, however, a great survivor. He overcame chronic physical problems by sheer determination; he dealt with his fear of inadequacy over the Hawarden rectorship by developing the qualities of both strong leadership and sensitive co-operation; and, aided by his beloved wife, he won through wretched personal bereavement to a peaceful acceptance of what he perceived to be the will of God.

BIBLIOGRAPHY

Unpublished Works:

Eton College
The Eton Admissions Book.
The Eton School Lists for the years 1856–1862.

Flintshire Record Office
Boxes of ephemera relating to Hawarden (p/28/1/91)
Minutes of the Hawarden Institute (D/DM/523/3)
Catherine Gladstone's Diaries (GGMS 1773)
Letters from the Glynne Gladstone archive (all GGMS): Mary to Herbert, 948–951; the Rev. W. M. Church to Catherine, 757; Agnes to Catherine, 809; Annie to Herbert, 953; Mary to Catherine, 759; Mary to Gladstone, 603; Harry Drew to Harry Gladstone, 847; various correspondence on publishing Gladstone's speeches, 2061; Agnes to Herbert, 975; Harry Gladstone to Agnes, 980; Mary to Harry Gladstone, 848–850; Stephen to Harry Gladstone: 895–900; Stephen to Herbert, 971–973; Stephen to Catherine, 768; Harry Gladstone to Stephen, 839; Gladstone to Stephen, 840–841; Stephen to John Gladstone, 230; Stephen to Robertson Gladstone, 579; Stephen to Sir Stephen Glynne, 27; Stephen to Gladstone, 670–673; Stephen to Mary, 983; Catherine to Gladstone, 611, 613–615; various letters on the death of Stephen, 1058, Catherine to Stephen, 841.

Lincolnshire Archives
Barrowby Parish Records (BARROWBYPAR/1/7, 1/8, 1/10. 1/17, 5/1, 5/2, 5/6, 6/3, 19/1, 22/1.
1911 Census returns for Barrowby

Bibliography

London Metropolitan Archive
Parish records for St Mary the Less, Lambeth, 1868–1872.

In Private Ownership
Assorted papers (uncatalogued), property of Sir William Gladstone.

Websites
<<http://freespace.virgin.net/sound.houses/Manley%20
memories.txt>> accessed June 2012.
(The Village of Manley: Stories, Recollections, Glimpses of the Past. Collected from Manley residents. Ed. Andrew Rudd, 2007.)
<<www.britishpathe.com/record.php?id=51938>>
<<www.lincstothepast.com>>
<<www.peoplescollectionwales.co.uk>>
<<www.stbarnabaspimlico.org.uk/St_Bs/Welcome.html>>
<<www.stgite.org.uk/history.html>>
<<www.uk1891census.com>> (1891 Census returns for Hawarden.)
<<www.visionofbritain.org.uk/place>>

Published Works:

Magazines and Newspapers
Additional Curates' Society centenary pamphlet, 1937.
Barrowby Parish News, 1905.
Brixton, Clapham & Streatham Post, 1871–1872.
Clapham Observer, Tooting & Balham Times & Surrey Advertiser, 1869–1872.
Grantham Journal 1905–1911.
Hawarden Parish Magazine, 1873–1905 and 1910.

Books and Pamphlets

Ainger, Arthur Campbell, with contributions from Neville Gerald Lyttleton & John Murray, *Memories of Eton Sixty Years Ago*, London, John Murray, 1917.

Atkinson, Rev. J. C., *Forty Years in a Moorland Parish*, London, Macmillan & Co, 2nd ed. 1891.

Ball, Thomas Isaac, *A Pastoral Bishop. A Memoir of Alexander Chinery-Haldane D.D., Sometime Bishop of Argyll and the Isles*, London, Longmans, Green & Co, 1907.

Battiscombe, Georgina, *Mrs Gladstone: the Portrait of a Marriage*, London, Constable, 1956.

Bellamy, Martin, *Millport & the Cumbraes*, Stroud, Tempus Publishing Ltd, 2003.

Bennett, F., *The Story of W. J. E. Bennett, Founder of St Barnabas, Pimlico*, London, Longmans, Green & Co, 1909.

Brinsley-Richards, James (Ed.), *Seven Years at Eton, 1857–1864*, London, Richard Bentley and Son, 2nd ed., 1883.

Brock, Michael, & Curthoys, Mark, *History of the University of Oxford, Vols 6 & 7*, Oxford, Clarendon Press, 2000.

Card, Tim, *Eton Established, a History from 1440 to 1860*, London, John Murray, 2001.

Bibliography

Card, Tim, *Eton Renewed, 1860 to the Present Day*, London, John Murray, 1994.

Chadwick, Owen, *The Founding of Cuddesdon*, Oxford University Press, 1954.

Chadwick, Owen, *Edward King Bishop of Lincoln 1885–1910*, Lincoln Minster Pamphlets, Second Series no 4, Friends of Lincoln Cathedral, 1968.

Chadwick, Owen, *The Victorian Church*, 2 vols, London, Adam and Charles Black, 1966 & 1970.

Chadwick, Owen, *The Secularization of the European Mind in the 19th Century*, Cambridge, Cambridge University Press, Canto edition 1990.

Chapman, Mark D., *Ambassadors of Christ. Commemorating 150 Years of Theological Education in Cuddesdon 1854–2004*, Aldershot, Ashgate Publishing Ltd, 2004.

Checkland, Sydney, *The Gladstones. A Family Biography, 1764–1851*, Cambridge, Cambridge University Press, 1971.

Cox, Jeffrey, *The English Churches in a Secular Society. Lambeth 1870–1930*, Oxford, Oxford University Press, 1982.

Crowther, M. A., *Church Embattled: Religious Controversy in Mid-Victorian England*, Newton Abbot, David & Charles, 1970.

Drew, Mary, *Catherine Gladstone*, London, Nisbet & Co. Ltd, 1919.

Drew, Mary, *Mr Gladstone's Library at Hawarden*, London, Spottiswoode & Co Ltd, 1906.

Gladstone, Penelope, *Portrait of a Family, the Gladstones 1839–1889*, Distributed by Thomas Myster, 1989.

[Gladstone, Stephen E.], *The Ecclesiastical Parish of Hawarden, 1872–1895, by the Rector for the Time*, Hawarden, 1895.

Gladstone, William, *The Hawarden Events Book 1864–2008*, Great Malvern, Capella Archive Limited Edition, MMIX.

Gladstone, W. E. G., *The Gladstone Diaries – with Cabinet Minutes and Prime Ministerial Correspondence 1825–1896: editors Vols 1–2 M. R. D. Foot; 3–4 M. R. D. Foot & H. C. G. Matthew; 5–14 H. C. G. Matthew*, Oxford, Clarendon Press, 1968–1994.

Gooddie, Sheila, *Mary Gladstone. A Gentle Rebel*, London, Wiley, 2003.

Gregory, Robert, *Robert Gregory, 1819–1911, Being the Autobiography of Robert Gregory, D.D., Dean of St Paul's. Prepared for the press, with notes, by W. H. Hutton*, London, Longmans, Green & Co, 1912.

Hammond, J. L. & Foot, M. R. D., *Gladstone and Liberalism*, London, English Universities Press Ltd, 1952.

Heeney, Brian, *A Different Kind of Gentleman; Parish Clergy as Professional Men in Early and Mid-Victorian England*, published for the Conference on British Studies at Wittenberg University, North Haven, CT, Archon Books, 1976.

Hoppen, K. Theodore, *The Mid-Victorian Generation: 1846–1886 (New Oxford History of England)*, Oxford, Clarendon Press, 1998.

Houghton, Walter E., *The Victorian Frame of Mind 1830–1870*, New Haven, Yale UP, 1957.

Inglis, K. S., *Churches and the Working Classes in Victorian England*, London, Routledge & Kegan Paul, 1963.

Isba, Anne, *Gladstone and Women*, London, Hambledon Continuum, 2006.

Jalland, Pat, *Women, Marriage and Politics 1860–1914*, Oxford, Clarendon Press, 1986.

Kilvert's Diary. Selections from the Diary of Rev. Francis Kilvert. Chosen, edited and introduced by William Plomer. 3 Vols. London, Jonathan Cape, 1938–1940.

Lawrence, P. S. H., *An Eton Camera*, Salisbury, Michael Russell, 1980.

Liddon, H. P, *The Work and Prospects of Theological Colleges: A Sermon*, Preached at the Cuddesdon Anniversary Festival, on June 10, 1868, London, Rivingtons, 1868.

Lyttleton, Neville Gerald, *A Sketch of Another Preparatory School*, in *Ainger, Memories of Eton Sixty Years Ago*, London, John Murray, 1917.

Maccoll, Malcolm, *Memoirs and Correspondence*, ed. G. W. E. Russell, London, Smith, Elder & Co, 1914.

Mallet, Sir Charles, *Herbert Gladstone. A Memoir*, London, Hutchinson & Co, 1932.

Marlow, Joyce, *Mr and Mrs Gladstone: an Intimate Biography*, London, Weidenfeld and Nicolson, 1977.

Mason, Paul F. & Rolfe, Phyllis, *Historic Hawarden*, Clwyd Record Office, 1985.

Masterman, Lucy (ed.), *Mary Gladstone (Mary Drew.) Her Diaries and Letters*, London, Methuen & Co Ltd, 1930.

Matthew, Colin, *Gladstone*, 2 vols, Oxford, Oxford University Press, 1986–1995.

Pantin, W. A., *Oxford Life in Oxford Archives*, Oxford, Clarendon Press, 1972.

Perry, W., *Cumbrae College. The Oxford Movement in Scotland*, Cambridge, Cambridge University Press, 1933.

Pritchard, T. W., *A History of St Deiniol's Library*, Hawarden, Monad Press, 1999.

Pritchard, T. W., *A History of the Old Parish of Hawarden*, Wrexham, Bridge Books, 2002.

Pritchard, T. W., 'The Reverend S. E. Gladstone (1844–1920)', *The Flintshire Historical Society Journal*, Vol. 35, 1999, pp. 191–241.

Ragg, Lonsdale, *Memoir of Edward Charles Wickham, Dean of Lincoln, formerly Headmaster of Wellington College*, London, Edward Arnold, 1911.

Roebuck, Janet, *Urban Development in 19th century London, Lambeth, Battersea & Wandsworth 1838–1888*, London and Chichester, Phillimore, 1979.

Russell, George, W. E., *Harry Drew. A Memorial Sketch*, Oxford, Oxford University Press, 1911.

Sage, Lorna, *Bad Blood: A Memoir*, London, Fourth Estate, 2000.

Shannon, Richard, *Gladstone: Peel's Inheritor 1809–1865*, Harmondsworth, Penguin, 1999.

Shannon, Richard, *Gladstone: Heroic Minister 1865–1898*, Harmondsworth, Penguin, 1999.

Thomas, Ivor, *Gladstone of Hawarden*, London, John Murray, 1936.

Thompson, Henry, L., *Henry George Liddell D.D., Dean of Christ Church, Oxford*, London, John Murray, 1899.

Thompson, Henry L., *University of Oxford College Histories: Christ Church*, Oxford, Oxford University Press, 1900.

Thomson, John, *Victorian London Street Life in Historic Photographs,* Dover Publications Inc., New York, 1994.

Trench, M., *Charles Lowder. A Biography,* London, Kegan, Paul Trench & Co, 1882.

Trevelyan, G. M., *English Social History,* London, The Reprint Society, 1944.

Various, *Essays and Reviews,* London, 1860.

Veysey, A. Geoffrey, *Mr Gladstone and Hawarden,* Clwyd Record Office, 1982.

de Ville, Eileen, *Guide to Barrowby Parish Church All Saints, Grantham,* printed by Journal Commercial Printers, 1977.

INDEX

Index